Inland Waterways of Germany

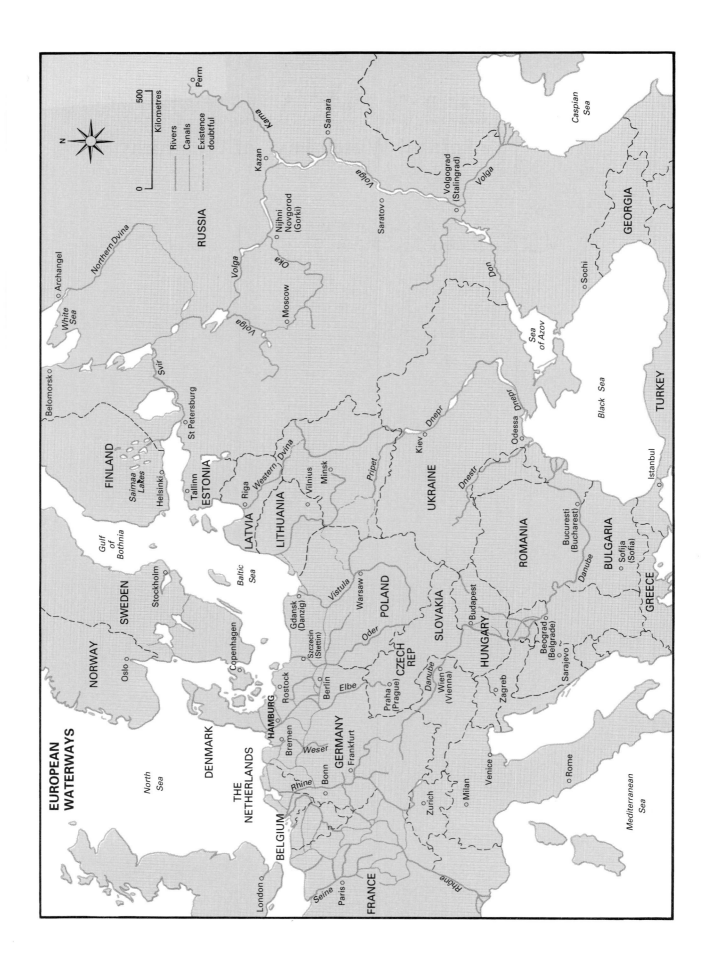

Inland Waterways of Germany

BARRY SHEFFIELD

Imray Laurie Norie & Wilson Ltd
St Ives Cambridgeshire England

Published by
Imray Laurie Norie & Wilson Ltd
Wych House, St Ives, Huntingdon
Cambridgeshire PE17 4BT, England
☎ +44 (0) 1480 462114 *Fax* +44 (0) 1480 496109
1995

The last input of technical information was November 1995.

Printed in Great Britain by
The Bath Press, Avon

British Library Cataloguing in Publication Data.
A catalogue record for this book is available from the British Library.

ISBN 0 85288 283 1

CAUTION
Every effort has been made to ensure the accuracy of this book. It contains selected information, and thus is not definitive and does not include all known information on the subject in hand; this is particularly relevant to the plans, which should not be used for navigation. The author and publishers believe that it is a useful aid to prudent navigation, but the safety of a vessel depends ultimately on the judgement of the navigator, who should assess all information, published or unpublished, available to him.

CORRECTIONS
The author would be glad to receive any corrections, information or suggestions which readers may consider would improve the book. Letters should be addressed to the publishers. The more precise the information the better, but even partial or doubtful information is helpful, if it is made clear what the doubts are.

CORRECTIONAL SUPPLEMENTS
Imray pilot books are amended at intervals by the issue of correctional supplements. Supplements, if available, are supplied free of charge with the books when they are purchased. Further supplements are available from the publishers. The following should be quoted:

1. Name of book
2. Date of edition (above)
3. Date of last supplement (if applicable)
4. Name and address to which supplement should be sent on a stamped addressed A4 envelope

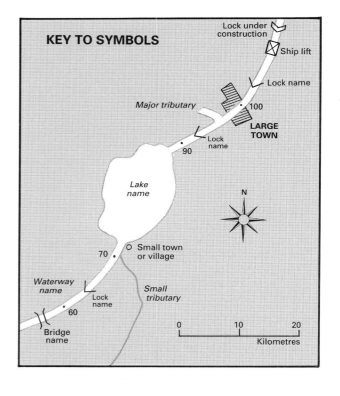

Contents

Preface

Germany has a thriving water transport system which exists for commercial purposes, but for those of us who cruise in small boats it also provides an extensive and up-to-date waterway network which makes it possible for us to explore an attractive country in an interesting way. It enables us to meet its people and extend our interests in history, architecture, music, wildlife, food or wine in a new context. Furthermore, occupying as they do the central part of Europe, the German rivers and canals provide through routes which make it possible to travel in comfort to new cruising areas in far-off places such as the Baltic, eastern Europe and the Black Sea.

The aim of this book is to enable more boat owners and charterers to enjoy the pleasures of cruising in Germany. Part I discusses cruising in Germany generally, provides an introduction to the German waterway system and deals with the specific issues relating to cruising in a small boat. Part II, the main bulk of the book, contains a detailed description of every navigable inland waterway route in Germany.

The route descriptions in Part II are intended to provide enough information to enable the skipper of a small boat to navigate any waterway he wishes. It might be considered advantageous, however, to use the book in conjunction with the appropriate sheets of the 1:200,000 general touring maps known as *Die General Karte*, which can be bought cheaply in almost any book shop in Germany.

ACKNOWLEDGEMENTS

It would not be realistic to believe that every detail of a guide such as this could derive from personal knowledge. Although I have spent a considerable amount of time travelling the German inland waterways, I have also been fortunate in having many friends in Germany who have generously helped me by checking my material and in some cases providing additional information.

I would especially like to thank Kapitän Konrad Nussbaum in Frankfurt for spending a great deal of time checking my work so thoroughly and so diligently. I am greatly indebted to him. The late Fred Evers of Petershagen and Wolfgang Peiler from Berlin also helped me with their extensive knowledge based on practical boating experience.

I would also like to thank Herr Heesch of WSD-Nord and the staff of all the other WSD regions for the helpful way they answered my queries.

Finally I would like to express my gratitude to Willie Wilson and his staff at Imrays, and to Sue Pepper for her constant encouragement.

Barry Sheffield
Falmouth, November 1995

Pastoral scene on the Untere Havel.

Part I. Cruising in Germany

Modern Germany

There is something satisfactory about being in Germany. It is well organised. Everything works. The people one meets in the streets are friendly and helpful. Most of them seem to speak English. They are self-confident without being arrogant. Hardly any of them are poor. Even in eastern Germany, until recently under a corrupt totalitarian regime, conditions are improving rapidly, although (hardly surprisingly in view of the rapid pace of change) not without some degree of tension.

Perhaps the 'clean sweep' following World War II, with the setting up of a new system of government designed to meet present-day needs and not handicapped by history and tradition, made it possible for Germany to achieve prosperity without sacrificing good humanitarian principles. Whatever the reason, the Germans do seem to have found a way of achieving a well balanced society, of which realism, logic and hard work seem to be the hallmarks. Their electoral system produces a legislature whose range of hues fairly reflects those of the electors. Their welfare system is effective but does not overburden the taxpayer. They understand the importance of a good infrastructure and manage to invest adequately in it. And although there is considerable delegation of power to the sixteen *Länder* (semi-autonomous states), most Germans appear to recognise the importance of European collaboration and know that Germany must play its part in an increasingly united Europe.

The first thing that hits you as a visitor from Britain (at least in the former West Germany) is the feeling of prosperity. There is a noticeable absence of old cars, poor-quality buildings or badly maintained public facilities. Town (and country) planning seems to be very effective in achieving an aesthetically pleasing environment. There is surprisingly little visible evidence of heavy or unsightly industry in spite of Germany's success as a supplier to the markets of the world. It would seem that the public want 'green' policies – and the political system is capable of translating the wishes of the public into reality.

The Reichstag: central to the recent history of Germany.

The Brandenburg Gate – the old dividing line between East and West.

Geography

It is possible to find almost every type of terrain in Germany. The *Bodden* (salt-water lagoons) and islands of the northern coastline exude a feeling of wildness and mystery. The beautiful lakes of Mecklenburg-Vorpommern are full of old-world charm. The low-lying agricultural lands of Lower Saxony are lush and fertile. The wooded hills and valleys of central Germany have a warmth which contrasts with the Wagnerian splendour of the hill-top castles of Rheinland, the jagged peaks of Saxony and the alpine ranges of the extreme south.

The grim fortress of Diez.

History

The history of Germany effectively begins in the 9th century, when Charlemagne forced together a number of tribes in central Europe during the formation of the Holy Roman Empire. Over the following centuries the Empire became less unified and five feudal states, or duchies, emerged: Bavaria, Swabia, Franconia, Lorraine and Saxony. It is in these that some of the 16 present-day *Länder* (a *Land* is a semi-autonomous region similar in concept to one of the states in the USA) had their origins. The diagram on page 1 shows these important political regions as they are today (together with their anglicised names where these exist).

Gradually the Empire became a loose federation of German princedoms, but to create a greater collective strength an overall emperor, Albert of Habsburg, was elected in 1438. The Habsburgs held the throne almost continuously until the final dissolution of the Holy Roman Empire in 1806 following the Napoleonic wars. At this point there were some 39 German states, which became united as the German Confederation, although in practice most of the sovereignty lay in the hands of the member states.

In 1866 Bismarck, prime minister of Prussia, defeated Austria and annexed most of the northern German states. The southern states soon joined this confederation and in 1871 the German Empire was formed with King William I of Prussia as emperor. By 1900 the unified Germany had become the leading industrial nation in Europe.

At the end of World War I William II abdicated and under the Treaty of Versailles Germany lost the overseas colonies which it had by now established. The resulting collapse of the economy and the ensuing massive unemployment and social discontent led to the rise of the National Socialist (Nazi) party. In 1933 Adolf Hitler became chancellor and a year later president of what became known as the Third Reich. Hitler's ambition and fanaticism led to Germany's defeat in World War II, and its occupation by the Allies in four zones. In 1949 the United States, Britain and France consolidated their zones into the Federal Republic of Germany and the Soviet Union set up the German Democratic Republic under communist rule.

West Germany very rapidly developed its industrial capabilities and achieved a leading position as a world industrial nation. East Germany meanwhile suffered severely from the corruption arising from its non-democratic totalitarian government. Civil unrest became rampant, and in 1961 the Berlin wall was built in order to reduce the number of defections to the West.

Following the ending of the Cold War, the Berlin wall was demolished in 1989 and Germany became reunited in 1990, with the five eastern *Länder* joining the existing eleven of the Federal Republic. However, the task of reconstructing eastern Germany is huge, and it is likely to require many further years of struggle and hardship before the people of the East gain full equality with their more fortunate compatriots of the West.

Architecture

To the visitor the visible evidence of this fascinating history is a wealth of historic buildings and other relics left behind by countless kings, princes, dukes, counts and bishops, and scattered throughout the land. There are important buildings from all ages: ruins from the times of Caesar, churches and monasteries from the period of the Holy Roman Empire, and magnificent baroque palaces and castles. There are also many uncomfortable reminders of the mass destruction of the Second World War.

Most of the beautiful old buildings are carefully preserved and often on show to visitors – as if with a sense of pride. Elegant churches, castles standing dramatically on hill tops and mediaeval houses clustered in picturesque groups just as they were centuries ago all demonstrate the rich history of the country.

In rural areas farms, equipped though they may be with the latest technology, blend architecturally with their surroundings as harmoniously as they have always done. Clearly new building is carefully controlled, with a responsible eye to the environment. While on the one hand out-and-out modern architecture is encouraged in Frankfurt, the exciting and vibrant centre of banking and commerce, on the other hand in the many historic towns and villages where new buildings need to coexist with the old there is an emphasis on traditional materials such as clay tiles and red bricks, creating a satisfactory sense of overall harmony. Trees too are clearly a very important factor in planning, and their use to enhance modern developments almost seems obligatory. Presumably it is this same sensitivity towards the environment which also limits the extent of outdoor advertising – so disfiguring and alien to nature in many countries.

Transport

With the natural coming together of the countries of western Europe, travelling to Germany is very little different from travelling to other parts of the British Isles. There are direct flights to many German airports, travel by rail and coach is very easy and there is no difficulty in driving, crossing the Channel by ship, hovercraft or tunnel. Formalities are few, and although – as in any country – politeness requires at least some effort at speaking the language, it is possible to cope with the basic necessities of life without knowing any German at all.

Arriving by boat with the intention of cruising on the German inland waterways involves fewer options, but there are still a number of choices, depending on the departure point, the area to be explored and the type of boat. These matters will be discussed later.

For travel inside Germany, whatever your method of transport, you will find order and efficiency. The airports are designed for practicality, and domestic services are good. Rail transport is excellent: trains are comfortable, punctual and not expensive. Possibly because of this, intercity coaches are not as numerous as in some countries.

Church at Bad Wimpfen on the Neckar.

The standard of local bus and tram services in most cities is a good incentive to leave your car on the outskirts. The system is normally to buy a ticket from a kiosk or automatic machine, and to validate it by inserting it into a stamping machine as soon as you board the bus. Penalties for not doing so are quite steep, and are collected on the spot. In some areas, but by no means all, tickets can be bought from the bus driver, but still need validation.

The bicycle is widely accepted as a cheap, healthy, rapid and environmentally friendly method of local transport and cycling is encouraged everywhere by the provision of good cycle tracks, usually safely segregated from road traffic, with special traffic lights at crossing points and good provision for storing bicycles wherever it is needed. Indeed, outside most railway stations you will see hundreds of bicycles neatly stored in specially designed racks, often covered. Bicycles can also be hired at many railway stations.

Renting a car is very straightforward, with prices similar to those at home, but shop around: it is nearly always possible to find local rental companies whose rates undercut the well known international operators by half. Long-distance road travel is catered for by the constantly evolving autobahn network. There are often bitter battles between environmentalists and planners over new autobahn routes, and it is perhaps because of this that the end result seems to be roads which do not disfigure the countryside – at least after the inevitably ugly construction phase has been completed. Roads are generally well. maintained and roadworks seldom seem to be a problem. There are no speed limits on the autobahns, and on other roads the speed limits for cars are generally 100kph on the open road and 50kph in built-up areas, although other limits may be indicated where appropriate. On the whole, speed limits tend to be realistic but well enforced, and road discipline is generally of a high order.

It is not only the motorist who is subject to discipline: pedestrians are forbidden to jaywalk, and anyone seen dropping litter in a public place also risks a fine.

Over 20% of heavy freight is transported by river and canal (in western Germany). This remarkable achievement, relieving the roads of a considerable volume of heavy lorries, is undoubtedly the result of strategic planning and adequate investment in the facilities which make it attractive for industry to ship its non-urgent bulk cargoes by water. Interestingly, as can be seen from the diagram below, this percentage is holding relatively steady, even though the proportion carried by rail is gradually declining.

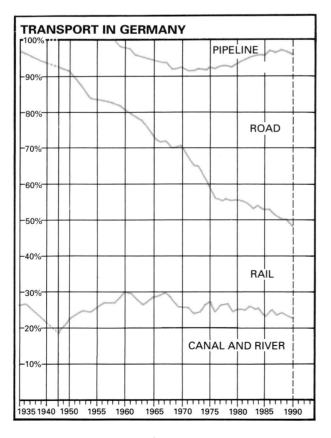

TRANSPORT IN GERMANY

Accommodation

There is plenty of overnight accommodation at whatever price level is required, from youth hostels to Hilton hotels. But if the visitor wishes to get to know and understand German people there is no doubt that bed-and-breakfast accommodation in private houses (there are *Zimmer Frei* signs everywhere except perhaps in the centre of large towns and cities) offers an excellent way of gaining an insight into the everyday lives of ordinary people. This type of accommodation is also without doubt the best value for money. Do try to arrive in time for an evening meal, and do try to speak in German, no matter how rudimentary your linguistic skills may be.

Money

Apart from the fact that one is using Deutschmarks instead of sterling, there is little difference between the arrangements for getting and spending money in Germany and in the UK. It is good sense to be equipped with Eurocheques, obtainable from all major UK banks, as these are generally accepted in shops throughout Germany. The accompanying cheque-guarantee card can also be used, with the correct PIN number, to obtain cash from automatic teller machines, which are widely available throughout the western part of the country and being rapidly introduced in the east too. These machines normally have the ability to give on-screen instructions in English as well as German.

The use of credit seems to be less popular amongst shoppers in Germany than in the UK, and as a consequence credit cards are not as widely used, although their popularity is increasing quite fast. If you are driving, it is not always safe to assume that every garage or filling station will accept your credit card. Again, this is a problem which is more acute in the eastern part of the country than elsewhere.

Banking hours are normally 0900 to 1230 and 1430 to 1600, with an extension to 1730 on Thursdays. Banks do not open on Saturdays. It should be remembered that German bank holidays are not all coincident with ours, and it is easy to be caught out by unexpected closures of banks and shops or – perhaps more importantly – by the non-operation of locks. The normal bank holidays in Germany are listed below.

Public holidays

New Year's Day	*Neujahr*	1 January
Epiphany	*Heilige Drei Könige*	6 January
Good Friday	*Karfreitag*	variable
Easter Monday	*Ostermontag*	variable
Labour Day	*Tag der Arbeit*	1 May
Whit Monday	*Pfingstmontag*	variable
Corpus Christi	*Fronleichnam*	variable
Day of German Unity	*Tag der Deutschen Einheit*	3 October
All Saints' Day	*Allerheiligen*	1 November
Day of Prayer and Repentance	*Buß- und Bettag*	17 November
Christmas	*Weinachten*	25–26 Dec

Shopping

If, as with many people in the western world, shopping is one of your major hobbies you will not be disappointed in Germany. The range of shops and goods in them is enormous, although it is noticeable that the huge hypermarkets of Britain and France are slow in spreading to Germany. Why this should be so might well be a very interesting sociological phenomenon, but it is a fact. The big department stores of the large cities are remarkably similar to those in the high streets of our own towns, and the specialist food shops (cake shops in particular) are a sight for sore eyes. Unfortunately, with the gradual downward movement of the value of sterling over the last few decades, prices seem generally high to British eyes.

There are excellent markets in most places, and for economical shopping it is as well to locate one of these. The range and quality of goods are always excellent, and prices tend to be lower than in the larger stores.

Shop opening hours vary, but they can usually be expected to be open Mondays to Fridays from 0800 to 1830. On Saturdays most stores close at 1400, and there is little opportunity for shopping on Sundays at all. Many smaller shops close for lunch from 1200 to 1400 on weekdays. In large cities, however, you often find a good range of shops in or around the main railway station which open later on weekday evenings and also on Sundays.

Laundry

For boat people that often problematic matter of laundry is easily dealt with, as there is no shortage of spotless, well equipped laundrettes. Dry-cleaning shops are in every main street.

Telecommunications

Germany's telecommunication systems are superb, as might be expected in a nation so successful in international markets. For the visitor, this means that telephoning or faxing home is no problem. It is possible to make international telephone calls from almost any call box in any street. The access code for international calls is 00 and there is no need to wait for a second dial tone before dialling the country code. It is very convenient to use phonecards. Sending a fax is easy: nearly every copy bureau and post office has a fax machine, except of course in eastern Germany, where it is taking a little time to catch up. Even here, however, one of the first priorities has been the replacement of the antiquated telephone system, and it will not be long before the telecommunications services of eastern Germany are up to the standard of those of the west.

Radio

If your German is good enough, there is no problem in keeping in touch with world affairs via the German broadcasting services, but even if your linguistic abilities are not up to this there is always a wide selection of broadcast music which can be heard by tuning in to local or national services.

On the western side of Germany it is very easy to pick up Radio 4 on 198Khz. As you progress eastwards, however, if your German is limited and you want to keep in touch with world and British news you will find it necessary to use the excellent shortwave broadcasts of the BBC World Service. It is well worth investing in a small transistor radio (preferably with digital tuning) capable of receiving short wave.

Food

There is a widespread myth that German food is dull. This is far from the truth. For the adventurous there is a very wide range of new tastes to try, and for the more conservative there are many traditional meat, fish and vegetable dishes. It is certainly true that the Germans eat well and heartily: you are unlikely to leave the table feeling unsatisfied – but few people will find this a matter to complain about. Desserts do not feature a great deal on German menus, although their wonderful cakes and pastries, often eaten with coffee in the morning or afternoon, more than amply make up for this.

There is a very wide choice of restaurants if you feel like eating out. There are plenty of expensive restaurants if money is not a limitation, but it is perfectly possible to eat out at reasonable cost by choosing the less pretentious restaurants – which is most of them. Most yacht clubs have a modest restaurant, and even where this is not the case it would be surprising if there were not a *Gaststätte* (a cross between a pub and a restaurant) in the locality. The *Gasthof* (guest house) usually provides good value too. Always look for the *Tagesmenu* (fixed-price menu of the day).

Wine

It is fashionable to dismiss German wines as sweet and perhaps even of poor quality. This again is quite unjust. There are of course few red German wines, but there are many magnificent whites, and by choosing with care – and perhaps a little local advice – it is possible to find wines of an almost infinite variety of tastes, including some rated amongst the best in the world. Do not think that all German wines are like the cheap *Liebfraumilch* which is sold in large volumes in British supermarkets.

Beer

Germany is often said to be the home of beer. The variety is enormous – and the arguments about the relative merits of different brands never-ending. Beer can be drunk everywhere, from the traditional *Biergarten* (beer garden) or *Bierkeller* (beer cellar) to the most sophisticated of restaurants. It is worth taking local advice on which type of beer to choose. Try to avoid sticking to the mass-produced brands; some of the local brews are not to be missed, but as at home the smaller breweries are gradually being gobbled up by the large groups and local individual flavours are sadly disappearing.

Festivals

Wherever you are in Germany you are almost certain to stumble across a festival. There are festivals of beer, of wine, of food, of music. For the boat traveller it can be most enjoyable to get involved in a local beer or wine festival. A small amount of alcohol works wonders with language problems and is excellent for promoting international understanding! The *Oktoberfest* (which starts in September in spite of its name) in Bavaria is probably the best known beer festival; it is regarded as a bad year if fewer than 6,000,000 litres of beer are consumed. It is well worth while checking the list of festival dates at the German tourist office before deciding your cruise plan.

Culture

The popular image of Germans as excessive beer drinkers is, however, misleading. They are in fact a very cultured nation. Classical music has a much larger following than in many countries, and even medium-sized towns have opera houses and concert halls as well as art galleries. The Wagner festival at Bayreuth (July/August) is world-famous. The Bach festival at Leipzig and the Handel festival at Halle are important events in the international music calendar. There are also international drama, film and folk festivals.

Etiquette

If you are lucky enough to be invited into a German home – or boat – for a meal, you should recognise that the Germans are somewhat more formal than we are. Take flowers (preferably not roses), and do not too quickly assume that you can call your hosts by their first names.

Cost of living

Unfortunately for us, the relative prosperity of the Germans, coupled with the intermittent devaluation of sterling over the years, means that by our standards the cost of living in Germany is high. However, if care is taken to avoid some of the more expensive products, with prudent shopping in supermarkets and by eating in yacht clubs or modest restaurants it is possible to live in Germany at only a slightly higher cost than at home.

Climate

Germany's climate is not enormously different from our own. The winters are somewhat colder and the summers are perhaps slightly hotter than ours. The rainfall is a little lower.

Wildlife

Germany is rich in wildlife of a wide variety of types, but to the boat traveller it is the birds which haunt the rivers, canals, lakes and estuaries that are a constant source of interest. Needless to say, swans and ducks (of many types) are constantly in attendance, and herons can always be seen at the water's edge. In some areas storks and egrets are much in evidence; hoopoes can be spotted amongst the trees, and on the desolate *Bodden* of the Baltic coast thousands of geese and swans collect, unapproachable by human beings. It is also a common sight whilst travelling the canals and rivers to see kites, harriers and occasionally eagles wheeling overhead in search of prey. Do not forget to take a book which will help you to identify the birds of central Europe.

The German waterways

The German waterway network offers enough interest in its own right to justify many years of enjoyable cruising. It also provides opportunities for ambitious long-distance cruising. The frontispiece map shows the scope of the German waterway system itself and gives some idea of the extent of the sheltered-water cruising opportunities which exist, not only in central Europe but further afield in southern Scandinavia, Russia and the Black Sea.

The atmosphere on the *Bundeswasserstrassen* (national waterways) is one of purposefulness. The waterways are alive: they exist for a practical purpose, and the skippers and crews of the barges, push-tows, hotel ships, car transporters, tugs and ferries form a very special community. But it is far from being a closed community, and a *Sportboot* (any boat used for leisure purposes) will be readily accepted as part of this fraternity of the waterways – provided the skipper is judged to be competent. It should be remembered that barge skippers, river police and lock-keepers are professionals with a job to do and time schedules to meet. It is hardly surprising that their tolerance can easily become stretched if they discern that a *Sportboot* skipper is incompetent, or thoughtless about the needs and the problems of large unwieldy commercial vessels. Much of the pleasure of travelling on the German waterways is the satisfaction of being for a time part of this waterways fraternity.

The skippers of German pleasure boats also have a good sense of camaraderie, and this is willingly extended to visitors from other countries whom they identify as like-minded. An overnight stop at a German yacht club is usually a friendly and pleasant experience, especially if the visitor is willing to try his or her hand at speaking German.

It is noticeable that there is a very strong European feeling everywhere. A high proportion of vessels now carry the European Union ensign, with the German flag inset in the top corner, instead of their own national ensign. Clearly there is a feeling amongst the waterways community that national boundaries and excessive demonstrations of national pride have become anachronistic. The much-publicised behaviour of some of the minority nationalist groups in Germany is certainly no reflection of national attitudes.

As well as the *Bundeswasserstrassen*, there are also many delightful smaller waterways, originally built for trading purposes but no longer used to any great extent by commercial ships. Nevertheless, many of them continue to be maintained for the benefit of pleasure craft. By contrast with the huge modern commercial waterways, these smaller waterways (such as the Lahn, the northwestern canals and the waterways throughout the Mecklenburg lake district) have an atmosphere not unlike that of the French canals: they are generally rural in character, they provide peace and tranquillity, and the lock-keepers are friendly and helpful. And there is still that same spirit of friendship from the skippers and crews of the other pleasure craft one meets.

Administrative matters

The German waterways are freely available to visitors. On arrival by boat at a German border or port, the visitor should report as soon as possible to the authorities. Unless there are any suspicious circumstances, there will be a minimum of formalities, and the customs and police officers will complete the small amount of paperwork rapidly and courteously. Usually passports and a boat-registration document are the only documents required, although it is possible that one might be asked to produce a helmsman's qualification such as the RYA International Certificate of Competence. This is not legally necessary, as the rule is that the skippers of vessels under 15 tonnes displacement need a certificate of competence only if such a document is required in their own country. However, as German *Sportboot* skippers are required to have an official 'sport-boat driving licence' it is regarded as the norm, and undue argument may be avoided if a suitable certificate is carried. For vessels over 15 tonnes displacement a full-scale Master's Certificate is required for navigation on the Rhein (Rhine) or the Donau (Danube).

All boats must be registered, but for British boats registration on the Small Ships Register is adequate. If VAT has been paid on the vessel it is sensible to carry documentary evidence of this. If VAT has not been paid, advice should be obtained from the RYA before arrival in Germany. Boats are expected to carry normal safety equipment such as life buoys, life jackets, first-aid kit, fire extinguishers and an anchor. It is believed that at some stage a regulation will be introduced requiring all vessels using the inland waterways to have holding tanks, and discharging toilets overboard will be prohibited. There is, however, no indication as yet of when this will become a requirement.

After clearing into Germany there are no further formalities, although the presence of the *Wasserschutzpolizei* (river police), or WSP, will be noticeable from time to time. Normally, however, the crews of WSP patrol vessels are nothing but helpful – and this can be very comforting to know in case of serious problems. It goes without saying, of course, that visiting sport boats – like everyone else on the water – should be careful to take proper notice of the rules of the road, speed limits, etc. These are working waterways, and not unreasonably all users are expected to behave responsibly.

For navigation on the Rhein, vessels over 20m long are required to have on board the *Rheinschiffahrtpolizeiverordnung* (Rhine river police regulations).

The *Bundeswasserstrassen* are administered by the German ministry of transport, through the agency of the *Wasser- und Schiffahrtsdirektion* (water and shipping authority), WSD for short, which has seven regions: WSD-Nord (Kiel), WSD-Nordwest

THE GERMAN WATERWAYS

DENMARK

North Sea

Baltic Sea

31

30 KIEL

30

Stralsund 54

Wolgast

Cuxhaven

LÜBECK 32

52

53

SZCZECIN (STETTIN)

28

HAMBURG

Schwerin

Waren

29

Bremerhaven

33

Lauenburg

45

44

51

Emden

Wilhemshaven

17

15 18

20

29

33

27

33

36

43 42 38

40

39

POLAND

NETHERLANDS

14

19 21

22

22

24

BREMEN

25

38 41

37

BERLIN 48

51

16

13

24

Celle

26

36

47

46

Frankfurt/ Oder

Minden

HANNOVER

Braunschweig

35

Brandenburg

49

50

51

Osnabrück

Hameln

24

MÜNSTER

13

Salzgitter

33

MAGDE- BURG

Wittenberg

4 Wesel 11

12 Hamm

34

Göttingen

10

13 DORTMUND

Halle

33

DUIS- BURG

9 ESSEN

24

KASSEL 23

LEIPZIG

Krefeld

DÜSSELDORF

Erfurt

DRESDEN

Chemnitz

KÖLN

4

BONN

Limburg

KOBLENZ 6

FRANKFURT/MAIN

7

4

MAINZ

Schweinfurt

3

Bamberg

Bayreuth

PRAHA (PRAGUE)

Trier

3

Würz- berg

Pilsen

CZECH REPUBLIC

8

LUDWIGSHAFEN

MANN- HEIM

NÜRNBERG

SAARBRÜCKEN

4

Heidel- berg

2

REGENSBURG

KARLSRUHE

5

Kelheim

STRASBOURG

Kehl

STUTTGART

1

Passau

FRANCE

4

Ulm

Augsburg

SALZBURG

Freiburg

MÜNCHEN

4

BASEL

ZURICH

AUSTRIA

SWITZERLAND

0   100

Kilometres

GERMAN WATERWAYS MAP – KEY TO FIGURES

1. Donau (Danube)
2. Main–Donau–Kanal (MDK)
3. Main
4. Rhein (Rhine)
5. Neckar
6. Lahn
7. Mosel
8. Saar
9. Ruhr
10. Rhein–Herne–Kanal (RHK)
11. Wesel–Datteln–Kanal (WDK)
12. Datteln–Hamm–Kanal (DHK)
13. Dortmund–Ems–Kanal (DEK)
14. Unter Ems
15. Ems–Seitenkanal
16. Haren–Rütenbrock–Kanal
17. Ems–Jade–Kanal
18. Nordgeorgsfehnkanal
19. Leda
20. Jümma
21. Elisabethfehnkanal
22. Küstenkanal (KK)
23. Fulda
24. Weser
25. Aller
26. Mittellandkanal (MLK)
27. Elbe–Seitenkanal (ESK)
28. Schiffahrtsweg Elbe–Weser
29. Oste
30. Nord–Ostsee–Kanal (NOK) (Kiel Canal)
31. Eider
32. Elbe–Lübeck–Kanal (ELK)
33. Elbe
34. Saale
35. Elbe–Havel–Kanal
36. Untere Havel–Wasserstrasse
37. Havelkanal
38. Havel–Oder–Wasserstrasse
39. Hohensaaten–Friedrichstaler–Wasserstrasse
40. Ruppiner Wasserstrasse
41. Finowkanal
42. Obere Havel–Wasserstrasse
44. Müritz–Havel–Wasserstrasse
45. Müritz–Elde–Wasserstrasse
46. Spree–Oder–Wasserstrasse
47. Teltowkanal
48. Müggelspree
49. Dahme–Wasserstrasse
50. Obere Spree–Wasserstrasse
51. Oder
52. Peene
53. Uecker
54. Strelasund

(Aurich), WSD-Mitte (Hannover), WSD-West (Münster), WSD-Südwest (Mainz), WSD-Süd (Würzburg) and WSD-Ost (Berlin). Each region of the WSD is further subdivided into smaller areas known as WSAs (*Wasser- und Schiffahrtsamt*), each responsible for the physical maintenance of the waterway system within its own area. A list of addresses of these organisations is included in the Appendix. There are normally no charges for foreign sport boats using waterways administered by the WSD, provided they are willing to use the locks in company with commercial shipping. Where this is impossible, perhaps because of time constraints, a small charge may be levied on some waterways (e.g. the Mosel) at each lock. It should be noted that although use of the WSD-controlled waterways is free to foreign yachtsmen, all German yacht clubs pay a substantial fee each year towards their upkeep, and German boat owners therefore share this cost. This fact should not be forgotten when visiting yacht clubs or mixing with local boat owners.

The smaller waterways are generally not controlled by the WSD and are usually operated by the appropriate *Land*. Most *Länder* make a nominal charge for using them.

Navigation

The normal rules of the road apply to users of the German waterways. Speed limits are clearly displayed and actively enforced by the WSP. Offenders are required to pay a substantial fine on the spot. Language is no excuse, and credit cards are not taken. All requisite warnings and other items of information are displayed by means of sign boards which conform to international standards. The more important of these signs are illustrated in the Appendix.

In general there are few problems in navigating these waterways, but there are several important matters which should be borne in mind. For example, when steering along a busy river, considerable concentration is called for, not only to be constantly aware of all traffic both ahead and astern, but also to observe all oncoming ships carefully to find out as early as possible whether they are 'blue-flagging'. All commercial vessels on the Rhein and other major waterways are required to carry a large square blue board (the 'blue flag') on the starboard side of the bridge. This board is normally carried horizontally, and is therefore virtually invisible to vessels approaching in the opposite direction. Should the helmsman wish, however, he or she has the option of turning the board vertical and therefore making it visible to oncoming vessels, indicating that he or she wishes to pass starboard to starboard. This option is very commonly used on rivers, especially the Rhein, where the vagaries of current and depth may make it

Around Bingen the Rhein seems to go wild.

Container barge with telescopic bridge.

Never release mooring lines until all the big ships have left.

Entering a deep lock can be a daunting experience.

difficult for large vessels to stick to the normal conventions. At busy times, when there may be as many as ten ships in your vicinity, you have to be aware not only of the channel markers (to avoid straying into shallow water), but also of the movements of all nearby ships, some of which will be blue-flagging and some not. This can cause the adrenaline to flow on occasion.

It is also important to be aware of some of the hydrographic effects of large power vessels moving through the water. When meeting a barge or other large vessel on a narrow canal, the width often dictates that you must pass within a few metres of the oncoming ship to avoid running aground. The natural reaction is to slow down to minimise the danger of grounding. However, the propeller of a large vessel creates a powerful suction, pulling water in from ahead and from both sides, ejecting it astern. A small vessel close abeam can therefore find itself sucked into collision with the larger one, and the slower the speed of the smaller vessel the more likely this is to happen. Some degree of skill may be required to judge the speed of your boat under these conditions. In practice, it is probably best to steer as close to the bank as possible with safety and to slow down almost to a standstill before the arrival of the ship, and then to open the throttle quite hard just before its bow is level with yours. If carried out skilfully this procedure will result in the boat having minimum speed but maximum manoeuvrability during the critical seconds while the two vessels are alongside each other.

Barges and other large vessels tend to travel at 6–7kn through the water, and if your cruising speed happens to be a little below this you will find that from time to time you are overtaken by a large vessel. Your natural reaction is to slow down to allow the other vessel to pass more quickly, but as you may be only a few metres from the ship the suction effect of the ship's propeller can be a danger if you slow down too much and lose steerage. Sometimes in this situation the barge skipper will help by closing his throttle at the critical point when his stern is almost abeam of you, thereby reducing the suction effect – but it might be unwise to assume that this will necessarily happen.

Similarly, if you come up behind a sizeable ship which is travelling at a slightly lower speed than you and you wish to overtake it you should take into account the fact that because the ship's propeller is constantly sucking in water from abeam and ahead, as your boat comes alongside your speed over the ground will reduce because of this artificial adverse current, and unless you have enough reserve of power to accelerate you may find that overtaking is impossible. At this point you will find that you are also unable to close your throttle for fear of losing control and being sucked into the stern of the vessel you have been trying to overtake. The secret is to slow down only slightly and to wait patiently for the barge to draw ahead. But keep an eye out for the over-helpful barge skipper who, recognising your predicament, closes his throttle to help you – just at the moment when you decide to give up the attempt and slow down yourself.

It is perhaps worth pointing out that the suction from passing ships applies equally well when a small boat is anchored at the side of the stream. In the event of engine trouble, or other emergency requiring the boat to anchor, it is essential to anchor both fore and aft. Unless the river is very wide, lying to a single anchor is not sufficient, as the scope of the anchor cable may be enough to allow you to be sucked helplessly into collision with a passing barge.

Locks

On the main waterways, because of the size and cost of the locks needed to accommodate the large vessels which need to use them, the tendency is to build as few locks as possible. It follows, therefore, that the average height of the locks is quite large. Some locks are well over 20m in height, and entering one of these can be a daunting experience. In practice, however, negotiating large locks is far less frightening than it might seem at first sight.

The Germans categorise the locks according to their type, and this is often reflected in the official name of a lock, for example *Doppelschleuse* Vogelgrün or *Schleusengruppe* Griesheim, indicating that the locks are double or multiple respectively. Some of the deeper locks are of a type resembling a vertical shaft with a guillotine gate at the bottom. This type of lock is known as a *Schachtschleuse* (shaft lock), for example *Schachtschleuse* Minden. However, even though the official name may include this categorisation, unless there is a possibility of confusion it is usual to refer to the lock (for example over VHF) simply as *Schleuse* Vogelgrün or *Schleuse* Griesheim. These categorisations have therefore been ignored in the route descriptions in this book.

Major locks on the commercial waterways are equipped with red and green lights (or in a few cases semaphores) to signal the state of the lock to waiting vessels and to give permission to enter. The signals are self-evident. If your German is sufficiently fluent you can also talk to the lock-keeper on VHF to discover the state of the lock and perhaps find out how long it will be necessary to wait before entering. In most cases small boats are expected to wait until any commercial vessels have entered, and then to tuck into any available space (if any) at the back of the lock. The normal practice therefore is either to tie up to some convenient mooring place or to hover, well clear of the lock gates but near enough to be able to enter quickly if and when the opportunity occurs. Generally it is advisable to approach the lock gates whilst the last ship is entering, to be able to enter the lock as soon as the turbulence from the ship has subsided. Lock-keepers cannot wait for sport boats if they are too far away.

A few locks have special mooring stages for sport boats, sometimes even with their own light signals to indicate when the lock is clear for entry. Or there may be an extension to the lock public address system for the benefit of waiting sport boats.

Amidships mooring to a floating bollard.

Once inside the lock, the technique used will undoubtedly vary from boat to boat according to personal preferences, although there are certain basic principles. Also, the method used when ascending will differ somewhat from that used when descending.

The locks on the main waterways are designed for large ships, with mooring bollards too widely spaced to allow a small boat to moor fore-and-aft. Instead, it is necessary to moor to a single bollard amidships. In tall locks, the mooring bollards are set in recesses in the lock wall in a vertical line, spaced at vertical intervals of about 1·5m, so that as the level of water rises or falls, the mooring warps can be shifted at intervals onto the next higher or next lower bollard. It is not difficult to develop a drill for this operation, and it is not normally hazardous except on rare occasions when strong turbulence is being experienced. Many of the larger and more modern locks are equipped with *Schwimmpoller* (floating bollards), which rise and fall with the level of the water, making life much simpler for a small craft. It should be borne in mind, however, that floating bollards have been known to stick before reaching the end of their travel, so it is wise to have some way of allowing lines to run if this should happen.

Mooring amidships is usually accomplished either by using a breast rope from a strong amidships mooring cleat or by bringing bow and stern lines together onto the same bollard. A single amidships line is undoubtedly quicker and easier to use, especially if it can be led back to a winch in the cockpit, but the strain on the fixing point can be very severe if there should be turbulence, and it may be considered prudent to use this arrangement as a convenient way of picking up the mooring, but then add bow and stern lines afterwards to ease the strain on the amidships point and to make the mooring doubly secure. Some locks, such as some of those on the Mosel, have very convenient vertical bars fixed to the stepladders which are set into the lock walls. By mooring amidships to these the mooring lines can be slid up or down, somewhat more convenient than moving them from one bollard to another as the water level changes.

When ascending, there will always be some risk of turbulence whilst the chamber is filling, and mooring lines should therefore be hauled tight before the lock starts to fill to minimise the extent to which turbulence can push the boat away from the lock wall. The engine should be kept running and if serious turbulence is experienced the strain can be reduced by engaging whichever gear is appropriate to counteract the flow of water. If the lock is an older one, the water inlet is usually via sluices in the top gate, and it is always best if going upwards to choose a bollard fairly close to the lower gate, as far away from the likely source of turbulence as possible. Even in the largest of German locks it is unusual for turbulence to be severe enough to be dangerous, but it is important to know that it can occur and that if appropriate precautions are not taken serious damage could be incurred. With many modern locks, such as those on the Main-Donau-Kanal, the water inlets are along the floor of the chamber, which usually makes for a much quieter flow. Even so it is not safe to assume that turbulence cannot exist, as water is admitted in distinct bursts, and at each burst turbulence can be created. Normal precautions should still be taken.

Descending is usually far less problematical than ascending, as the emptying of the chamber creates little turbulence within it. The biggest problem is that sometimes on entering a lock which is full (and not equipped with floating bollards) it may be difficult to know where on the lock wall the fixed bollards are located. It could be dangerous if it is discovered when the chamber starts to empty that the boat is not positioned over a line of bollards down the lock wall. If in doubt, ask – even if it is only in sign language.

Whether the lock is up or down, it is very important to be aware of the potential danger of turbulence from the propellers of large ships. The force of the water pushed out by the propeller of a 3,000-tonne ship or a powerful push-tow as it begins to move out of a lock, even under low power, is easily capable of wrenching a sturdy mooring cleat off the deck of a small boat. Do not be tempted to release mooring lines until all big ships have left the lock. Be aware also that this propeller wash can circulate from the stern of the vessel creating it around the closed end of the lock chamber and *forwards* along the wall opposite to the ship. This powerful reverse flow of water can take the skipper of a small boat off his or her guard and put immense strain on mooring cleats or even force the boat into collision with the lock wall.

On some rivers, for example the Mosel and the Main, many of the commercial locks have self-actuated boat locks alongside them, and sport boats, usually up to a maximum beam of 3·5 or 4 metres, are required to use these instead of the main locks. The procedure is to enter the lock, moor to a vertical rod, then climb onto the lock side, where a control box is situated. The control box has a lever which must be moved up or down to indicate the direction of travel, and a large knob which actuates the lock. When you are ready to leave, you press the knob again to open the appropriate gate. Full instructions are displayed on the control box.

At several places where a very deep lock would have been required, a *Hebewerk* (ship-lift) has been built instead. A ship-lift is essentially a moveable dock in which several ships can be moored. The gate is closed and the whole dock, complete with water and ships, is raised or lowered to the appropriate level. The other gate is then opened and the ships continue their journey. There are four of these mammoth lifts in Germany, two on western canals and two in the east. The two western lifts are modern, but the two eastern ones are gigantic monuments to the engineering feats of the past. Nevertheless they work perfectly well and, like their western equivalents, handle very large volumes of traffic, at the same time providing an irresistible spectacle for tens of thousands of onlookers every year. For the small pleasure boat they at first sight appear to present a daunting prospect, but in fact it is normally simpler and easier to use a ship-lift than to use an equivalent lock (or series of locks). The only practical problem is that most of the lifts are extremely busy and waiting times for barges are long. The secret is to tuck into a convenient corner within earshot of the Tannoy, so that if space can be found to accommodate a small boat behind a group of commercial ships you may be lucky enough to be called into the lift well ahead of your proper place in the queue. Listen to the Tannoy or VHF for the word *Sportboot*.

In the locks on the smaller waterways the situation is somewhat similar to that in France. Most of the locks are mechanised, but they are usually operated by a lock-keeper. You simply moor to bollards on the lock side, taking care to keep as far away from the upper gate as possible if you are going upwards, and let out or take in the lines as the lock empties or fills.

Overnight stops

On some of the major waterways commercial traffic continues throughout the night. Under no account should this be attempted in a small boat. The barge skippers know the waterways intimately and understand each other's habits, but for the foreign cruising skipper, navigating at night on the Rhein (for example) in the midst of heavy barge traffic is a nightmare. On most lakes around Berlin navigation at night is forbidden for pleasure boats.

Finding a place to stop for the night sometimes requires a little planning. On the smaller and less busy waterways it is usually very easy to find a quiet corner as dusk begins to fall, but on the larger rivers and canals this cannot be relied upon. Here it is best to think ahead and aim for a known harbour or yacht club which can be reached by 5 or 6 pm, and to have a contingency plan for an alternative stopping place which can still be reached during daylight hours in case there is a problem with the first choice. The problem is perhaps most acute on the more modern canals, such as the Main-Donau or the Elbe-Seiten, where there are often very long stretches without convenient moorings, and where it is forbidden to moor anywhere other than in a designated harbour. In eastern Germany too the choice of places to stop is slightly more restricted than in the western part of the country, simply because there are fewer yacht clubs. In other respects, however, the situation is similar.

Clearly the type of mooring place preferred is a matter of taste, and there is a wide variety to choose from. In the main most people find that it is best to look for a yacht club or yacht harbour away from the main stream if the waterway is likely to be in constant use during the night, where for a modest fee (usually £3–£4 a night) one gets a quiet berth, showers, the opportunity of a meal in the clubhouse – and usually a warm welcome.

Another convenient type of overnight stop is in a harbour provided by the local town council. These are usually safe and comfortable, but the facilities are often somewhat sparse compared with those at most yacht clubs. Nevertheless, as they are often situated close to town centres they can be extremely convenient.

One of the many harbours which exist for use by large commercial vessels can also provide a satisfactory overnight stop, but facilities for a small cruising boat are usually fairly non-existent and great care is required to find a spot in the harbour where you are unlikely to be a nuisance to larger vessels or to be damaged by them. Needless to say, one should always make an attempt to seek permission from the harbourmaster (if you can find one) before settling down for the night or leaving the boat to go to a restaurant.

On the main waterways there are quite often harbours operated by the WSAs (water authorities) to house their own work boats. Officially these are not available for sport boats, but it is sometimes possible to obtain permission to stay in one of these if there are no other mooring places in the vicinity. Sometimes too it is possible simply to anchor in a lake or backwater off the main channel, or to tie up alongside a vessel which is not in use and moored in an out-of-the-way corner. Similarly there are many industrial harbours at manufacturing plants on the side of the waterway where, in an emergency, it may be possible to stay for a brief overnight stop.

Probably the most satisfactory type of stopping place, however, is the quiet rural corner of a small canal or river, perhaps tied up to a grassy quay along the bank, moored in an out-of-the-way corner near a lock or anchored in some tranquil backwater.

Except when the boat is safely in a marina berth, a white anchor light should be displayed to warn other vessels of your presence. It is not unknown for a barge to turn up mysteriously in the middle of the night, expecting its regular mooring place to be free. A small vessel without a light could be very vulnerable.

If it is required to keep the boat in one place for a longer time, perhaps even over a winter, there are excellent secure storage facilities afloat or ashore at many yacht clubs. It would be advisable, however, to make enquiries well ahead of the time when the boat is to be left, as many such places tend to become over-subscribed and last-minute arrivals may be unlucky.

Fuel and water

On the whole, throughout the former West Germany there are few problems in finding convenient supplies of diesel fuel, either from bank-side fuelling stations or from the bunker boats which exist for the benefit of commercial shipping. On the rare occasions when it is not possible to find a means of refuelling alongside, there is almost certain to be a reasonably accessible street filling station for an emergency top-up. Note that when refuelling at a bunker boat it may occasionally be found that the delivery nozzle is too large for the normal small boat, as the prime purpose of these bunker boats is the refuelling of barges and other large vessels. Nor can it be guaranteed that a bunker boat will always be on station, as from time to time they may be taken to a fuel depot to replenish their supplies.

In the former East Germany, although things are steadily improving, it is advisable to ensure that your tanks are full before entering the area. If an emergency arises and a fuelling station cannot be found, it is best to contact a yacht club and explain your predicament. It would be unusual if help were not forthcoming.

Users of petrol will find the situation more difficult, and will frequently have to rely on carrying cans of fuel from the nearest roadside filling station.

Water supplies are not a problem, and tanks can be replenished either at bunker stations whilst refuelling or from hosepipes at yacht clubs, locks or harbours. Facilities for emptying holding tanks are becoming increasingly widespread, and enquiries will usually enable the necessary service to be located (except perhaps in the former East Germany, where such facilities are less common).

Depths and bridge clearances displayed on the Havel.

Channel depths

For most of the German waterways a *Tauchtiefe* (maximum permitted draught) is stipulated, either for the whole length of the waterway or for predetermined segments of it. Waterway users are legally required to observe the *Tauchtiefen*, and failure to do so could result in insurance and legal problems in the event of an accident in which grounding was a factor. In some cases, notably rivers subject to varying levels, *Tauchtiefen* change from day to day; they are published daily in a variety of ways, and usually related to the *Pegelstand* (level of water at a *Pegel* (depth gauge)). *Pegels* are situated at strategic intervals along each major waterway whose level is not constant.

On the Rhein, instead of quoting *Tauchtiefen* a slightly different system is used, based on a stated *Gleichwertiger Wasserstand-Fahrrinnentiefe* (normal channel depth) for each stretch of the river. It is important always to be aware of the current situation for the waterway in use, especially during dry periods when water levels are low. The system applicable to each waterway is outlined in the relevant route description in Part II.

During times of flood, all traffic may be banned if the water level exceeds a certain level. Such conditions normally occur only during winter or early spring, and if the situation arises it will be made amply evident that navigation is prohibited.

VHF radio

On all the major waterways there is a well organised *UKW* (VHF) radio communication system, heavily used by the skippers of commercial vessels. Conventions vary slightly, but in general Ch 10 is used for calling and safety purposes, much as Ch 16 is used at sea. The general channel allocations on the Rhein and the Elbe are given in the introductory information for each river in Part II. The channels for communicating with locks are given on a lock-by-lock basis in the route descriptions. In many cases it will be found that the *UKW* channel for the next lock is displayed on a board at the side of the waterway.

Boats and equipment

Few normal cruising boats are unsuitable for the German waterways. The ideal, perhaps, is the type of boat which has evolved over the years as almost the standard boat used by the Germans (and the Dutch). This is a steel motor cruiser, usually between 8–12m in length, with a draught of 1–1.2m, a centre bridge, an exterior steering position, a single propeller and a diesel engine giving a normal cruising speed of 7–8kn but capable of 10kn if the need arises. However, although such a boat may be most suitable, any boat with a draught of less than 1.8m and capable of sustaining a speed of 4–5kn will be able to cruise widely in Germany with only a few limitations. It is not really practicable to think of going upstream in the Rhein or the Donau in any boat which cannot cruise at a steady 8–10kn. Nor is it likely that any boat drawing more than 1.2m would be suitable for exploring a number of waterways in the eastern part of Germany in late summer.

Converted barges, ideal for inland waterway cruising in so many ways, usually have a displacement of more than 15 tonnes, and will therefore require a fully qualified captain for use in Germany.

There is considerable debate about the relative merits of single- and twin-propeller configurations. The advantage of the additional manoeuvrability provided by twin propellers may be offset by the increased probability of grounding against the shelving sides of canals, especially if, as is standard practice in the building of many canals, the profile of the canal bottom is constructed of broken rocks. With the emergence of bow thrusters, however, it seems likely that the ideal configuration will become a single propeller in combination with a bow thruster.

Wasserstände displayed at Mühlheim lock.

Sailing boats with their masts carried horizontally are an increasingly common sight on German inland waters, as boat owners begin to realise that an inland route can be a more interesting and comfortable way of reaching the Baltic or Eastern Europe than the usual offshore route. Provided care is taken to avoid damage to the overhanging spars there are no real problems to this. There are plenty of yacht clubs (or boatyards – but they tend to be more expensive) with cranes suitable for stepping and unstepping masts, and it is not difficult to construct two or three wooden crutches for carrying the spars horizontally.

For those who do not have the good fortune to own their own boat, or for boat owners who do not have the time for the lengthy journeys to and from Germany, it is very easy to charter a boat in Germany. A selection of charter companies is given in Appendix III.

Apart from the needs of safety, mentioned earlier, there are no special requirements for boat equipment, although for long journeys involving wide rivers and perhaps lakes or coastal waters it is very useful to have an autopilot. For exploring some of the smaller canals and rivers where (as in France) there is a danger of weed blocking the cooling-water intake, some form of audible or visible engine-overheating alarm has its advantages. In any case, it makes good sense to inspect the water-intake strainer daily to guard against clogging. A horn, although not likely to be used regularly, should be instantly available for use in an emergency.

From the earlier discussion on using locks, it should go without saying that good fendering is essential. Many small boats carry several car tyres for this purpose, but unless they are suitably covered they can be very unsightly and leave almost indelible black marks on the boat's topsides. Many people prefer simply to carry several extra large conventional fenders, which may be less offensive to the eye. It is also extremely useful to carry a good strong plank with a line attached to each end. By hanging this outside the fenders it is possible to moor alongside piled walls without difficulty. Indeed, you will find occasional locks with piled walls, and without a plank there may be a considerable danger of damaging the topsides of the boat. It need hardly be mentioned that the image of a well managed boat will be enhanced if fenders are taken up and stowed on deck promptly on leaving a lock.

All cruising boats accumulate a collection of hose fittings and electrical adapters. There is, surprisingly, no sign of standardisation in Germany so far as hose fittings are concerned, but *Strom* (electricity) outlets are usually either two-pin, with earth contacts on the sides, or the blue European standard fittings.

Camping Gaz is widely available on an exchange basis, and propane cylinders can usually be refilled at major depots. The further east one goes, the less easy it is to obtain *Camping Gaz*, and it is wise to have a propane regulator on board.

A powerful push-tow without barges.

It is useful but by no means essential to carry a dinghy for use on the odd occasion when it is desirable to anchor away from the shore, but by far the most useful accessory is undoubtedly the bicycle. A couple of small bikes make shopping and exploration so much easier and more enjoyable, especially as cyclists are so well catered for throughout Germany. It is quite unnecessary to invest in expensive folding bikes. The standard cheap 'shopping bicycle' is perfectly satisfactory and a good deal less attractive to potential thieves.

A car transporter near the Dutch border.

Routes

By general consensus, the favourite cruising grounds are (in no particular order) the Neckar, the Rhein Gorge, the Lahn, the Mosel, the Saar, the Main, the Donau, the upper Weser, the upper Elbe, Berlin, the Spree with its associated waterways, the Mecklenburg lake district and the *Bodden* of northeast Germany. In addition, there are many through routes which provide connections between these areas and also make it possible to reach the waterways of other countries.

The major through routes are:

A From the North Sea to the Baltic via the Nord-Ostsee-Kanal (fixed-mast route). A more interesting variation is to use the Eider for the first part of the journey.

B From the Netherlands upstream along the Rhein.

C From France into the Rhein via the Rhone-Rhein-Kanal, the Rhein-Marne-Kanal or the Mosel, then northwards into Holland or Routes D to I.

D From the Rhein to the Black Sea via the Main, the Main-Donau-Kanal and the Donau.

E From the Rhein to the North Sea via the Rhein-Herne or Wesel-Datteln-Kanal and the Dortmund-Ems-Kanal (masts up at Ditzum).

F From the Rhein to the Baltic via the Rhein-Herne or Wesel-Datteln-Kanal, the Dortmund-Ems-Kanal, the Mittellandkanal, the Elbe-Seiten-Kanal and the Elbe-Lübeck-Kanal (masts up in the Passathafen at Travemünde).

G From the Rhein to the Baltic via the Mittellandkanal, the Elbe, the Elbe-Havel-Kanal, the Havel-Oder-Wasserstrasse and the Oder (masts up in Marina Marco at Szczecin).

H To the Czech Republic via a modification of Route F, turning upstream in the Elbe at Magdeburg.

I To the Polish rivers via another modification of Route F, branching off at Berlin through the Spree to the Oder.

The main factors which influence the planning of routes in Germany are the currents and depths of the major rivers.

In the Rhein the current is quite strong throughout the year, and very strong in the spring. It is normally best to use the French canals in such a way as to avoid any travel upstream in the Rhein, unless of course the boat is capable of the necessary speed. A downstream passage is usually trouble-free at least up to the end of July, or even later for shallower-draught boats or in wet summers. An upstream passage through the Rhein Gorge and further up to Iffezheim is difficult at the best of times, and for most boats impossible before the end of May, as the current along this stretch can be anything up to 10kn.

In the Donau the current is very strong in the spring, and unless speeds of 10kn or so are possible an upstream journey should not be contemplated until early July at least. For downstream passages in times of flood, it is wise to make enquiries along the river to ensure that bridge clearances are adequate.

The currents in the Elbe are on the whole less of a problem than those in the Rhein and the Donau, but in most years vessels drawing more than 1·2m may have problems above Lauenburg after about the end of June. The short stretch of the Elbe connecting the Mittellandkanal to the Elbe-Havel-Kanal may have as little as 1·2m of water by the end of July, depending on rainfall.

The length of time required for any given journey naturally depends on the speed of the boat, the length of time travelled each day, the number of locks on the route, the number of days allowed for exploration ashore and of course the assistance (or otherwise) gained from any current. As a rough guide, it should be possible to cover an average of 50km a day, given a boat capable of cruising at 5–6kn, without having to get out of bed at the crack of dawn each day. This means that in practice it is possible to travel the 320km from the Rhein to the Elbe comfortably in about six days. By contrast, with the help of a moderate current in midsummer, a journey of some 630km downstream along the Rhein from Niffer to Wesel can be accomplished in a mere five days.

Part II. Waterways guide

Introduction

This section of the book is made up of detailed route descriptions for every navigable waterway in Germany. The information provided should enable a small-boat skipper to navigate any waterway he or she wishes without further documentation, but it will undoubtedly be useful to use the book in conjunction with the appropriate 1:200,000 sheets of the general touring map sold under the title of *Die General Karte* and easily available in almost any book shop in Germany.

Waterways are not necessarily described in the same direction as the kilometre markings. The height of each lock is quoted as a rise or a fall according to the direction in which the waterway is described. The terms 'left bank' and 'right bank' are used in a conventional sense (i.e. when pointing downstream) in connection with rivers only. In the case of canals, where 'left' and 'right' may cause confusion, the banks are called, for example, 'north' or 'south'. All waterway features referred to in the route descriptions are identified by their kilometre locations, reflecting the fact that all waterways have clearly marked kilometre posts along their banks.

Most of the major waterways in Germany have designated *Tauchtiefen* (maximum permitted draughts), which are legal requirements, but there are slight variations in the systems used for different waterways, and for the sake of simplicity a 'maximum draught' is quoted for each waterway, whether or not this is technically a *Tauchtiefe*.

Speed limits for pleasure craft are quoted in the section on each waterway. Where not otherwise stated, the speed limit on lakes is 25km/h at a minimum distance of 100m from the shore.

All lock operating hours relate to the summer months if not otherwise stated.

Since by far the greater number of German place names have no English translation, in the interests of consistency only the German versions of place names are used in Part II.

South

DONAU

The Donau, Europe's second-longest river after the Volga, rises on the eastern edge of the *Schwarzwald* (Black Forest) and flows northeastwards through the picturesque but little-known *Schwäbische Alb* (Swabian Mountains) to Ulm, the upper limit of navigation.

From Ulm to Kelheim the river flows through attractive Bavarian countryside. It is navigable only by small boats. Its 16 dams each have a lock and a hydroelectric generating plant.

Downstream from Kelheim, the Donau is an international waterway used for transport purposes by cargo vessels and passenger ships from many countries. The opening of the Main-Donau-Kanal completed the link between East and West, fulfilling a dream several centuries old. This part of the Donau valley is wide and flat, full of cornfields and livestock farms. To the north lies the *Bayerischer Wald* (Bavarian Forest), an area of outstanding natural beauty. Here and there along the river stand many fine examples of Bavarian Baroque abbeys. The brown waters of the Donau, although far from fulfilling the image evoked by Johann Strauss, do seem to carry you past a magical backdrop of beautiful countryside and picturesque towns like Regensburg, Straubing and Passau and on into Austria.

The river is administered by WSD-Süd from Kelheim to the Austrian border, and there are no fees for pleasure craft using this section.

1. ULM TO KELHEIM
Km 2585–Km 2411

Total distance 174km
Locks 16 (one more lock is planned, at Neustadt)

Ulm, although technically in the *Land* of Baden-Württemberg, is undoubtedly Bavarian in nature. The birthplace of Einstein, Ulm's historic centre has been superbly restored. The *Fischerviertel* (fishermen's quarter), with its narrow cobbled streets and half-timbered houses, the riverside gardens, and the *Münster* (cathedral), with its 161m-high steeple, are all Bavarian in character.

Downstream from Ulm, the old fortified town of Donauwörth stands on a hill overlooking the confluence of the Wörnitz with the Donau. Ingolstadt, the home of the Audi car, also has a well restored *Altstadt* (old town), with the remains of a city wall, half-timbered houses and exquisite Renaissance façades. 5km before reaching Kelheim the river runs through the spectacular Donaudurchbruch, a rocky gorge with 120m-high limestone cliffs, and passes the isolated Benedictine monastery of Weltenburg.

This part of the Donau is really only navigable by boats with a maximum height of 2·00m and draught of 1·00m, and special permission from the Burgermeister of Ingolstadt must be obtained if you wish to take your boat from Ulm to Kelheim. Liability insurance is obligatory, as is a technical inspection of the boat. When you apply for permission for the journey you are sent a list of dangers along the river, the chief of which are low bridges on the Ulm–Donauwörth stretch. As this part of the river is controlled by the *Land* of Bayern (Bavaria), and not by WSD, there is a charge. A permit costs DM 40, needs three weeks' notice and can be obtained only once a year. The address to write to is Stadt Ingolstadt, Postfach 21 09 64, Spitalstrasse 3, Ingolstadt, Germany. Boats with engines more powerful than 136hp are not allowed. There are no navigation marks and the current is very strong. The boat locks are 20x4m. Upstream passages are not permitted.

Schleuse Böfinger Halde is operated by lockkeepers. All others are self-service.

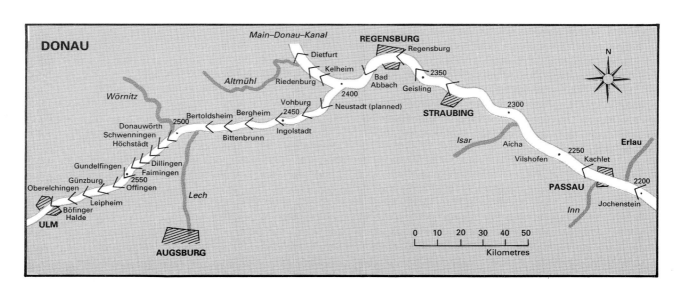

Km
ca2585 **Ulm.**
2581·5 *Schleuse Böfinger Halde*
Fall 6·50m.
2578·8 Motor-Yacht-Club Ulm.
2575·0 *Schleuse Oberelchingen*
Fall 5·75m.
2568·4 *Schleuse Leipheim*
Fall 5·85m.
2562·8 *Schleuse Günzburg*
Fall 5·40m.
ca2560 **Günzburg.**
2556·3 *Schleuse Offingen*
Fall 4·55m.
2551·9 *Schleuse Gundelfingen*
Fall 4·55m.
2545·5 *Schleuse Faimingen*
Fall 5·60m.
2539·0 *Schleuse Dillingen*
Fall 4·65m.
ca2537 **Dillingen.**
2530·8 *Schleuse Höchstädt*
Fall 5·75m.
2522·3 *Schleuse Schwenningen*
Fall 5·15m.
2511·9 *Schleuse Donauwörth*
Fall 5·15m.
ca2510 **Donauwörth.**
2490·1 *Schleuse Bertoldsheim*
Fall 4·85m.
2480·2 *Schleuse Bittenbrunn*
Fall 5·15m.
ca2480 **Neuburg.**
2470·0 *Schleuse Bergheim*
Fall 6·00m.
2459·2 *Schleuse Ingolstadt*
Fall 5·10m.
ca2458 **Ingolstadt.** Strong current.
2444·1 *Schleuse Vohburg*
Fall 6·80m.
ca2438 Schloss Wackerstein.
ca2432 **Neustadt.**
2431·6 Harbour of Neustadt water authority.
2422·5 Possible anchorage.
ca2421 **Kloster Weltenburg.**
2420 to
2416 **Donaudurchbruch.** Spectacular rocky gorge.
Nature reserve. No anchoring. Strong current.
Beware tripper boats.
2414·7 Entrance to old Ludwig-Donau-Main-Kanal.
ca2414 **Kelheim.**
2411·5 Junction with Main-Donau-Kanal.

2. KELHEIM TO AUSTRIAN BORDER
Km 2411–Km 2202

Total distance 209km
Maximum draught 1·70m
Maximum height 4·6m
Current 4–20km/h
Locks 6

The enchanting city of Regensburg began life as a garrison town in Roman times, and over the ages maintained a level of prosperity which can still be seen in the well preserved mediaeval buildings of the old town. It is dominated by the twin spires of St Peter's Cathedral, a superb example of Gothic architecture, and the *Steinerne Brücke* (stone bridge), built in 1146, is a masterpiece of early engineering.

Perched high on a wooded hillside overlooking the river a short distance downstream from Regensburg is the famous Walhalla, a replica of a Grecian temple built in 1842 by Ludwig I of Bavaria. Beyond Wörth, with its eight-turreted castle, the river winds its way to the charming old town of Straubing, also a major centre for the thriving agricultural area surrounding the town.

Deggendorf, another attractive old Bavarian town, has colourful market stalls and a delightful promenade. Its annual *Volkfest* at the end of July and the music week in August are important events in the area.

Passing the Benedictine monastery of St Mauritius, the river flows near to Osterhofen, with the elaborate Baroque monastery church of St Margaretha, past Hilgartsberg Castle at Hofkirchen, through Vilshofen and Windorf, where there is a bird reserve on a large island, to the city of Passau, dramatically situated on a spit of land between the Donau and its broad tributary, the Inn.

With its narrow streets, elegant squares and many mediaeval buildings, Passau is a major tourist centre, but it is also a modern city with excellent facilities for sport and the arts. It hosts an annual music and drama festival, and every day at noon in summer vast crowds flock to hear a recital on the famous 17,000-pipe organ in St Stephen's Cathedral, which dominates the whole city.

At Schleuse Jochenstein, 20km below Passau, the Donau crosses the border into Austria on its long journey to the Black Sea via Vienna, Budapest and Belgrade.

The German part of the river is administered by WSD-Süd and there are no fees. Two new locks between Straubing and Kachlet (Waltendorf and Osterhofen) are planned in order to reduce the strength of the current. All locks are of a size suitable for commercial ships, but there are also boat locks at Bad Abbach and Regensburg, with a width of 4m, albeit with depth restrictions in both cases. There are fixed bollards on all locks but there is little turbulence whilst the chamber is filling, except of course near the top gates.

The river is well buoyed where appropriate, using the normal convention of reds to starboard and greens to port downstream. Kilometre signs and warning signs are also provided.

Hydrology

As with most rivers, the strength of the current and the depth of the channel vary with the rainfall in the catchment area. The river is notionally divided into four stretches, and for each stretch a depth known as the *Regulierungsniederwasserstand* (regulated lower water level), or *RNW*, is quoted daily. This depth corresponds to a specific depth measured at a *Pegel* (water-level gauge) situated within the stretch. The variation from this water level at the *Pegel* is then made widely available at locks, over VHF and on local radio, so that the actual depths of water along the river can easily be calculated. Unlike those along the Rhein, however, the depths thus arrived at are not guaranteed. The *RNW* values together with the corresponding *Pegel* readings are set out below.

DONAU CHANNEL DEPTHS

Kelheim to Lazarettspitze-Regensburg (via Northern branch)
RNW 2·90m when *Pegel* Oberndorf 1·78m

Lazarettspitze-Regensburg to Geisling
RNW 2·90m when *Pegel* Regensburg-Schwabelweis 2·95m

Geisling to Deggendorf
RNW 1·70m when *Pegel* Pfelling 2·98m

Deggendorf to Vilshofen
RNW 2·00m when *Pegel* Hofkirchen 2·15m

Vilshofen to Kachlet
RNW 2·70m when *Pegel* Hofkirchen 2·15m

Kachlet to Jochenstein
RNW 2·70m when *Pegel* Passau-Donau 4·14m

Note also:
Bad Abbach boat lock to end of lock cut
RNW 0·90m when *Pegel* Oberndorf 1·78m

Southern branch from Regensburg boat lock to iron bridge Regensburg
RNW 0·90m when *Pegel* Regensburg-Schwabelweis 2·95m

Note that in times of drought water levels can be below the *RNW* figures.

At *RNW*, the current along most of this part of the Donau is between 1km/h and 10km/h. The fastest-flowing section is in the region of Passau, Km 2230–Km 2222, where the surface water speed is around 7km/h even at low water levels. In times of flood it can run at 20km/h, and some ships may be unable to pass under several of the bridges, notably the railway bridge at Deggendorf. At such times the strength of the current can make cruising in a small boat hazardous.

From the Austrian border to the mouth of the river on the Black Sea coast the minimum depth in mid-channel is quoted as 2·30m.

Km
2411·5 Junction with Main-Donau-Kanal.
2411·0 Marina Saal on right bank. Depth 2·5m. Operated by Boote Rammelmeyr KG. Water, electricity, showers, fuel, repairs, crane, restaurant.
2403·5 Sportboothafen Donautal Kapfelberg on left bank. Operated by Motorsportclub Kelheim. Water, electricity, showers, fuel by arrangement, slip, shops in village.
2397·5 *Schleuse Bad Abbach*
Fall 5·7m.
VHF Ch 19.
Hours 0600–2200.
Boat lock on right bank. Entrance 40m above top gate of main lock. Check headroom at boat lock if water level is high.
2386·9 Sportboothafen Sinzing on left bank. Depth 1·4m. Operated by Motorboot- und-Wasserski-club Regensburg. Water, electricity, showers, slip, crane, bar, shops and restaurant 10 minutes.

Northern branch
2379·7 *Schleuse Regensburg*
Fall 5·2m.
VHF Ch 82.
Hours 0600–2200.

Southern branch
2381·3 *Bootschleuse Regensburg*
Fall 5·2m.
Check headroom if water level is high.
2380·8 Regensburger Motorboot- und Wassersport-verein. Water, electricity, showers, repairs, crane, holding-tank emptying. Fuel from nearby filling station. Shops and restaurants in town.
ca2380 **Regensburg**.
2379·6 Steinerne Brücke (stone bridge). Height 3·0–3·8m. Beware strong currents and eddies.
2377·7 Branches reunite.
2377 to
2372 Port of Regensburg.
2368·7 **Walhalla**. Mooring difficult because of tripper-boat traffic.
2354·3 *Schleuse Geisling*
Fall 7·3m.
VHF Ch 22.
Hours 24hrs.

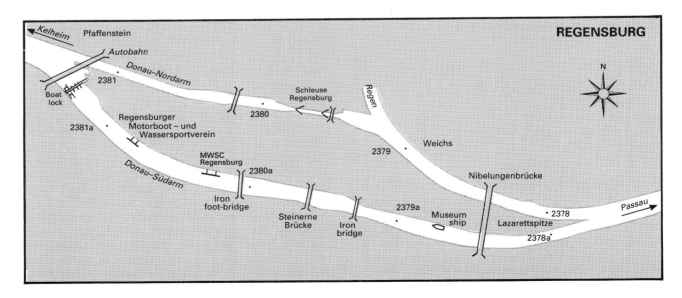

2343 to	
2315	River narrow and with many sharp bends. Keep clear of commercial traffic.
2324·3	*Schleuse Straubing* *Fall 5·4m.* *VHF Ch 18.* *Hours 24hrs.*
ca2321	**Straubing**.
ca2319	Entrance to weir stream, navigation permitted up to Schlossbrücke. Access to town from ferry jetty. Camp site with kiosk.
2314·0	Motorboot- und Wasserskiclub Straubing on right bank. Water, electricity, showers, slip. Small repairs, holding-tank emptying. Shops and restaurants 2km.
2309·0	**Hermannsdorf**. Anchorage by right bank opposite entrance to Bogener Altwasser (entry forbidden) on left bank.
2305·8	**Pfelling**. Possible mooring at ferry ramp.
2297·3	**Mariaposching**. Possible anchorage near ferry by left bank.
2289·5	**Metten**. Possible anchorage at entrance to Mettener Altarm, the backwater behind Mettener island, which is a nature reserve.
2288·6	Staging of Motorbootclub Deggendorf. Rudimentary facilities.
ca2285	**Deggendorf**.
2284·0	Donau-Yacht-Club Deggendorf. Water, electricity, fuel 200m, restaurant.
2270·0	**Mühlham**. Small overnight mooring place for up to three boats.
2261·2	Langer Haufen. Anchor at entrance to backwater at downstream end of island on right bank. No facilities.
2257·0	**Hofkirchen**. Motorbootclub Hofkirchen. Water and electricity on the pontoon. Showers in nearby restaurant Hafenstüberl. Fuel from nearby filling station. Shops.
2249·2	**Vilshofen**. Possible mooring at commercial pontoons in river.
2237·9	Restaurant Fischerstüberl. Pontoon in river. Water. Showers in restaurant.
2232·5	**Heining**. Motor-Yacht-Club Passau on right bank. Boats up to 7m long in harbour. Larger boats moor outside. Water, electricity, showers, bar, slip, crane, small repairs.
2230·6	*Schleuse Kachlet* *Fall 9·8m.* *VHF Ch 20.* *Hours 0500–2300.*
2228·3	Hafen Passau-Racklau on right bank. Water authority harbour, but permission may be obtained for overnight mooring. No facilities.
2226·0	**Passau**. Possibility of mooring on left bank at the Luitpoldbrücke.
2225·5	Junction with River Inn. Entry forbidden.
2224·0	Restaurant Aschenberger on left bank. Staging in river.
2223 to	
2203	Right bank Austria, left bank Germany.
2222·1	Tankschutzhafen Passau-Lindau on left bank. Possible overnight mooring with harbourmaster's permission.
2215·0	Junction with River Erlau on left bank. Possible anchorage in mouth of Erlau.
2211·4	Sportboothafen Obernzell. Two small harbours on left bank. Guest berths just inside upstream harbour. Water, electricity, showers, slip, fuel from nearby filling station.
2209·8	Customs. Austrian on right bank near ferry, German on left bank opposite.
2208·4	Sportboothafen Kasten on right bank. Water, electricity, showers, slip, crane. Fuel 150m. Shops nearby.
2205·6	Harbour of European Sea Scouts on left bank.
2203·3	*Schleuse Jochenstein* *Fall 10·2m.* *VHF Ch 22.* *Hours 24.* Note that the lock is on the border. Boats enter in Germany and exit in Austria.

MAIN–DONAU–KANAL

Total distance 171km
Maximum draught 2·50m
Maximum height 5·50m
Maximum beam 11·4m
Current Negligible
Speed limit 13km/h
Locks 16
Hours 0600–2200 weekdays. 0600–1330 Sundays.

The first attempt to link the Rhein and the Donau was ordered by Charlemagne. Work started on a short canal connecting their tributaries, the Altmühl and the Rednitz, in the year 793, but the project was abandoned after a few months. Parts of the canal are still to be seen near Weissenburg.

The Bavarian king Ludwig I revived the idea, and work started in 1837 with a workforce of 6,000. The canal, linking Bamberg to Kelheim, was opened

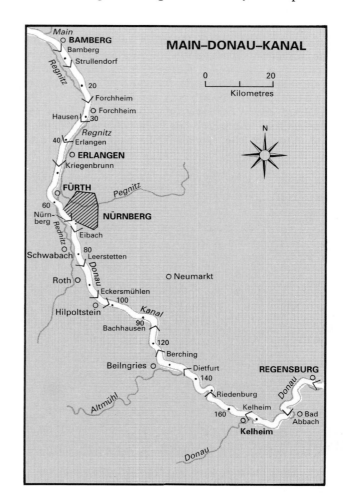

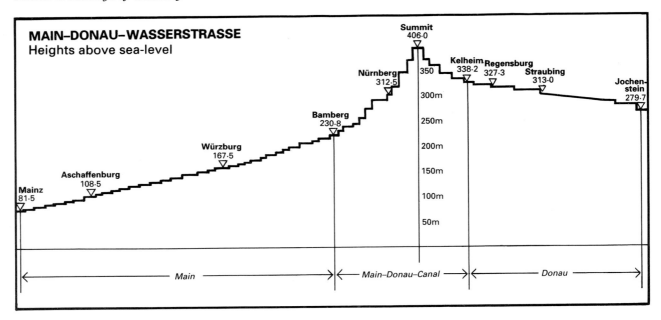

MAIN–DONAU–WASSERSTRASSE
Heights above sea-level

Summit 406·0
Nürnberg 312·5
Kelheim 338·2
Regensburg 327·3
Straubing 313·0
Jochenstein 279·7
Bamberg 230·8
Würzburg 167·5
Aschaffenburg 108·5
Mainz 81·5

350
300m
250m
200m
150m
100m
50m

← Main → ← Main–Donau–Canal → ← Donau →

fully in 1846. By 1850 the Ludwig-Donau-Main-Kanal was carrying almost 200,000 tonnes of freight a year. However, because the horse-drawn canal barges were not really suitable for the as yet poorly regulated Main and Donau, the canal could not compete with the booming railways. Although it remained in use until the 1940s, it is now merely an interesting relic of a bygone age.

The present Main-Donau-Kanal came into being as a result of the founding in 1892 of the Deutscher Kanal- und Schiffahrtsverein Rhein-Main-Donau (German Rhein-Main-Donau Canal and Shipping Association). After many political attacks and uncertainties, the project finally came to fruition on 25 September 1992 with the opening of the complete link between the North Sea and the Black Sea. The diagram above demonstrates the magnitude of the engineering task which has been achieved in linking the Rhein to the Donau: 555km of waterway, 50 locks and a summit level of 406m (over 1,300ft) above sea level.

The canal, which is under the control of WSD-Süd, has been built to carry both the standard 1,350-tonne 'Europa' barge and the two-unit pushed train carrying up to 3,300 tonnes. Because of the shortage of water along the route, the most recent locks are of the water-saving variety, using side ponds into which 60% of the water from the lock flows when the lock empties. This means that only 40% of the water used flows into the downstream reach. The canal is also used to transport water from the Donau basin to the Regnitz-Main area, where water is less plentiful.

The traffic forecasts for the Main-Donau connection predict volumes of between 4,000,000 and 15,000,000 tonnes per annum, and the new waterway is expected to compete strongly with existing means of transport.

The canal traverses the central part of Bayern (Bavaria), with beautiful rolling countryside and historic towns and cities, of which Bamberg and Nürnberg are the most famous.

Bamberg is a historic town of great interest, mercifully untouched by the bombs of World War II. Amongst its many treasures, the amazing town hall stands in the centre of the river like an anchored ship, whilst downstream from it old fishermen's houses crowd the river bank at Klein Venedig (Little Venice).

The handsome city of Nürnberg (Nuremberg), with its close associations with Adolf Hitler and the Third Reich, suffered very badly from Allied bombing in World War II, but has been carefully reconstructed to its former glory. Unfortunately the northern outskirts, through which the canal passes, are somewhat industrial.

Note the major restrictions on anchoring and mooring along the canal. It is necessary to plan ahead carefully to ensure safe arrival at a comfortable harbour by nightfall. It is not permitted to leave boats unmanned on the Main-Donau-Kanal.

French ship leaving Schleuse Hilpoltstein on the Main-Donau-Kanal.

Km

0·0 **Bamberg**. Start of canal.

2·5 Motorbootclub Regnitz-Main. In entrance to non-navigable western arm of Regnitz. Water and electricity but no sanitation.

2·6 Hafen Bamberg – *Hafenbecken* (Basin) 2. Depth 2m. 30 minutes' walk to city centre, but bus stop 2 minutes away. No facilities, but repairs can be arranged at nearby firms.

7·4 *Schleuse Bamberg*
Rise 10·9m.
Bollards Fixed.
VHF Ch 20.

7·4 to
22·2 Anchoring forbidden.

13·3 *Schleuse Strullendorf*
Rise 7·4m.
Bollards Fixed.
VHF Ch 22.

25·1 Motoryachtclub Forchheim, 0·8km into weir stream. Water, electricity, showers, slip, bar. Shops, filling station and restaurants 2·5km in Forchheim.

25·9 *Schleuse Forchheim*
Rise 5·3m.
Bollards Fixed.
VHF Ch 78.

ca28 **Forcheim**.

28·4 Yachtclub Forchheim. In entrance to old river immediately before footbridge. Water, electricity, showers, slip, bar, supermarket nearby, filling station 2km in Forchheim.

32·9 *Schleuse Hausen*
Rise 12·0m.
Bollards Fixed.
VHF Ch 79.

32·9 to
114·7 Anchoring forbidden.

41·1 *Schleuse Erlangen*
Rise 18·3m.
Bollards Fixed.
VHF Ch 81.

ca45 **Erlangen**.

47·8 Bunker boat for diesel, water and gas (propane).

48·7 *Schleuse Kriegenbrunn*
Rise 18·3m.
Bollards Fixed.
VHF Ch 82.

57·5 Sportboothafen Fürth-Unterfarrnbach. Tiny harbour on west bank. No facilities.

ca58 **Fürth**.

65·2 Motor-Yacht-Club Nürnberg. Finger pontoons. Water, electricity, showers, slip, bar, shops and restaurants nearby. Bus to Nürnberg. Fuel by arrangement or from filling station 10 minutes' walk away.

ca66 **Nürnberg**.

69·0 Bunker boat for diesel and water.

69·1 *Schleuse Nürnberg*
Rise 9·4m.
Bollards Fixed.
VHF Ch 18.

72·0 Hafen Nürnberg. Commercial harbour only.

73·0 *Schleuse Eibach*
Rise 19·5m.
Bollards Floating – east wall only.
VHF Ch 20.

84·5 *Schleuse Leerstetten*
Rise 24·7m.
Bollards Floating – east wall only.
VHF Ch 22.

95·1 *Schleuse Eckersmühlen*
Rise 24·7m.
Bollards Floating – east wall only.
VHF Ch 78.

ca98 **Hilpoltstein**.

99·1 *Schleuse Hilpoltstein*
Rise 24·7m.
Bollards Floating – east wall only.
VHF Ch 79.

99·1 to
115·6 Summit reach.

115·6 *Schleuse Bachhausen*
Fall 17·0m.
Bollards Floating – east wall only.
VHF Ch 81.

120·0 Berchinger Yacht-Club. Moor stern to buoy. Water, electricity on staging. Showers nearby. Shops and restaurants in Berching (1km). Fuel by arrangement.

121·0 Steganlage Berching. Staging on east bank in town. No facilities.

122·6 *Schleuse Berching*
Fall 17·0m.
Bollards Floating – east wall only.
VHF Ch 82.

128·5 Sportboothafen Beilngries. Water, electricity on staging. Showers in nearby restaurant.

ca129 **Beilngries**.

135·4 *Schleuse Dietfurt*
Fall 17·0m
Bollards Floating – east wall only.
VHF Ch 18.

136·6 Sportboothafen Dietfurt. Anchor in tiny basin or moor to bank. Minimal facilities.

149·5 Sportboothafen Riedenburg. Small harbour without facilities on west bank.

149·8 to
151·0 Anchoring forbidden.

151·0 *Schleuse Riedenburg*
Fall 8·4m.
Bollards Floating – west wall only.
VHF Ch 20.
Boat lock 20x4m on east side of main lock.

152·6 **Riedenburg**. If not in use by passenger vessels moor to staging on west bank. Close to centre of town but no facilities.

161·5 **Essing**.

161·5 to
166·1 Anchoring forbidden.

166·1 *Schleuse Kelheim*
Fall 8·4m.
Bollards Floating – east wall only.
VHF Ch 78.
Boat lock 20x4m.

168·0 **Kelheim**. Staging on west bank near *Altstadt* (old town). Uncomfortable and no facilities. It is preferable to moor at Marina Saal in the Donau.

171·0 Junction with Donau Km 2411·5.

MAIN

Total distance 384km
Maximum draught Kostheim–Aschaffenburg 2·60m.
  Aschaffenburg–Bamberg 2·30m.
Maximum height 4·8m (except boat locks)
Current Negligible (can be 5km/h after prolonged
  heavy rain)
Speed limit None (except 8km/h in canal at
  Gerlachshausen)
Locks 34
Hours Kostheim–Kleinostheim 24hrs.
  Obernau–Viereth 0600–2200 weekdays,
  0600–1400 Sundays.

The Main valley is very beautiful and very interest-ing. The exciting modern city of Frankfurt is the financial centre of Germany. Würzburg, 250km upstream, is one of the finest of Europe's historic cities. Most of the route, however, is amongst vine-covered slopes, attractive villages and forested hills. This is perhaps the heartland of German tradition, famous for its artists and craftsmen, but with all these riches it is off the beaten tourist track.

The waterway is controlled by WSD-Süd, and there are no fees. There were originally 37 locks between the Rhein and Bamberg, but the number was reduced to 34 by building new locks with greater lift. There is little turbulence in the locks, and all locks except two have boat locks. Some of the more modern locks have floating bollards, but in some cases whilst the channels for floating bollards exist, the bollards themselves have not been in-stalled in them. Kleinostheim, for example, has a full set of channels, but only a few of them contain bollards.

There are many potential mooring places along the river banks, but the wash from passing ships can make many of them extremely uncomfortable. This guide does not attempt to give details of all such moorings, concentrating mainly on moorings pro-tected from the hurly-burly of the river and thus more suitable for overnight stops.

Km

0   Junction with Rhein, Km 496·6.
1·2   Moorings at Haupt-Boot boatyard.
3·2   *Schleuse Kostheim*
      Rise 3·0m.
      VHF Ch 20.
      Boat lock size 22x3·5m. *Headroom* 3·2m.
      Boat lock between main lock and the weir. Care is required when entering downstream owing to the proximity of the weir to the entrance of the lock.
11·5 Yachtclub Untermain. Small harbour on left bank with 2m depth. Stern to buoy. Water (not drinkable) and electricity on staging.
15·6 *Schleuse Eddersheim*
      Rise 3·6m.
      VHF Ch 78.
      Boat lock size 22x3·5m. *Headroom* 3·2m.
      Boat lock on opposite side of river to main lock.
24·7 Moorings at Speck boatyard. Depth 3m. Water and electricity on staging.

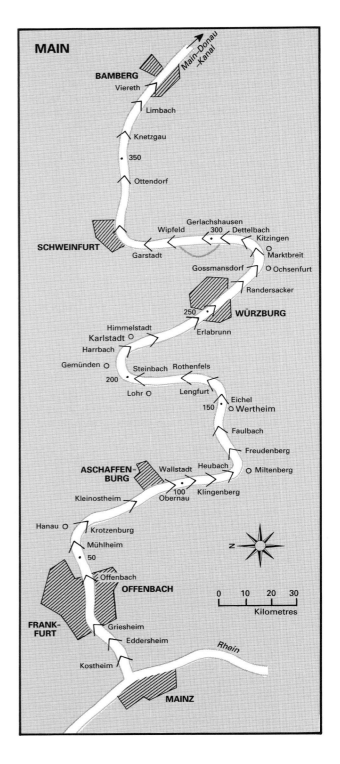

28·7   *Schleuse Griesheim*
         Rise 4·5m.
         VHF Ch 79.
         Boat lock size 22x3·5m. *Headroom* 3·2m.
         Boat lock on opposite side of river to main lock.
29·5   **Frankfurt**. Staging provided by Speck boatyard.
31·3   Frankfurter Yachtclub. One of several stagings on
         left bank, with 3m depth.
33·1   Westhafen on right bank. Speck boatyard. Quiet
         but not very attractive. Convenient for city
         centre. 500m from main railway station. Water
         and electricity provided.
33·5   Bunker station for diesel.
38·5   *Schleuse Offenbach*
         Rise 3·2m.
         VHF Ch 81.
         Boat lock size 22x3·5m. *Headroom* 3·2m.
         Boat lock between main lock and weir.
40·0   Frankfurter Osthafen on right bank. Bunker boat
         for diesel and chandlery.
ca40   **Offenbach**.
47·1   Sportboothafen Mainkur. 2m depth, alongside
         moorings in quiet harbour on right bank. Water,
         electricity, showers.
53·2   *Schleuse Mühlheim*
         Rise 3·8m.
         VHF Ch 82.
         Boat lock size 22x4·0m. *Headroom* 3·7m.
         The newest lock on the river, built in the late
         eighties. It was built with only one main chamber
         as an economy measure. Boat lock between main
         lock and weir.
55·8   **Hanau**. Automobil und Motorbootclub Hanau.
         Staging in river. Water, electricity, showers, slip.
63·9   *Schleuse Krotzenburg*
         Rise 2·7m.
         VHF Ch 18.
         Boat lock size 22x4·0m. *Headroom* 3·7m.
         Boat lock between main lock and weir.
67·0   **Kahl**. Quiet mooring on right bank. Water,
         electricity, showers, laundry. Engine repairs at
         Lässig-Motor company. Fuel by arrangement.
         Depth 2m.
77·9   *Schleuse Kleinostheim*
         Rise 6·8m.
         VHF Ch 20.
         Boat lock size 13·8x3·5m. *Headroom* 3·2m.
         Second newest lock on river, built in the early
         eighties. Some sliding bollards. Boat lock
         between main lock and weir.
87 to 88 **Aschaffenburg**. Four water-sports clubs with
         staging in backwater on right bank. The furthest
         upstream, Boots-Sport-Club Nautilus, has most
         facilities for visiting boats. Fuel is obtainable
         from a filling station close by.
92·9   *Schleuse Obernau*
         Rise 4·0m.
         VHF Ch 22.
         Boat lock size 12x2·5m. *Headroom* 2·2m.
         Boat lock between main lock and weir.
101·2   *Schleuse Wallstadt*
         Rise 4·0m.
         VHF Ch 78.
         Boat lock size 12x2·5m. *Headroom* 2·2m.
         Boat lock between main lock and weir.
107·0   **Erlenbach**. Erlenbacher Wassersportclub in well
         protected basin on right bank. Depth 2m. Water,
         electricity, showers. Shops and restaurants 15
         minutes' walk. Filling station 1km.

Schleuse Griesheim, on the Main at Frankfurt.

Frankfurt's uncompromising modern skyline.

Boat lock at Schleuse Offenbach, on the Main.

113·2 *Schleuse Klingenberg*
Rise 4·0m.
VHF Ch 79.
Boat lock size 12x2·5m. *Headroom* 2·2m.
Boat lock between main lock and weir.

122·4 *Schleuse Heubach*
Rise 4·0m.
VHF Ch 81.
Boat lock size 12·5x2·5m. *Headroom* 2·2m.
Boat lock between main lock and weir.

ca 125 **Miltenberg**.

125·1 Yachtclub Miltenberg. Yacht harbour on right bank with 1·8m depth at entrance, reducing to 1·2m at the innermost end. Maximum length 10m. Water, electricity and showers. Town quay on left bank has 3m depth, but no protection and no facilities.

133·9 *Schleuse Freudenberg*
Rise 4·5m.
VHF Ch 82.
Boat lock size 12·5x2·5m. *Headroom* 2·2m.
Boat lock between main lock and weir.

144·0 Hafen Stadtprozelten. Small harbour on right bank, operated by boatyard Hock. Depth 2m. Water, electricity. Showers at boatyard. Filling station 50m.

147·1 *Schleuse Faulbach*
Rise 4·5m.
VHF Ch 18.
Boat lock size 12·1x2·5m. *Headroom* 2·2m.
Boat lock between main lock and weir.

156·5 **Wertheim**. Motor-Yacht-Club Wertheim entrance to R. Tauber. Depth 1·5m. Water, electricity, showers.

160·5 *Schleuse Eichel*
Rise 4·5m.
VHF Ch 20.
Boat lock size 12·5x2·5m. *Headroom* 2·2m.
Boat lock between main lock and weir.

167·0 Yacht harbour of Wassersportverein Wertheim-Bettingen on left bank. Water, electricity, showers, laundry. Well sheltered. Shops, restaurants and filling station 1km.

174·5 *Schleuse Lengfurt*
Rise 4·0m.
VHF Ch 22.
Boat lock size 12·5x2·5m. *Headroom* 2·2m.
Boat lock between main lock and weir.

185·9 *Schleuse Rothenfels*
Rise 5·3m.
VHF Ch 78.
Boat lock size 12·5x2·5m. *Headroom* 2·2m.
Boat lock between main lock and weir.

198·0 **Lohr**. Town quay on right bank. Depth 2m. Filling station 300m.

200·7 *Schleuse Steinbach*
Rise 5·2m.
VHF Ch 79.
Boat lock size 12·5x2·5m. *Headroom* 2·2m.
Boat lock between main lock and weir.

210·5 Schutzhafen Gemünden. Permission needed. No facilities.

ca211 **Gemünden**.

216·5 **Wernfeld**. Yachtclub Wernfeld-Main in inlet on left bank. Two basins. Visiting boats should use the upstream basin, which has a depth of 2m. Water, electricity, showers. Shops and restaurants in town on right bank (ferry).

219·5 *Schleuse Harrbach*
Rise 4·9m.
VHF Ch 81.
Boat lock size 12·5x2·5m. *Headroom* 2·2m.
Boat lock between main lock and weir.

226·0 **Karlstadt**. Staging close to town centre.

232·3 *Schleuse Himmelstadt*
Rise 4·3m.
VHF Ch 82.
Boat lock size 12·5x2·5m. *Headroom* 2·2m.
Boat lock between main lock and weir.

241·2 *Schleuse Erlabrunn*
Rise 4·1m.
VHF Ch 18.
Boat lock size 12·5x2·5m. *Headroom* 2·2m.
Boat lock between main lock and weir.

248·0 Bunker boat for diesel and chandlery at entrance to commercial harbour on right bank.

252·5 *Schleuse Würzburg*
Rise 2·8m.
VHF Ch 20.
No boat lock.

252·8 **Würzburg**. Yacht-Club Würzburg immediately above lock with pontoon on right bank. Convenient for town centre. Water, electricity, showers. Shops, restaurants and filling station nearby.

253·2 Bootshaus Seubert. Entrance between posts on left bank immediately above bridge. Depth 1·5m. Water, electricity. Engine repairs.

258·9 *Schleuse Randersacker*
Rise 3·3m.
VHF Ch 22.
Boat lock size 12·5x2·5m. *Headroom* 2·2m.
Boat lock between main lock and weir.

262·3 **Eibelstadt**. Marina Levandowski on right bank. Good shelter. Depths 1·5–1·8m. Water, electricity, showers, bar. Shops and restaurants 10 minutes away. Fuelling berth (depth 1·5m). Engine repairs.

269·0 *Schleuse Gossmannsdorf*
Rise 3·4m.
VHF Ch 78.
Boat lock size 12·5x2·5m. *Headroom* 2·2m.
Boat lock between main lock and weir.

270·8 **Ochsenfurt**. Ochsenfurter Bootsclub at upstream end of commercial harbour. Depth 1·5–2m. Water, electricity, showers. Shops, restaurants and filling station a few minutes' walk.

275·7 *Schleuse Marktbreit*
Rise 3·3m.
VHF Ch 79.
Boat lock size 12·5x2·5m. *Headroom* 2·2m.
Boat lock between main lock and weir.

277·2 **Marktbreit**. Small harbour on left bank. Depth 2m. No facilities, but shops, restaurants and filling stations nearby.

284·0 *Schleuse Kitzingen*
Rise 3·6m.
VHF Ch 81.
Boat lock size 12·5x2·5m. *Headroom* 2·2m.
Boat lock between main lock and weir.

286·5 **Kitzingen**. Convenient quay on right bank.

290·6 **Mainstockheim**. Motor-Yacht-Club Anspach in small harbour on right bank. Depth 2m. Water, electricity, showers. Showers at camping site. Shops and restaurants close by.

295·4 *Schleuse Dettelbach*
Rise 5·5m.
VHF Ch 82.
Boat lock size 12·5x2·5m. *Headroom* 2·2m.
Boat lock between main lock and weir.

The Pfalz: one of the Rhein's most famous landmarks.

The spectacular Rhein Gorge.

Shrimper in Ditzum harbour at the mouth of the Ems.

Schwerin.

298·5 Bootshafen Mainblick. Staging and slip at camping site.

299·8 Pleasant anchorage in old river below Gerlach-hausen lock. Depth uncertain.

300·5 *Schleuse Gerlachshausen*
Rise 6·3m.
VHF Ch 18.
Lock is in 5km cut (speed limit 8km/h). No boat lock.

313·5 **Obereisenheim**. Yacht harbour of Yachtclub Frankonia on left bank.

316·3 *Schleuse Wipfeld*
Rise 4·3m.
VHF Ch 20.
Boat lock size 12·5x2·5m. *Headroom* 2·2m.
Boat lock between main lock and weir.

316·5 Motoryachtclub Nürnberg. Immediately above weir, on opposite side of river to Wipfeld lock. Water, electricity, showers (open-air), slip. Fuel by arrangement. Shop and restaurant in village.

322·4 **Garstadt**. Schweinfurter Yacht- und Wasser-sportclub in harbour on right bank. Depth 1·5m. Water, showers. Shop and restaurant 10 minutes.

323·5 *Schleuse Garstadt*
Rise 4·8m.
VHF Ch 22.
Boat lock size 12·5x2·5m. *Headroom* 2·2m.
Boat lock between main lock and weir.

330·4 Fuelling berth in commercial harbour.

332·0 *Schleuse Schweinfurt*
Rise 4·6m.
VHF Ch 78.
Boat lock size 12·5x2·5m. *Headroom* 2·2m.
Main lock is in centre of river. Boat lock is close to right bank.

333·0 **Schweinfurt**. Town quay on right bank. Depth 2m. Quiet mooring, but no facilities.

345·3 *Schleuse Ottendorf*
Rise 7·6m.
VHF Ch 79.
Boat lock size 12·5x2·5m. *Headroom* 2·2m.
Boat lock between main lock and weir.

350·4 Motorbootclub Obertheres on right bank. Depth 1·1m in entrance.

355·5 **Hassfurt**. Quay on right bank.

359·8 *Schleuse Knetzgau*
Rise 4·3m.
VHF Ch 81.
Boat lock size 12·5x2·5m. *Headroom* 2·2m.
Boat lock between main lock and weir.

367·2 *Schleuse Limbach*
Rise 5·3m.
VHF Ch 82.
Boat lock size 12·5x2·5m. *Headroom* 2·2m.
Boat lock between main lock and weir.

369·7 **Eltmann**. Yacht-Club Eltmann on left bank. Suitable for boats under 5 tonnes. Depth 2m. Water, electricity, showers, slip, crane.

380·7 *Schleuse Viereth*
Rise 6·0m.
VHF Ch 18.
No boat lock.

380·8 Motorboot- und Wasserskiclub Bamberg. Pon-toon on right bank immediately above weir. Depth 3m. Water, electricity, showers, slip.

381·9 Motorboot- und Segelclub Coburg. Small har-bour on left bank. Depth 3m. Water, electricity, showers, slip.

382·9 Sportboothafen Trosdorf. Attractive small har-bour on left bank. Depth 2m. Water, electricity, showers, slip.

384·0 **Bamberg**. Junction with Main-Donau-Kanal Km 0·0.

Klein Venedig, at Bamberg.

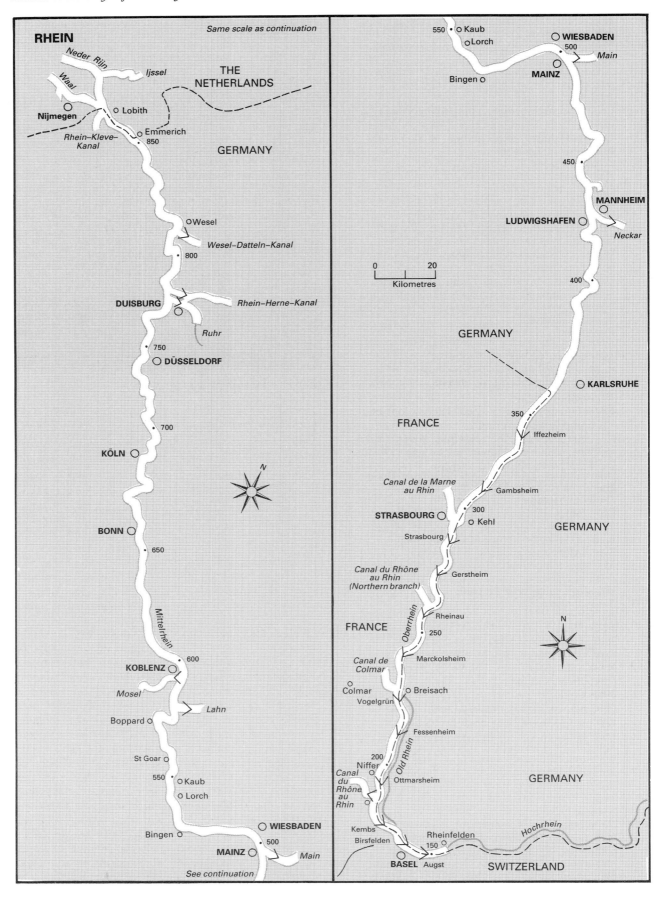

RHEIN

Same scale as continuation

Neder Rijn

Ijssel

THE NETHERLANDS

Waal

Nijmegen

○ Lobith

GERMANY

Rhein–Kleve–Kanal

Emmerich
• 850

○ Wesel

Wesel–Datteln–Kanal
• 800

DUISBURG

Rhein–Herne–Kanal

Ruhr

• 750

○ **DÜSSELDORF**

• 700

KÖLN ○

BONN ○

• 650

Mittelrhein

• 600

KOBLENZ ○

Mosel

Lahn

Boppard ○

St Goar ○

550 • ○ Kaub

○ Lorch

Bingen ○

○ **WIESBADEN**

MAINZ ○ • 500

Main

See continuation

N

0   20
Kilometres

550 • ○ Kaub
• Lorch

○ **WIESBADEN**
500

Bingen ○   **MAINZ**   *Main*

GERMANY

450 •

MANNHEIM

LUDWIGSHAFEN ○ •

Neckar

400 •

GERMANY

○ **KARLSRUHE**

350 •

FRANCE

• Iffezheim

Canal de la Marne au Rhin

Gambsheim

STRASBOURG ○ • 300

○ Kehl

GERMANY

Strasbourg

Canal du Rhône au Rhin (Northern branch)

Gerstheim

FRANCE

Rheinau

Oberrhein

• 250

Canal de Colmar

Marckolsheim

○ Colmar

○ Breisach

Vogelgrün

Fessenheim

Old Rhein

200 •
Niffer ○

Canal du Rhône au Rhin

Ottmarsheim

N

GERMANY

Kembs

Rheinfelden
Hochrhein

Birsfelden

○ 150

Augst

BASEL ○

SWITZERLAND

28

Southwest

RHEIN

The Rhein is the third-longest waterway in Europe, after the Volga and the Donau, but by far the busiest. To cruise the full length of the Rhein, just under 900km from Rheinfelden to the sea, can take as little as seven days in a typical small cruising boat capable of travelling at a steady 5–6kn through the water. But to do it at this rate is to ignore much of the richness of interest which the river can provide. Such a journey can be a feast of history, of architecture, of art, of literature, of sociology, of food, of wine, of engineering and of transport. With so much to experience, it is a pity to hurry.

Although the source of the Rhein lies high in the Swiss Alps, the Rhein proper is generally considered to start at Konstanz on the Bodensee (Lake Constance). The Bodensee, bordered by Germany, Austria and Switzerland, is a major inland waterway, carrying a considerable amount of waterborne traffic. It has a number of major harbours and is the home of a very large number of pleasure craft. But it has no through connections to any other waterway, and therefore cannot be visited except by boats capable of being towed overland.

From Konstanz, the picturesque first 149km stretch to Rheinfelden lies partly in Switzerland and includes the dramatic Rheinfall (Rhine Falls), probably the most powerful waterfall in Europe. Until Rheinfelden the river is not navigable for anything other than small craft, and although plans for a major canalisation project to extend the navigable Rhein to the Bodensee have existed for many years, there seems little chance that they will ever come to fruition.

From Rheinfelden to the sea the river becomes a huge transport artery, carrying freighters, tankers, container ships, passenger ships, hotel ships, small seagoing ships, hydrofoils and even car-transporter ships, as well as large numbers of privately owned pleasure craft. Almost a quarter of Germany's freight travels by water, and the Rhein accounts for the biggest slice of this by far.

The Rhein flows through countryside of many types, from the meadows and windmills of the low-lying countryside near the Dutch border to the spectacular rocky crags overhanging the river in the Rhein Gorge between Wiesbaden and Koblenz; it passes through magnificent cities like Strasbourg, Köln and Bonn. It is flanked sometimes by industry and sometimes by agriculture. It traverses widely varying cultures. Its picturesque tributaries, the Neckar, the Main, the Lahn and the Mosel, are all excellent cruising grounds in their own right.

Furthermore, with its through-route connections to the French, Dutch, Polish, Czech and Austrian inland waterway systems it is also an important link in the thoroughly international waterway network which now exists in Europe.

The Rhein above Bonn is administered by WSD-Südwest, and below Bonn by WSD-West. There are no charges for pleasure boats.

Hydrology

The upper sections of the Rhein have for many years been tamed by canalisation, but in the lower stretches the water levels and the currents vary widely during the year. It is therefore desirable to understand the hydrology of the river when planning a trip along it.

The primary factor in the mind of anyone involved in navigation on the Rhein is the depth of water. To enable the depth of water to be described in a way which is useful to river users, the following system is used.

For the canalised part of the river, above Iffezheim (Km 334) and below Basel (Km 179), specific minimum depths are quoted: 4·50m above Breisach (Km 227) and 3·00m between Breisach and Iffezheim. These depths are maintained throughout the year.

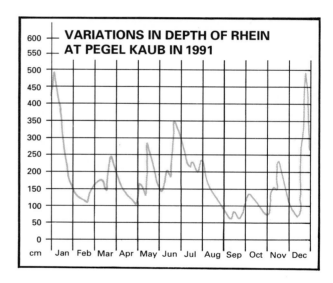

Below Iffezheim and above Basel the depth of water varies over a wide range during the course of the year. To demonstrate this, the variations in depth as measured at Kaub (above Köln) during 1991 are shown graphically above. The river is notionally divided into *Strecken* (stretches); for each *Strecke* there is a published *Gleichwertiger Wasserstand-Fahrrinnentiefe* (normal minimum depth), and the depth is not expected to fall below this for more than 20 days in any year. Somewhere in each stretch is a master *Pegel* (water gauge) which has a known *Pegelnullpunkt* (datum level at the *Pegel*) corresponding to the *GlW-Fahrrinnentiefe* for the stretch of river. The actual depth of water in each stretch can therefore be calculated by taking the known *GlW-Fahrrinnentiefe* and adding the difference between the current *Wasserstand* (water level) at the *Pegel* and the *Nullpunkt*. As *Wasserstände* are displayed at locks, made available over VHF radio, broadcast over local radio and even shown on local teletext services on television, it is seldom difficult to obtain the information necessary for your journey. The maximum draught quoted for each section of the river in the following route descriptions is based on the published *GlW-Fahrrinnentiefe* for that stretch. The *Pegels*, together with the corresponding *Null-punkt* for each, are listed in the following table.

RHEIN *PEGELS* AND CHANNEL DEPTHS

Strecke	Pegel	Nullpunkt	GlW F
Km 166–Km 179	Rheinfelden	1·70m	2·50m
Km 179–Km 334	Guaranteed minimum depth		2·50m
Km 334–Km 384	Maxau	3·50m	2·10m
Km 384–Km 412	Speyer	2·15m	2·10m
Km 412–Km 431	Mannheim	1·60m	2·10m
Km 431–Km 462	Worms	0·70m	2·10m
Km 462–Km 511	Mainz	1·70m	1·90m
Km 511–Km 540	Bingen	0·60m	1·90m
Km 540–Km 566	Kaub	0·85m	1·90m
Km 566–Km 601	Koblenz	0·95m	2·10m
Km 601–Km 624	Andernach	1·05m	2·10m
Km 624–Km 660	Bonn	1·55m	2·10m
Km 660–Km 716	Köln	1·50m	2·50m
Km 716–Km 763	Düsseldorf	1·25m	2·50m
Km 763–Km 794	Ruhrort	1·95m	2·50m
Km 794–Km 837	Wesel	1·70m	2·50m
Km 837–Km 857	Emmerich	1·10m	2·50m

At times of flood (most likely late spring), if the *Wasserstand* for each stretch reaches a predetermined level, *Marke I* (high-water mark 1), vessels are required to announce their movements on VHF. Vessels without VHF are not allowed to move. If the *Wasserstand* reaches a second predetermined level, *Marke II* (high-water mark 2), all traffic in the stretch is prohibited from moving. In the unlikely event of either situation arising during a cruise, appropriate warnings will be issued by WSP patrol vessels and displayed at relevant locks.

During exceptionally dry periods, most likely September or October, the water level may fall below the *GlW-Fahrrinnentiefe*. If this occurs barges may be forced to operate at half load, and it may become difficult for some vessels to enter many of the smaller harbours.

If the strength of the current is crucial, it is possible to find out from the appropriate WSD office the strength of the stream likely to be experienced for various water levels at the *Pegel* for each stretch. From these the current likely to be found in other stretches can be deduced.

Navigational marks

The Rhein is well buoyed wherever appropriate, using the normal convention of green to port and red to starboard when travelling downstream. It is also sufficiently well lit to enable commercial traffic (in most parts of the river) to keep going all through the night, but it is extremely dangerous for a small vessel to travel after dark. Experience of night passages at sea is not relevant to night operations on the Rhein, and skippers of pleasure craft are warned against attempting night passages.

The river is also amply provided with kilometre marks and conventional navigation marks on banks and bridges (see Appendix VI).

VHF radio

The main channel allocations on *UKW* (VHF) are listed below. Ship-to-lock channels are given for each lock in the route descriptions.

Channel	Purpose
10	Safety and calling channel
13	Ship-to-ship and harbourmasters
15, 17	On-board communications, closed for small craft
73, 77	Ship-to-ship
18, 20, 22, 78, 79, 80, 81, 82	Nautical information (WSD/WSA)

Stopping places

As set out in the descriptions of the individual segments of the river, there is an abundance of harbours, yacht clubs and other places to tie up for the night (or a few days or weeks – or even for wintering). It is essential, however, to plan ahead carefully because of the strength of the current. It is easy to overshoot a harbour, and getting back upstream to it can be extremely hard going.

Along the canalised section of the river, in addition to normal harbours and yacht clubs, there are many places where access can be obtained to the Altrhein (Old Rhein). Although frequently shallow and perhaps unbuoyed, some of these stretches of the old river often provide attractive anchorages. Some of them too have become the homes of yacht clubs. Where possible, such places are indicated in the route descriptions which follow.

1. RHEINFELDEN TO BASEL
Km 149–Km 170

Total distance 21km
Maximum draught 3·20m
Maximum height 4·80m
Current 4–6km/h
Locks 2

This short stretch is the highest navigable part of the river. It runs westwards between the Black Forest in Germany and the mountains of Switzerland into the urban surroundings of Basel.

The left bank is Switzerland and the right bank is Germany, and the river is administered jointly by the Swiss authorities and WSD-Südwest.

Km
149·8 **Rheinfelden**. Hafen Rheinfelden. For commercial shipping.
152·4 Possible mooring.
155·6 *Schleuse Augst*
Fall 4·6–6·6m.
VHF Ch 79.
Hours 0500–2100.
163·4 *Schleuse Birsfelden*
Fall 5·9–9·3m.
VHF Ch 22.
Hours 0500–2100.
ca167 **Basel**.
170·0 Hafen Kleinhüningen. Mooring may be possible by negotiation with harbourmaster. Bunker station for diesel.

2. BASEL TO BREISACH
Km 170–Km 227

Total distance 57km
Maximum draught 4·50m
Maximum height 6·70m
Current 4–6km/h
Locks 4

Between Basel and Iffezheim, 40km below Strasbourg, the Rhein is canalised. The stretch from Basel to Breisach is one continuous canal, with the old river running a parallel course immediately to the east. To the French this section is known as the Grand Canal d'Alsace. To the Germans it is known as the Rhein-Seitenkanal. It is wide and somewhat featureless, but the moderate current makes a downstream passage relatively fast. It is possible, for example, to complete the passage from the junction with the Canal du Rhône au Rhin at Niffer to Strasbourg well within one day.

The locks operate 24 hours a day for the benefit of commercial shipping, but it is strongly recommended that pleasure craft should not travel after dark. All locks are equipped with sliding bollards, although the amount of turbulence while the lock is filling is not serious (except of course close to the upper gates). Note that the Niffer lock, in the entrance to the Canal du Rhône au Rhin, has a lift of around 5m, and has neither sliding nor stepped bollards. It is necessary to make fast to the top of the lock.

Km
172·4 Motor- und Yacht-Club Weil. Landing stage in river.
173·7 Start of Grand Canal d'Alsace.
179·1 *Schleuse Kembs*
       Fall 13·2m.
       VHF Ch 20.
185·4 **Niffer**. Entrance to Canal du Rhône au Rhin via Niffer lock (*VHF* Ch 22). Port de Plaisance Kembs in Canal de Huningue through Niffer lock. Depth 2m. Water, electricity, showers, fuel, shops and restaurants 1·5km.
193·6 *Schleuse Ottmarsheim*
       Fall 14·7m.
       VHF Ch 22.
210·5 *Schleuse Fessenheim*
       Fall 15·1m.
       VHF Ch 20.
224·5 *Schleuse Vogelgrün*
       Fall 11·8m.
       VHF Ch 22.
225·7 Motorboot- und Yachtclub Breisach in old river below weir on right bank. Depth 2m. Good shelter. Water, electricity, showers, slip. Shops and restaurants nearby.
226·0 Hafen **Breisach**. On right bank at entrance to old river below weir. Commercial harbour.
226·3 End of Grand Canal d'Alsace. On left bank, entrance to Canal de Colmar (23km long, depth 1·5m, 3 locks).

3. BREISACH TO IFFEZHEIM
Km 227–Km 334

Total distance 107km
Maximum draught 3·00m
Maximum height 6·70m
Current 5–6km/h
Locks 6

Still canalised along this stretch, until Strasbourg the river continues to be somewhat featureless, but not far away to the west lies the beautiful wine-growing area of Alsace, centred on Colmar, with its own canal connecting it to the Rhein at Breisach.

It is as if the undramatic nature of the countryside along the canalised river is specially planned to enhance the drama of arriving at Strasbourg. This city must surely be one of the most attractive places to visit in Europe. Not only the cultural and economic centre of its own region, it has become the home of both the European Parliament and the Council of Europe. It has the atmosphere of a thoroughly modern cosmopolitan city, whilst successfully preserving the charm of its long history. No cruise down the Rhein should omit a leisurely stay here.

The huge locks are all equipped with floating bollards and operate 24hrs a day for the benefit of commercial shipping.

Km
227·6 Marina Schumacher on right bank. Depth 2·5m. Water, electricity, showers, restaurant. Shops 2·5km. Small repairs.
234·4 Associated water-sports clubs of Burkheim on right bank above weir at Marckolsheim. Staging in river. Depth 2m. Electricity. Shops 1·5km.
239·9 *Schleuse Marckolsheim*
       Fall 13·8m.
       VHF Ch 20.
249·0 Associated water-sports clubs of Weisweil on right bank above weir at Rhinau. Staging in river. Depth 2m. Water, electricity. Shops and restaurants 2km, but kiosk nearby.
256·1 *Schleuse Rhinau*
       Fall 12·3m.
       VHF Ch 22.
257·9 Entrance on left bank to northern branch of the Canal du Rhône au Rhin, which has a depth of 1·8m and runs parallel to the Rhein to join the Canal de la Marne au Rhin in Strasbourg. It has 12 manually operated locks.
268·4 Yachtclub Lahr on right bank. Staging in river above Nonnenweier weir. Depth 2m. Water, electricity. Shops 3km.
272·2 *Schleuse Gerstheim*
       Fall 11·0m.
       VHF Ch 20.
287·4 *Schleuse Strasbourg*
       Fall 10·8m.
       VHF Ch 22.
289·8 Club du Port de Plaisance de Strasbourg in Bassin Adrien Haelling on left bank. Depth 2m. Water, electricity, showers, restaurant. Shops 2km.
291·3 Southern entrance to port of **Strasbourg**, with connection to Canal de la Marne au Rhin and northern branch of Canal du Rhône au Rhin, leading to Rhinau.

291·3 Grand Garage Ruhlmann – Base Nautique adjacent to southern entrance to port of Strasbourg. Water, electricity, repairs. Shops 2km.

293·8 Harbour of Nautic-Club Kehl on right bank. Depth 2m. Water, electricity, showers, restaurant, fuel, repairs. Shops and restaurants 1km.

295·6 Northern entrance to Strasbourg commercial harbour and to Canal de la Marne au Rhin. Mooring possible in port area.

308·2 Karcher boatyard in Altrheinarm Grossenwasser on right bank above Gambsheim weir. Depth 2m. Water, electricity, showers, repairs, slip, crane. Shops and restaurants 2km.

308·8 *Schleuse Gambsheim*
Fall 10·4m.
VHF Ch 20.

312·4 Entrance to Petersee (Baggersee Freistett) on right bank. Narrow channel leads to deep tree-lined lake, once a gravel pit, with a sandy beach. There are two yacht clubs, a sailing school and a boatyard. Most facilities, but shops and restaurants are 2km away.

313·7 Entrance to Baggersee Offendorf, once a gravel pit, on left bank. Ignore sign 'Wassersport Verboten'. Good overnight mooring at Marina Offendorf at far end of basin. Water, electricity, showers, restaurant (weekends only), repairs. Shops and restaurants 2·5km.

321·3 Hafen Greffern on right bank. Motor-Yacht-Club Greffern staging on port hand. Water, electricity, bar. Shops and restaurants 1km.

334·0 *Schleuse Iffezheim*
Fall 10·3m.
VHF Ch 18.

4. IFFEZHEIM TO KARLSRUHE
Km 334–Km 360

Total distance 26km
Maximum draught 2·10m (at normal minimum water level)
Maximum height 9·00m (at normal minimum water level)
Current 6–8km/h (at normal minimum water level)
Locks 0

The canalisation of the Rhein stops at Iffezheim, and from here downstream navigation requires more care, but the river becomes more interesting. Its banks are at once more mature, with woods, seemingly well established communities and interesting buildings. The countryside is mostly green and rural; the land, relatively low-lying and fertile, is increasingly devoted to intensive farming.

Leaving behind the canalised part of the river, immediately the channel width reduces from around 200m to 90m, and the depth (at normal minimum water level – normally exceeded for most of the year) drops from 3·00m to 2·10m. Consequently the current increases dramatically. From Km 336 to Km 420 the rush of water over the uneven gravel bottom creates turbulence, with boiling eddies and whirlpools clearly visible; buoys and bridge supports all have vigorous bow waves, but in practice the speed of the current has little effect on small-boat navigation downstream.

The strength of the current does, however, vary considerably with the water level, reaching as much as 15–18km/h in times of flood. Hand-in-hand with the variations in current, the height of water too varies by several metres according to the volume of water in the river. During times of drought the depth can reduce to below the normal minimum depth of 2·10m. In bad years barges are even forced to operate at half load because of the lack of water. Deep-draught boats, for which these reduced depths might constitute a danger, are advised to plan their journeys so as to complete this stretch of the river before mid-August, the time at which in a dry summer water levels may become exceptionally low.

There are numerous flooded gravel pits along this stretch of river, usually connected to the river by a narrow channel. Some of these have been developed for water sports and now have yacht clubs based in them, and others may be suitable as emergency overnight stops, although there is often an element of uncertainty about the depth of water. Nevertheless, as far as possible the entrances have been noted in the route description.

Km
335·4 Hafen Beinheim. Leaving Iffezheim lock downstream, pass under the railway bridge, then turn to port and go back upstream under the bridge into the river below the weir. The entrance to Hafen Beinheim is immediately to starboard. There are two yacht clubs, with good facilities. Restaurant in club-ship of MYC Baden-Baden. Other restaurants and shops in Beinheim (2km).

339·0 Entrance to gravel pit on left bank.

339·7 Entrance to gravel pit on left bank.

341·1 Entrance to gravel pit on right bank.

341·6 Entrance to gravel pit on left bank.

347·1 Entrance to Goldkanal on right bank. Leads into gravel pit with rowing club.

349·2 Hafen Lauterbourg on left bank. Restaurant.

354·1 Customs post in entrance to Neuburger Altrhein on right bank. All boats should still report here when entering or leaving Germany, but formalities are minimal. Care needed, as entrance not obvious. Overnight mooring possible at Yacht-club Oberrhein, immediately beyond the customs post. Depth 1·8m. Water, electricity, shops 2km.

355·2 Entrance to Neue Lauter river. Entrance difficult due to current and underwater obstruction. Two yacht clubs. Water, electricity, cold showers, restaurant. Shops and filling station 2km.

359·9 Hafen **Karlsruhe** on right bank. Mooring prohibited.

5. KARLSRUHE TO BUDENHEIM
Km 360–Km 508

Total distance 148km
Maximum draught 2·10m (at normal minimum water level)
Maximum height 9·00m (at normal minimum water level)
Current 5–10km/h (at normal minimum water level)
Locks 0

Becoming more beautiful and more interesting with every kilometre, the Rhein now enters wine country. The two largest German wine-producing areas, the Rheinpfalz and Rheinhessen, lie near the left bank, and from the historic city of Worms northwards village names – like Nierstein and Oppenheim – take on the character of a wine merchant's list as vineyards begin to line the steepening slopes along the river.

Km

362·6 Hafen Maximiliansau on left bank. Commercial harbour. Mooring possible in northern part of harbour.
Bunker boat for diesel.

362·6 Hafen Maxau on right bank. Round tower at downstream side of entrance. Depth 2m. Motor-boot-Club Karlsruhe. Water, electricity, showers, restaurant in clubhouse on barge, fuel. Shops 2km.

365·8 **Karlsruhe**. Hafen Wörth on left bank. Commercial harbour. Mooring possible.

373·1 Hafen Leimersheim on left bank. Depth 1·0–1·2m. Club Nautico Karlsruhe. Water, electricity. Shops 2km.

376·7 Hochstetter Altrhein on right bank. Mooring possible. Two restaurants nearby.

385·3 Hafen Germersheim on left bank. Depth 1·5m. 3 yacht clubs. Water, electricity, showers, restaurant. Shops 3km.

386·6 Entrance to gravel pit on left bank.

389·2 Entrance to gravel pit on right bank. Small canoe and rowing club near a nuclear power station.

391·8 Entrance to Oberhauser Altrhein on right bank. Large shallow lagoon.

393·5 Berghauser Altrhein on left bank. Lagoon suitable for shallow-draught boats.

399·5 Neuer Hafen **Speyer** on left bank above bridge. Marina Braun. Water, electricity, showers, fuel, slip, crane, repairs, winter storage.

400·6 Alter Hafen Speyer on left bank below bridge. Mooring possible, but subject to wash from passing ships.

405·1 Entrance to gravel pit on left bank.

406·3 Reffenthaler (Angelhofer) Altrhein on left bank. 1km inside, 4 yacht clubs with good facilities, including travel-lift. No fuel.

411·0 Otterstätter Altrhein on left bank. Depth 3m. Anchorage and marina. Water, electricity, showers, restaurant. Shops 3km.

412·4 Harbour of Motoryacht-Club Kurpfalz Mannheim on right bank. Water, electricity, showers, restaurant, fuel, repairs, shops 1km.

ca415 Hafen **Mannheim**. Commercial harbour.

416·9 Motorboot-Club Altrip on left bank in Altriper Arm. Water, showers. Shops 1km.

418·9 Entrance to Kiefweiher on left bank. 4 yacht clubs. Water, electricity, showers, repairs.

420 to
430 **Ludwigshafen**.

421·4 Kaiserwörthhafen on left bank. Commercial harbour. Emergency mooring possible.

423·8 Luitpoldhafen on left bank. Emergency mooring possible.

424 to
428 Several bunker boats for diesel.

427·3 Mühlauhafen on right bank. Commercial harbour.

427·6 Bunker boat for diesel on right bank.

428·0 Bunker boat for diesel and provisions on right bank.

428·1 Junction with Neckar on right bank.

431·4 Entrance to Sandhofer Altrhein on right bank. Xylon-Werft boatyard. Repairs, travel-lift.

431·7 Nordhafen on left bank. Commercial harbour.

440·3 Lampertheimer Altrhein on right bank. Entrance to 4 yacht clubs. Water, electricity, slip, showers, crane. Shops 3km.

442·1 Entrance to Motor-Yacht-Club Worms on left bank. Depth 1·8m. Water, electricity, showers, restaurant, fuel, repairs. Shops 2km.

ca445 **Worms**.

462·1 Entrance to Hafen Gernsheim on right bank. Marina of Gernsheim harbour company. Water, electricity, showers, restaurant, fuel, repairs. Shops 2km.

466·0 Entrance to Eicher See on left bank. Flooded gravel pit with two sailing clubs and a restaurant. Ignore 'no entry' sign at entrance.

473·9 Entrance to Erfelder Altrhein on right bank. Navigable for 9km. Depths uncertain. Entrance needs care. Two yacht clubs.

480·4 **Oppenheim**. Hafen Oppenheim on left bank. Two small yacht clubs. Fuelling berth in harbour.

ca481 **Nierstein**.

484·8 to
488·4 Nackenheimer Mühlarm on left bank. Backwater behind two islands. Automobil- und Wasser-sport-Club Oppenheim-Nierstein.

484·8 Upstream entrance to Nackenheimer Mühlarm. Closed.

486·3 Middle entrance to Nackenheimer Mühlarm.

488·4 Downstream entrance to Nackenheimer Mühlarm.

492·9 Entrance to Ginsheimer Altrhein on right bank. Bootshaus Haupt, near centre of Ginsheim. Restaurant opposite.

495·9 Hafen Gustavsburg on right bank above bridge. Commercial harbour.

496·6 Junction with Main on right bank.

497·0 Bunker station for diesel on right bank just below entrance to Main.

497·2 **Mainz**. Winterhafen Mainz on left bank. 3 yacht clubs. Water, electricity, showers, fuel, repairs, slip.

497·8 Bunker station for diesel on right bank.

498·1 Entrance to Flosshafen Mainz-Kastel on right bank. Bootsclub Maaraue. Water, electricity, showers. Shops and restaurants 1km.

501·8 Leave island to port.

502·0 Downstream entrance to Kasteler Arm on right bank in backwater behind island. Note that upstream entrance is very shallow. Two small yacht harbours. Water and electricity. Shops and restaurants 1km.

505·8 **Wiesbaden**. Hafen Schierstein. 4 yacht clubs. Water, electricity, showers, restaurant, fuel, shops nearby.

506·7 Fuelling station on left bank.

507·9 Niederwalluf. Segelclub Rheingau in small harbour on right bank. Water, electricity, showers, slip, repairs. Shops and restaurants nearby.

6. BUDENHEIM TO ST GOAR
Km 508–Km 557

Total distance 51km
Maximum draught 1·90m (at normal minimum
    water level)
Maximum height No bridges
Current 5–7km/h (at normal minimum water level)
Locks 0

This is the climax of any Rhein journey. The Rhein
Gorge is the picture-book Rhein. On both banks
high craggy hills tower over the river. Vineyards
with names direct from wine merchants' shelves
stream past as the current once again gathers pace.
Buoys and rocks, often apparently in mid-stream,
tear their way through the water; those barges and
passenger boats heading upstream struggle with
wide-open throttles to make headway against the
current, whilst others dance their way downstream,
as if almost out of control. Picture-book castles
appear round every corner, perched on hill tops
high above the river. The 'Mouse Tower' at Bingen,
the Pfalz, the Loreley rocks – these are the images of
the Rhein which we all know.

Soon after Wiesbaden the river seems to go wild.
For most of the year the river is normally above
normal minimum level, and so the current is generally stronger than quoted, often running at around
10–12km/h. In a small boat there is now no turning
back; it feels like shooting rapids. But in fact there
are no great problems so long as the helmsman
looks well ahead to see the line of the channel markers and to anticipate the movements of upstream
ships, many of which will be blue-flagging to avoid
the strongest current as they toil upriver.

The excitement reaches its peak at Binger Loch
(Bingen Hole), the 1km stretch between Km 530
and Km 531, where the current is faster than anywhere else on the whole of the navigable part of the
river. After this the force diminishes, and the
helmsman can relax and settle down to enjoying the
drama of the terrain.

There is a long-term project in hand to dredge the
Budenheim to St Goar section to a uniform 2·10m
at normal minimum water level. When the work is
complete the whole length from Iffezheim to Köln
will have a normal depth of 2·10m. In the meantime, travellers along this stretch of the river should
take care to note the relevant *Pegelstand* information,
displayed at locks and broadcast on local radio
stations as explained earlier.

Km	
510·8	Burg Crass on right bank.
512·0	Leave island to port.
512 to 527	Nature reserves on islands.
513·3	Schloss Reinhartshausen on right bank.
516·7	Schloss Reichardshausen on right bank.
519·5	Hafen **Ingelheim**. Emergency mooring possible.
520·7	Entrance to backwater behind island at Winkel on right bank. Two yacht clubs. Possible moor-ing.
524·5	Leave island to port.
525·3	Hafen Rüdesheim. Marina and yacht club. Water, electricity, showers, restaurant, repairs. Shops 1km.
526·6	**Rüdesheim**. Brömser Burg. Bunker boat for diesel on right bank.
527·4	Hafen Bingen on left bank just below island. Motor-Yacht-Club Bingen. Water, electricity, showers, restaurant. Shops 3km. Beware ferries.
528·4	**Bingen**.
529·1	Junction with Nahe on left bank. Not navigable.
530 to 531	Binger Loch. The fastest current in the whole of the navigable part of the river. Current 8km/h at normal minimum water level – but often 10–12km/h and can be 20km/h at times of peak flood.
530·1	Mäuseturm (Mouse Tower) on upstream end of island near left bank.
530·5	Burg Ehrenfels on right bank.
533·0	Burg Rheinstein on left bank.
534·4	Burg Reichenstein on left bank.
537·1	Burg Sooneck on left bank.
539·0	Burg Hohneck on left bank.
539·7	**Lorch**. Small yacht club on right bank just below island. Entry difficult, but suitable for small boats.
540·8	Burg Nollig on right bank.
541·2	Burg Fürstenberg on left bank.
543·0	Burg Stahleck on left bank.
544·5	Leave island to starboard.
546·0	The Pfalz (Pfalzgrafenstein Castle) on down-stream end of island.
546·5	**Kaub**. Burg Gutenfels on right bank.
548·8	Burg Schönburg on left bank.
549·7	Entrance to Hafen **Oberwesel** on left bank. Overnight mooring if space available.
550·6	Signal station A on left bank (traffic signal for commercial shipping).
552·8	Signal station B on left bank (traffic signal for commercial shipping).
553·6	Signal station C on left bank (traffic signal for commercial shipping).
554·3	Signal station D on left bank (traffic signal for commercial shipping).
554·3	Loreley rock on right bank.
554·3	Loreleyhafen on right bank. Mooring possible but difficult.

The Rhein near St Goar: a dramatic river.

555·4   Signal station E on left bank (traffic signal for commercial shipping).
555·9   Burg Katz on right bank.
         Pilot station on left bank.
556·1   **St Goar**.
557·0   Hafen St Goar on left bank. New marina.

7. ST GOAR TO KÖLN
Km 557–Km 686

Total distance 129km
Maximum draught 2·10m (at normal minimum water levels)
Maximum height 9·0m (at normal minimum water levels)
Current 3–5km/h (at normal minimum water levels)
Locks 0

After the high drama of Binger Loch and the Loreley, the mountains become more rounded and less craggy. The steep hillsides are now covered with pine trees and terraced vineyards, but castles still cast their spells over the river. Below Koblenz the river still flows amid steep wooded hillsides, pretty villages and attractive towns.

The current remains strong, still running at 7–9km/h, not much less than in the more dramatic stretches a little higher upstream, but with much reduced turbulence.

Km
558·9   Burg Maus on right bank.
559·0   Hafen 'Am Hund' on left bank. Boats with draught greater than 1·50m should keep close to upstream side of entrance. Harbour not recommended when water levels are low.
559·8   Leave island to port.
566·2   Burg Liebenstein on right bank.
566·5   Burg Sterrenberg on right bank.
ca571   **Boppard**.
579·9   Burg Marksburg on right bank.
585·2   Burg Stolzenfels on left bank.
585·7   Junction with Lahn on right bank. Hafen Oberlahnstein at junction. Emergency mooring possible.
         Bootshaus Radermacher 0·5km into Lahn on starboard side between the two bridges. Water, electricity, restaurant. Shops and more restaurants 1km.
589 to
594   **Koblenz**.
590·0   Hafen Rheinlache on left bank. Wassersportfreunde Oberworth. Water, electricity, repairs.
591·3   Hafen Ehrenbreitstein on right bank. Emergency mooring possible.
591·6   Bunker boat for diesel on right bank.
592·0   Bunker boat for diesel on right bank.
592·3   Junction with Mosel on left bank.
594·0   Keep left, leaving island to starboard.
605·7   Yacht club staging on right bank. Subject to current. Water, electricity, restaurant.
606·0   Passage either side of island.
ca 608   **Neuwied**.
608·1   Bunker station for diesel on right bank.
ca612   **Andernach**.
617 to
618   Island near right bank. Nature reserve. Mooring between island and bank possible at two small yacht clubs. No facilities.
617·5   Burg Hammerstein on right bank.

Hafen Oberwinter.

621·6   Hafen Brohl on left bank. Emergency mooring possible.
624·8   Schloss Arenfels on right bank.
628·8   Schloss Dattenberg on right bank.
630·7   Burg Ockenfels on right bank.
635·6   Schloss Marienfels on left bank.
639·1   Hafen Oberwinter on left bank. Yacht-Club Mittelrhein and Bonner Yacht Club. Water, electricity, showers, restaurant, repairs, fuel, shops, slip, crane.
642·0   Yacht club behind island near right bank. Entrance below island. Water, electricity, showers, restaurant, slip. Shops 1km. Small repairs.
650 to
660   **Bonn**.
659·7   Hafen Mondorf on right bank. Two yacht clubs. Water, electricity, shops, restaurant, slip, repairs.
661·0   Upstream entrance to channel behind Herseler Werth island on left bank. Depth problematic. Water, electricity, shops 1km.
662·4   Downstream entrance to channel behind Herseler Werth. Anchorage possible.
677·3   Hafen Porz-Zündorf on right bank. Water, electricity, showers. Shops 1km.
680 to
700   **Köln**.
684·5   Bunker station for diesel on left bank.

The twin spires of Köln cathedral.

8. KÖLN TO DUISBURG
Km 686–Km 780

Total distance 94km
Maximum draught 2·50m (at normal minimum
water level)
Maximum height 9·00m (at normal minimum water
level)
Current 3–4km/h (at normal minimum water level)
Locks 0

The route now passes through the industrial heartland of Germany. But there is little ugliness. From the river the view remains remarkably rural until Düsseldorf, and even amidst the steelworks, power stations, petrochemical plants and chemical factories of the area around Düsseldorf and Duisburg the impression one gets is of modern, well planned industrial complexes and often exciting architecture.

Ruhrorter Yacht-Club, in the Eisenbahnhafen at Duisburg-Ruhrort.

Much of the dereliction we tend normally to associate with industrial areas seems to have been avoided. There are rumours of heavy pollution in the water, but this is not in any way evident to the crew of a small boat – and, to judge by the number of fishermen on the river banks, not to the fish either.

Km	
687·3	Hafen Deutz on right bank. Mooring only in emergency.
687·5	Rheinauhafen on left bank. Bridge at entrance opens on three long blasts. Water, electricity, showers, fuel, slip, repairs. Shops and restaurants. May be uncomfortable.
691·5	Hafen Mülheim. Emergency mooring possible.
695·7	Köln-Niehl commercial port. Emergency mooring possible in first basin.
707·0	Hafen Hitdorf on right bank. 4 yacht clubs. Water, electricity, showers. Shops and restaurants nearby.
709·6	Hafen Worringen on left bank. Commercial harbour. Not recommended.
718·1	Yacht harbour on left bank. Uncomfortable.
730 to 760	**Düsseldorf**.
735·0	Yacht harbour on right bank. Small yachts only.
735·7	Neusser Sporthafen (Napoleonshafen) on left bank. 3 yacht clubs. Water, electricity, slip, repairs. Shops and restaurants.
740·2	Entrance to Erftkanal on left bank. Neusser Yacht-Club in basin to port about 1km into canal. Water, electricity. Quiet mooring.
743·1	Entrance to Hafen Düsseldorf on right bank near television tower. Yacht club in *Becken* (Basin) A. Water, electricity. Bunker boat for diesel. Marina in Zollhafen at entrance to industrial harbour. Water, electricity, showers, crane, repairs. Shops and restaurants nearby. Convenient for centre of Düsseldorf.
746·0	Düsseldorfer Sporthafen on right bank. Small boats only.
747·2	Yachthafen Düsseldorf on right bank. 3 yacht clubs. Water, electricity, showers, slip, repairs, shops, restaurants.
748·9	Wassersporthafen Düsseldorf-Lörick (Paradieshafen) on left bank. 4 yacht clubs. Water, electricity, showers. Shops, restaurants 1km.
761·8	Entrance to yacht harbour of Krefelder Yacht-Club on left bank. Depth 2m. Water, showers, electricity, restaurant, repairs. Shops 1km.
763·9	Entrance to Hafen Krefeld-Uerdingen on left bank. Entry only from below bridge. Yacht club 2km into harbour. Water, electricity.
770 to 790	**Duisburg**.

9. DUISBURG TO LOBITH
Km 780–Km 863

Total distance 83km
Maximum draught 2·50m (at normal minimum
    water level)
Maximum height 9·00m (at normal minimum water
    level)
Current 3–4km/h (at normal minimum water level)
Locks 0

The heavy industry of Duisburg is soon left behind,
and the countryside becomes once more rural. But
it now begins to take on an increasingly Dutch
character, low-lying, verdant and with cattle grazing
on the river banks. The architecture too demonstrates the same shift in style as the Dutch border
approaches.

Km
780·1 Junction with Ruhr.
780·4 Junction with Rhein-Herne-Kanal.
780·6 Entrance to Duisburg Hafenmund and Kaiser-
       hafen on right bank under bridge. Bunker boat
       for diesel at end of harbour (1·5km). Special
       permit needed by pleasure craft.
781·0 Entrance to Eisenbahnhafen on right bank below
       bridge. Ruhrorter Yacht-Club. Water, electricity,
       showers, restaurant, diesel.
790·2 Hafen Schwelgern on right bank. Emergency
       mooring possible.
791·2 Südhafen Walsum on right bank. Emergency
       mooring possible.
793·0 Nordhafen Walsum on right bank. Emergency
       mooring possible.
813·2 Junction with Wesel-Datteln-Kanal on right
       bank.
814·6 Hafen **Wesel** on right bank. Emergency mooring
       possible.
816·5 Yachthafen Wesel on right bank. 2 yacht clubs.
       Water, electricity, showers, slip, crane, repairs.
       Shops 2km.
838·0 Entrance to gravel pit on left bank. Wassersport-
       verein Xanten. Water, electricity. Shops 1km.
842·7 Entrance to gravel pit on right bank. 3 yacht
       clubs. Water, electricity. Shops 5km.
851·7 Hafen Emmerich on right bank. Entry only in
       emergency.
851·8 *Zollhafen* (customs harbour) Emmerich on right
       bank. German and Dutch customs reporting
       point for vessels leaving the Netherlands and
       entering Germany.
853·7 Sporthafen **Emmerich** on right bank. Yacht
       club and marina. Water, electricity, showers,
       restaurant, slip, crane, repairs. Shops 2km.
857·7 Dutch-German border on right bank.
862·4 Zollstation **Tolkamer** (**Lobith**) on right bank.
       Dutch customs reporting point for vessels leaving
       Germany and entering the Netherlands.
863·3 Vluchthafen Lobith-Tolkamer on right bank.
       Bunker boat for diesel.
863·9 Junction with Rhein-Kleve-Kanal (Schiffahrtsweg
       Kleve) on left bank.
865·5 Dutch-German border on left bank.

Rhein-Kleve-Kanal
Navigable distance 10·0km
Maximum draught 2·30m above lock. Depth below
    lock depends on water level in Rhein.
Maximum height One lift bridge
Current Nil
Locks 1
Speed limit 5 km/h

This canal comprises the Griethauser Altrhein and
the Spoykanal. It exists purely to connect the industrial town of Kleve to the German waterway system.
    The lock works from 0700 to 1900 weekdays,
0700 to 1500 on Saturdays, and is closed on Sundays.

Km
10·1 Junction with Rhein Km 863·9.
4·7   Junction of Griethauser Altrhein with Spoykanal.
4·6   *Schleuse Brienen*. Lift bridge.
      Rise 4·6m.
ca1·0 Hafen Kleve.
0·4   End of canal.

Rhein (continued)
ca864 Bunker boats and provisioning ships on left bank.
864·3 Entrance to gravel pit De Bijland on right bank.
       Depth 1·7m at entrance even at lowest water
       levels. Keep close to stone groyne on upstream
       side of entrance to avoid shallow patch marked
       by buoy. Bunker boat immediately inside after
       bridge. Major yacht harbour 1km to starboard.
       Quiet mooring. Depth 3–4m.

Pegel Wesel.

NECKAR

Length 201km
Maximum draught Feudenheim–Lauffen 2·50m.
  Lauffen–Plochingen 2·30m.
Maximum height 5·50m.
Current Negligible except during flood conditions.
Locks 27. None equipped with floating bollards.
Speed limits 18km/h in river. 14km/h in canalised
  sections.

From its source, close to that of the Donau, in
Baden-Württemberg to the east of the Schwarzwald
(Black Forest), the Neckar makes its way through
Stuttgart, a modern city built almost from scratch
after being destroyed by Allied bombing, and
famous as the home of Mercedes and a centre of the
arts. Navigable from Plochingen, a little way above
Stuttgart, the river meanders northwards to Heilbronn and then winds majestically through the rolling wooded hills of the Odenwald (Oden Forest),
between steep hillsides covered with pine trees and
vines and with castles sitting on hill tops. Finally, it
runs through the legendary university city of Heidelberg to join the Rhein.

Heading upstream from the Rhein, Heidelberg is
the first of the many essential stopping places on the
Neckar. Although somewhat overrun by tourists,
Heidelberg is a wonder of preservation. It is difficult
to believe that the historic gabled buildings and
cobblestone streets of the *Altstadt* are real and not a
film set.

Continuing upstream towards Stuttgart, with
huge sweeping bends and spectacular tree-covered
hillsides, it is sheer joy to travel up the river: Neck-
arsteinach, with its four hill-top castles, Hirschhorn,
Burg Guttenberg, Bad Wimpfen: each one a delight
to the eye.

Since the river is entirely canalised along its navigable length, its depth is closely controlled. The
current too is normally slight, although heavy rain-
storms can cause a sudden swelling of the stream
and a strong current can be generated, taking the
unwary by surprise.

From Feudenheim to Heilbronn inclusive the
locks work from 0600 to 2200 weekdays and 0800
to 1600 Sundays. From Horkheim to Deizisau inclusive the weekday hours are 0600 to 2100 and on
Sundays 0800 to 1600.

The Neckar is administered by WSD-Südwest.
There are no charges.

Km	
0·0	Junction with Rhein Km 428·2.
6·2	*Schleuse Feudenheim*
	Rise 5·6–10m (depends on level in Rhein).
	VHF Ch 20.
17·7	*Schleuse Schwabenheim*
	Rise 8·7m.
	VHF Ch 78.
23 to	
27	**Heidelberg.**
ca24	3 yacht clubs on left bank. Pontoons in river. Water, electricity, showers, clubhouse, crane, repairs. Shops and restaurants nearby in city centre.

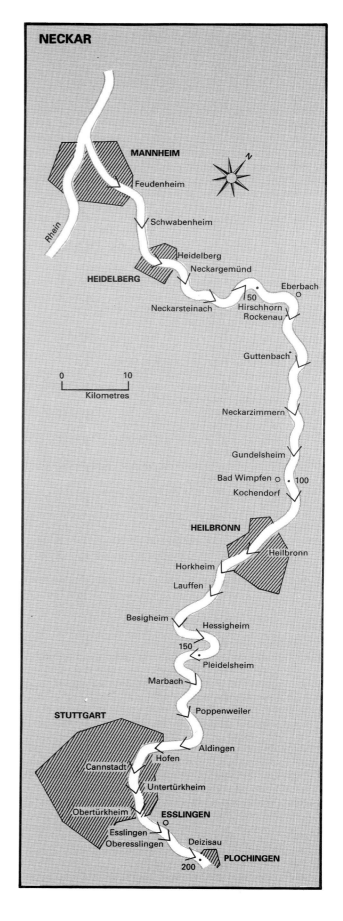

26·1	*Schleuse Heidelberg* *Rise* 2·6m. *VHF* Ch 79.
28·7	Motor-Boot-Club Heidelberg. Staging in river on left bank. Depth 2m. Water, electricity, showers. Bus stop to city centre.
30·9	*Schleuse Neckargemünd* *Rise* 3·9m. *VHF* Ch 81.
34·2	Neckargemünd. Junction with Elsenz on left bank. Bank mooring 2m.
ca38·5	Neckarsteinach. Possible but uncomfortable mooring at pleasure-boat landing on right bank if a vacant space can be found.
39·3	*Schleuse Neckarsteinach* *Rise* 4·7m. *VHF* Ch 82.
39·4	Good mooring at Dilsberg, immediately above lock on left bank.
40·1	Boatyard on right bank. Repairs.
ca47	Hirschhorn. Town quay on right bank below lock. Depth 2m. Beware strong currents from weir following heavy rain. No facilities.
47·7	*Schleuse Hirschhorn* *Rise* 5·3m. *VHF* Ch 18.
ca57·5	**Eberbach**. Small landing stage at camp site on left bank. Also possibility of mooring at down-stream end of town quay on right bank, out of the way of passenger ships.
61·4	*Schleuse Rockenau* *Rise* 6·0m. *VHF* Ch 20. Supermarket near lock.
63·1	Krösselbach. Mooring possible at private quay on left bank. Depth 2m. No facilities, but repairs possible at Neckarsport.
63·2	Possibility of mooring at Lindach on right bank close to ferry. No facilities.
66·2	Motor-Yachtclub Neckar. Staging on left bank. Deepest water 1·60m near ferry. Water, electricity, showers, clubhouse. Shops and restaurants nearby.
69·6	Neckargerach. Quay on right bank. Depth 2·50m. No facilities, but shops and restaurants nearby.
72·2	*Schleuse Guttenbach* *Rise* 5·3m. *VHF* Ch 22.
75·8	Binau. Staging at camp site on right bank. Water, electricity, showers, restaurant, swimming pool.
80·8	Obrigheim. Motor-Boot-Club Obrigheim on left bank. Depth 1·20m. Water, electricity, showers. Shops and restaurants nearby.
86·0	*Schleuse Neckarzimmern* *Rise* 5·6m. *VHF* Ch 78. Good mooring place above lock on left bank. Shops, including chandlery.
86·2	Boatyard on right bank. Depth 1·20m.
86·5	Burg Hornberg on right bank.
87·3	Possibility of using river authority harbour on left bank. Depth 1·50m. No facilities.
88·2	Hassmersheim. Possibility of mooring close to ferry.
88·6	Bunker boat for diesel on left bank.
91·2	Neckarmühlbach. Possibility of mooring in 2·5m at new quay on left bank. No facilities.
93·0	Gundelsheim. Quay on right bank. Depth 2·50m. No facilities, but shops and restaurants in village.
93·9	*Schleuse Gundelsheim* *Rise* 4·2m. *VHF* Ch 79. Long stretch of left bank with bollards above lock. Suitable for overnight mooring after barges stop for the night. Depth 2·5m. No facilities.
98·3	Offenau. Motorboot-Club Mittlerer Neckar. Staging on right bank.
ca100	**Bad Wimpfen**. Picture-book mediaeval town high above left bank. Possibility of mooring at end of passenger landing stage.
103·0	Yacht club in backwater on left bank. Depth 1·30m. No facilities.
103·9	*Schleuse Kochendorf* *Rise* 8·0m. *VHF* Ch 81.
108·0	Osthafen Heilbronn. Possibility of mooring if a space is vacant. Depth 2·00m. Water, electricity, repairs.
110·6	Old branch of river, leading to the 1821-built, self-operated *Wilhelmschleuse*, bypassing main lock (Schleuse Heilbronn). Suitable for boats of up to 1·20m draught.
112·0	**Heilbronn**. Bunker boat in old river on left bank below lock.
113·6	*Schleuse Heilbronn* *Rise* 3·2m. *VHF* Ch 82. Situated in new branch of river.
114·0	Württembergischen Motor-Boot-Club Heilbronn in old branch of river above Wilhelmschleuse. Depth 2·00m. Water, electricity, showers, clubhouse, repairs. Shops and restaurants nearby. The largest yacht club on the Neckar.
117·0	Entrance to old branch of Neckar on left bank below Schleuse Horkheim. Depth 2·00m. Mooring to bank.
117·5	*Schleuse Horkheim* *Rise* 7·3m. *VHF* Ch 18.
124·2	Entrance to old Neckar on left bank at entrance to lock cut. Depth 2·00m. Mooring to bank.
125·2	*Schleuse Lauffen* *Rise* 8·4m. *VHF* Ch 20.
136·0	Overnight mooring possible on left bank below lock.
136·3	*Schleuse Besigheim* *Rise* 6·3m. *VHF* Ch 22.
137·5	Bootshafen Walter on left bank. Cramped, but possibility of overnight stay. Water, electricity, showers. Shops and restaurants nearby.
143·0	*Schleuse Hessigheim* *Rise* 6·2m. *VHF* Ch 78.
150·1	*Schleuse Pleidelsheim* *Rise* 8·0m. *VHF* Ch 79.
155·5	Motor-Boot-Club Binningen on left bank. Depth 1·30m. Water, electricity, showers, clubhouse.
157·6	*Schleuse Marbach* *Rise* 6·0m. *VHF* Ch 81.
165·0	*Schleuse Poppenweiler* *Rise* 7·0m. *VHF* Ch 82. Mooring possible on right bank for 1km above lock.

166·5 Motor-Boot-Club Poppenweiler on right bank. Wash from passing vessels can be severe. Water, electricity, showers, clubhouse.

168·8 Boatyard on right bank. Depth 2·5m. Repairs. Wintering possible.

170·1 Small yacht club behind island near right bank. No facilities. Depth 2·00m.

170·5 Junction with Rems. Mooring to bank possible inside entrance. Shops and restaurants nearby.

172·0 *Schleuse Aldingen*
Rise 3·6m.
VHF Ch 18.

176·3 *Schleuse Hofen*
Rise 6·8m.
VHF Ch 20.

176·5 Bootshaus Sonder on right bank. Water, electricity, showers. Tram to Stuttgart centre.

178·5 Signal station for upstream and downstream traffic. Observe red and green lights.

180 to
190 **Stuttgart**.

182·7 *Schleuse Cannstadt*
Rise 5·4m.
VHF Ch 22.
Boat lock size 11·4x2·4m. Headroom 2·7m.
Self-service.

186·5 *Schleuse Untertürkheim*
Rise 3·7m.
VHF Ch 78.

ca188 Hafen Stuttgart. Very large commercial harbour.

189·5 *Schleuse Obertürkheim*
Rise 8·4m.
VHF Ch 79.

194·0 *Schleuse Esslingen*
Rise 5·2m.
VHF Ch 81.

194·8 *Schleuse Oberesslingen*
Rise 5·9m.
VHF Ch 82.

196·8 Harbour of Motor-Yacht-Club Esslingen. Behind island. Depth 2·00m. Water, electricity, showers, clubhouse. Tram to Esslingen and then S-Bahn train to Stuttgart centre.

199·6 *Schleuse Deizisau*
Rise 5·1m.
VHF Ch 18.

200·1 **Plochingen**. Yachtclub Plochinger Wassersportfreunde on right bank. Quay, water, electricity, showers, clubhouse. Shops and restaurants 1·5km.

201·5 End of navigation.

LAHN

Navigable length 67·3km
Maximum draught 1·50m
Maximum height 3·20m
Maximum beam 5·25m
Current Negligible except in times of flood.
Locks 12
Speed limit 12 km/h

The Lahn must be one of the most attractive waterways in Europe for cruising. With no commercial traffic (apart from three passenger vessels), the river winds its way along a beautiful valley amongst steep wooded hills. Postcard villages nestle at every bridge and castles tower over the valley from their hill-top

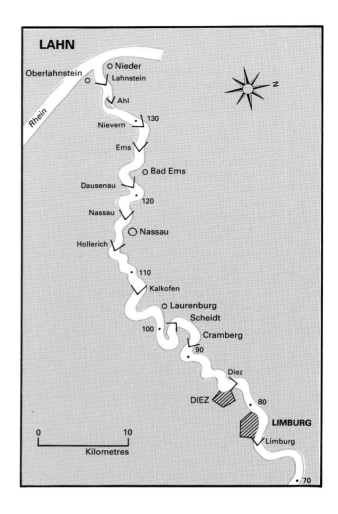

vantage points. There are several nature reserves in the vicinity of Nassau.

The waterway is still Federal, administered by WSD-Südwest, so there are no charges and all installations are meticulously maintained. There are 12 locks on the 67km of river, and with a minimum depth of 1·60m it is perfectly practicable for boats drawing 1·50m to navigate its waters. Boats drawing more than 1·20m are advised, however, to keep to the centre of the channel as far as possible. Boats with shallower draughts are expected to give way. There are plenty of excellent places for overnight mooring.

In summer there is normally very little current, but the river does swell rapidly after heavy rain. When *Pegel* Kalkofen reaches 3·60m all navigation is temporarily stopped.

The locks are not equipped with VHF radio. They operate from 1000 to 1830, daily in summer but weekdays only in winter.

Kilometering starts at Giessen, 70km above the practical navigable limit at Dehrn near Limburg. Although the locks on the river above Dehrn are maintained in good working order, the river is navigable only by canoes and small boats. There is also a staircase lock and a tunnel (the only one in Germany) at Weilburg.

Km	
137·3	Junction with Rhein Km 585·7.
136·7	Bootshaus Radermacher on left bank above railway bridge. Water, electricity, showers, repairs, restaurant. Shops nearby.
136·0	*Schleuse Lahnstein* *Rise* 6·0m. Depends on level in Rhein.
135·1	Boatyard on right bank. Water and electricity.
134·7	Yacht-Club Lahn on right bank.
133·1	*Schleuse Ahl* *Rise* 3·0m.
129·4	*Schleuse Nievern* *Rise* 3·4m.
127·0	*Schleuse Ems* *Rise* 3·1m.
126·8	Marina on left bank. Water and electricity.
126·5	Boatyard on left bank. Fuel, repairs.
ca125	**Bad Ems**. Mooring to bank through town centre. No facilities.
124·0	Motorboot-Club Bad Ems on right bank. Water, electricity. Shops and restaurants nearby.
122·4	*Schleuse Dausenau* *Rise* 3·5m.
121·0	Motor-Yacht-Club Siegerland on right bank. Water, electricity. Shops and restaurants nearby.
117·6	*Schleuse Nassau* *Rise* 3·8m.
ca117	**Nassau.**
113·1	*Schleuse Hollerich* *Rise* 5·2m.
113·0	Attractive yacht harbour above lock. Water, electricity, showers, restaurant.
106·5	*Pegel* Kalkofen on right bank.
105·8	*Schleuse Kalkofen* *Rise* 5·5m.
102·5	**Laurenburg**. Fuel available from filling station close to right bank. Mooring to bank above and below bridge.
98·6	Beware outflow from power station.
96·8	*Schleuse Scheidt* *Rise* 3·8m.
91·8	*Schleuse Cramberg* *Rise* 4·7m.
91·0	Mooring possible on right bank above lock. No facilities.
90·8	Motor-Yacht-Club Schaumburg on right bank. Water, electricity, showers, clubhouse.
85·6	Staging on right bank. No facilities.
ca84	**Diez**.
83·8	Pontoon on left bank. No facilities.
83·2	*Schleuse Diez* *Rise* 3·4m.
81·6	Staging on left bank. Diez town 1·5km.
76·6	*Schleuse Limburg* *Rise* 3·6m.
76·4	Mooring to bank above lock.
ca76	**Limburg**.
75·8	Nautic-Club Mittellahn. Staging on left bank. Convenient for town centre.
73·0	Dietkirchen. Boatyard and staging on right bank. Water, electricity, showers. Shops and restaurants nearby.
71·0	Dehrn. Bootsclub Limburg on right bank. Water, electricity, showers, repairs, clubhouse. Shops and restaurants nearby.
70·0	End of navigation.

Obernhof on the Lahn.

Schleuse Kalkofen, above Obernhof.

MOSEL

Navigable length 242km
Maximum draught 2·50m
Maximum height 3·10–5·20m (see text).
Current 0·5–1·0km/h
Locks 13
Speed limit 30km/h except where indicated.

All the way from the French border to the Rhein, the Mosel valley is gorgeous. The scenery is very nearly as dramatic as that of the Rhein Gorge, with hillsides rising steeply from the water's edge and covered in vineyards or pine forests, and throughout the whole length of the river picturesque towns and villages with names familiar to everyone who drinks wine.

The Mosel is administered by WSD-Südwest. The river is fully canalised and has a minimum depth of 2·70m when *Pegel* Cochem reads 2·20m. At normal times it flows at only 0·5–1·0km/h. When the river is in flood, the speed of the current increases. If *Pegel* Cochem reaches 6·00m all traffic must stop. The lowest bridge is just downstream of Schleuse Koblenz, with a height of 5·20m at the time of highest water on the Rhein.

Including Apach, which is on the border, there are 13 locks on the German part of the river. None of them has floating bollards, but most have vertical bars as well as fixed bollards at intervals down the lock wall, which is very convenient for small boats. At each lock there is a self-operated boat lock with a width of 3·20m and a least depth of 1·50m.

Use of the boat locks is free, and there is also no charge for using the main locks provided it is in company with other vessels. If it is necessary for a small boat to be locked through one of the main locks alone, a small charge is made. All locks operate 24 hours a day.

Owing to the heavy barge traffic in the Mosel, most moorings in the main river are extremely uncomfortable due to the violence of the wash from the barges. As many barges operate during the night, it is always best to make overnight stops in harbours protected from their wash, rather than on exposed quays or pontoons along the river banks. Unfortunately, suitable harbours are not always conveniently situated, and journeys should be planned with this in mind. However, it will be found that at many locks there are sheltered corners where the lock-keepers will allow a small boat to stay for the night.

Km
0·0 Junction with Rhein Km 592·3.
0·4 to
1·0 Waiting quays for barges and passenger ships. Small boats are not welcome.
1·8 Schleuse Koblenz
Rise 4·90m (when *Pegel* Koblenz = 2·53m).
VHF Ch 20.
2·5 to
6·0 Speed limit 8km/h.
3·7 Segel- und Motor-Yacht-Club Koblenz on left bank. Water, electricity, showers, clubhouse. Shops and restaurants nearby.

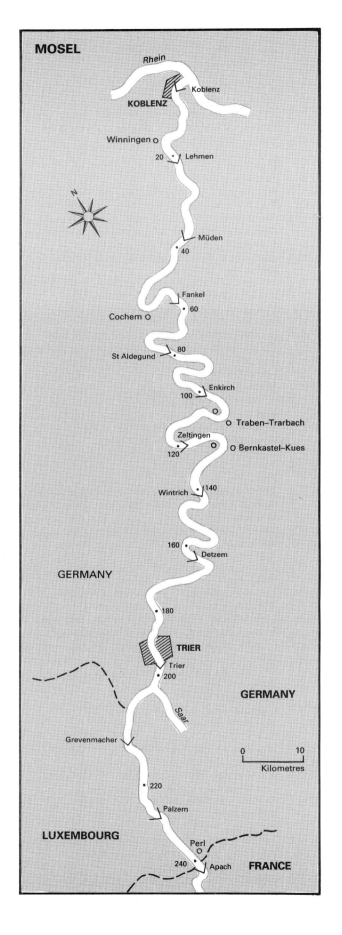

3·8   Motorboot- und Wasserski-Club Koblenz on left bank. Water, electricity, showers, clubhouse. Shops and restaurants nearby.

3·9   Yachtclub Rhein-Mosel-Koblenz on left bank.

4·5   Bootshafen Grühn on left bank. Fuel and repairs.

7·0   Marina Widenau on left bank. Repairs, wintering, restaurant.

11·3   Winningen. Fuel berth and railway station on left bank.

12·4   Marina Untermosel on right bank. Motorboot-Club Winningen. Water, electricity, showers, restaurant, fuel, repairs, crane.

13·5   Spectacular autobahn bridge.

20·8   *Schleuse Lehmen*
       Rise 7·5m.
       VHF Ch 78.

25·4   Filling station with staging on left bank.

26·7   Brodenbach. Yacht harbour on right bank. Depth 3m. Convenient for town centre. Water, electricity, showers. Shops and restaurants nearby.

32·0   Small yacht harbour at Burgen on right bank. Water, electricity, showers, restaurant.

37·1   *Schleuse Müden*
       Rise 6·5m.
       VHF Ch 79.

40·5   Large yacht harbour at Treis on right bank. All major facilities. Shops and restaurants nearby.

50 to

53   **Cochem**. Beautiful old town on left bank.

51·3   Cochem municipal yacht harbour on right bank.

59·4   *Schleuse Fankel*
       Rise 7·0m.
       VHF Ch 81.

60·8   Fuel berth on left bank.

61·0   Beilstein. Pretty village on right bank.

67·9   Senheim yacht harbour on right bank. Attractive setting. Pontoons. Good facilities.

78·3   *Schleuse St Aldegund*
       Rise 7·0m.
       VHF Ch 82.

82·1   River authority harbour on left bank near Alf. Possibility of overnight mooring with permission.

87·2   Zell. Town quay.

103·0   *Schleuse Enkirch*
       Rise 7·5m.
       VHF Ch 18.

103·7   Traben. Good yacht harbour on left bank, but close to railway. Water, electricity.

105·9   Fuel berth and river mooring place on right bank at Trarbach.

112·8   Kröv. Very attractive village on left bank, but no mooring place.

123·9   *Schleuse Zeltingen*
       Rise 6·0m.
       VHF Ch 20.

124·0   Possible mooring above lock.

128 to

132   **Bernkastel-Kues**.

130·8   Good harbour on left bank at Kues. Water, electricity, repairs, wintering. Shops and restaurants nearby.

141·4   *Schleuse Wintrich*
       Rise 7·5m.
       VHF Ch 22.

ca148   Piesport. Picturesque, but no mooring place.

166·8   *Schleuse Detzem*
       Rise 9·0m.
       VHF Ch 78.

178·4   Yacht harbour on left bank. Depth uncertain. Pontoon in river subject to severe wash. Water, electricity, showers, clubhouse, fuel. Restaurant.

Heavy traffic on the Mosel.

184·1   Hafen Trier. Commercial. Used for coal.

188 to

197   **Trier**. Fascinating town, but no satisfactory mooring places.

188·6   Shipyard on right bank.

191·2   Passenger jetty on right bank. Possibility of temporary mooring, but likely to be uncomfortable.

195·8   *Schleuse Trier*
       Rise 7·3m.
       VHF Ch 79.

196·3   Yacht club pontoons on right bank.

196·5   Bunker boat for diesel on left bank.

197·5   Trier municipal harbour for pleasure boats on left bank.

200·0   Konz municipal harbour. Marina and pontoons in river. Water, electricity, showers, clubhouse. Shops and restaurants nearby.

200·8   Junction with Saar.

205·9   Junction with Sauer. Left bank now Luxembourg.

206·0   Quay on left bank. Restaurant.

Bernkastel.

208·4	Hafen Mertert on left bank. Commercial harbour.
212·9	*Schleuse Grevenmacher* *Rise* 6·3m. *VHF* Ch 18.
215·0	Fuel station on left bank.
ca222	Wormeldigen. Quays on left bank.
229·8	*Schleuse Palzem* *Rise* 3·8m. *VHF* Ch 20.
233·4	Remich. Quay on left bank. No facilities. Shops and restaurants nearby.
237·5	Schwebsange. Large marina on left (Luxembourg) bank. Water, electricity, showers, fuel (cheaper than in Germany or France), chandlery.
242·2	French/German border on right bank.
242·4	*Schleuse Apach* *Rise* 4·4m. *VHF* Ch 20. Customs (French and German) at lock. Boat lock exists, but has not been operational for some time.

SAAR

Work has been in hand for many years to make it possible for Rhein barges to reach the coal-mining city of Saarbrücken, and to connect the Saar through to the *Saarkohlenkanal* (Saar coaling canal), which is known to the French as the *Canal des Houillères de la Sarre* (canal of the colliers of the Saar) and connects to the French waterway system via the Canal de la Marne au Rhin. However, partly due to environmentalist opposition, progress has been slow, and the expected completion date for the through route has had to be postponed repeatedly. At present, it is possible to navigate from the Mosel as far as Hostenbach (Km 73·3), and work is progressing with the final section to Saarbrücken, from where the old canal to the French border and beyond is still operational. Schleuse Lisdorf is already complete, and the new large lock at Saarbrücken is under construction. When the project is completed in 1997 the small locks at Völklingen, Luisenthal and Saarbrücken will no longer exist.

Apart from the industrial area around Saarbrücken, the canal's setting is idyllic, similar in character to that of the Mosel. The river winds its way along a beautiful valley, bordered by steep wooded hillsides. At each bend a new and dramatic vista unfolds.

The Saar is controlled by WSD-Südwest and passage is free.

1. KONZ TO HOSTENBACH
Km 0·0–Km 73·3

Navigable distance 73·3km
Maximum draught 2·7m
Maximum height 5·25m
Current Negligible at normal times.
Locks 5
Hours 24hrs daily Kanzem to Rehlingen, Lisdorf 0600–2200 after pre-advice in Rehlingen.
Speed limit 16km/h

Each of the first four locks on this stretch of the canalised Saar is in fact a pair of locks, the larger one having a width of 12m and the smaller 6·75m.

Km	
0·0	Junction with Mosel Km 200·8.
5·1	*Schleuse Kanzem* *Rise* 11·75m. *VHF* Ch 78.
8·2	Biebelhausen. Possible mooring on left bank.
10·2	Niederleuken. Water authority harbour on left bank. Possibility of mooring in emergency.
11·7	**Saarburg**. Possible mooring on left bank at quay near passenger landing point.
15·6	Possible mooring on right bank.
18·4	*Schleuse Serrig* *Rise* 14·5m. *VHF* Ch 82.
19·4	Hamm. Possible mooring on left bank.
30·4	Mettlach. Possible mooring place on left bank.
31·4	*Schleuse Mettlach* *Rise* 11·0m. *VHF* Ch 18.
41·1	Hafen Merzig. Commercial harbour.
ca44	**Merzig**.
44·2	Possible mooring place for pleasure craft.
54·1	*Schleuse Rehlingen* *Rise* 8·0m. *VHF* Ch 20.
56·4	Harbour on right bank for Wasser- und Wassersport-Club Dillingen/Saar. Water, electricity, slip, repairs. 35 minutes on foot to town centre.
58·8	**Dillingen**. Commercial harbour.
60·7	Saarlouis. Possible mooring place on right bank. 20 minutes to town centre.
66·1	*Schleuse Lisdorf* *Rise* 3·9m. *VHF* Ch 22.
73·3	Hostenbach. Temporary end of navigation.

2. GÜDINGEN TO SAARBRÜCKEN
Km 0·0–Km 8·4

Navigable distance 8·4km
Maximum draught 1·80m
Maximum height 5·25m
Current Very little under normal conditions.
Locks 1
Hours Mon–Fri 0830–1700, Sat/Sun 1000–1830.
Speed limit 12km/h

From the French border, 6km upstream from Saarbrücken, the canalised Saar enables French *péniches* to reach Saarbrücken. The minimum lock dimensions are the standard French 38·50x5·10m, but when the through connection to the Mosel is completed, downstream from Saarbrücken the minimum lock dimensions will be 185x12m.

Km	
0·0	French/German border on left bank.
1·1	*Schleuse Güdingen* *Rise* 2·3m. *VHF* Ch 79.
3 to 13	**Saarbrücken**.
3·9	Osthafen Saarbrücken. Commercial harbour.
6·8	Possible mooring on right bank.
8·4	*Schleuse Saarbrücken.* *VHF* Ch 78. Temporary end of navigation.

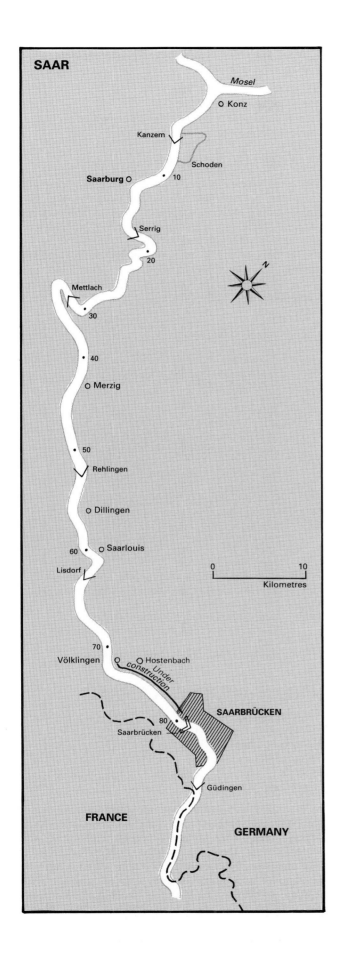

SAAR

Mosel

o Konz

Kanzem

Schoden

Saarburg o • 10

Serrig

• 20

Mettlach

• 30

• 40

o Merzig

• 50

Rehlingen

o Dillingen

60 • o Saarlouis

Lisdorf

0   10
Kilometres

70 •

Völklingen o   o Hostenbach

Under construction

SAARBRÜCKEN

80 •

Saarbrücken

Güdingen

FRANCE

GERMANY

West

RUHR

The Ruhr: the very name conjures up an image of industrial wastelands and ugliness. Maybe this was once an accurate picture of the area, but there are few such sights still existing. From the Rhein the first 12km stretch of the river Ruhr is indeed still industrial, but by no means ugly. Beyond Mülheim the river becomes pleasantly rural, used mostly for leisure purposes.

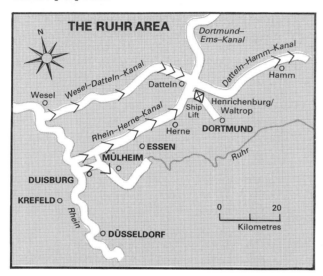

1. RHEIN TO MÜLHEIM
Km 0·0–Km 12·2

Navigable distance 12·2km
Maximum draught 2·60m
Maximum height 6·50m
Current Negligible
Locks 2
Speed limit 12km/h

The two locks operate from 0500 to 2100 on week-days and 0500 to 1300 on Sundays.

This stretch of the river is administered by WSD-West, and there are no charges.

Km
0·0   Junction with Rhein Km 780·1.
2·5   *Schleuse Duisburg*
        Rise 5m but varies with level in Rhein.
        VHF Ch 20.
4·3   Connecting link to Rhein-Herne-Kanal.
7·9   *Schleuse Mülheim-Raffelberg*
        Rise 6·9m.
        VHF Ch 78.
ca9   Hafen **Mülheim** on left bank. Large commercial port.
8·6   Harbour of Yachtclub Mülheim Ruhr on left bank. Water, electricity, clubhouse. Shops and restaurants nearby.
12·2 End of WSD-West jurisdiction.

2. MÜLHEIM TO ESSEN-RELLINGHAUSEN
Km 12·2–Km 41·4

Navigable distance 29·2km
Maximum draught 1·70m
Maximum height 3·2m (4·75m in centre of arches).
Current Negligible
Locks 3
Speed limit 12km/h (6km/h in narrow parts).

The river passes through some very interesting and attractive countryside. Between Baldeney-See and Rote-Mühle motorboats must stay in the marked channel. Mooring is not permitted in the Baldeney-See, above Schleuse Baldeney.

This part of the Ruhr is not operated by WSD: it is owned by the *Land* of Nordrhein-Westfalen, and a fee is charged for using it. The locks are not equipped with VHF radio.

Km
12·5 *Schleuse Mülheim*
        Rise 5·5m.
        Hours Mon–Fri 0700–1630, Sat/Sun 0730–2000.
ca13 Possible mooring place on right bank.
21·5 *Schleuse Kettwig*
        Rise 5·5m.
        Hours Mon–Fri 0730–1630, Sat/Sun 0900–1200 and 1500–2000.
22·1 Motorbootclub Kettwig on right bank. Water, electricity. Shops and restaurants nearby.
22·7 Camp site on left bank with moorings.
25·7 Essener Outboard-Club on left bank. Water, electricity.
26·1 Werdener-Yacht-Club on right bank.
29·3 *Schleuse Baldeney*
        Rise 9·2m.
        Hours Mon–Fri 0730–1630, Sat/Sun 0900–1200 and
        1500–2000.
        Note that in Baldeney-See it is not permitted to leave the marked channel or to land on the shore.
33·5 Private harbour on left bank.
38·4 *Schleuse Rote-Mühle.* Permanently open: no longer in operation. Restaurant and landing stage.
41·4 Essen-Rellinghausen. End of navigation.

RHEIN-HERNE-KANAL

Navigable distance 49·2km
Maximum draught 2·50m
Maximum height 4·50m
Current Nil
Locks 5
Speed limit 12km/h

At one time this canal was heavily industrial, but it has been transformed into a waterway which is now largely rural. There are still a few industrial plants in evidence, but they are mostly modern and clean. The canal itself is bordered for most of its length by trees; there is copious wildlife, and it is popular with anglers. In warm weather it is likely that swimmers too will be enjoying water which is presumably therefore not significantly polluted.

The first 3·6km of the canal is technically the Hafenkanal Duisburg, and Km 0·0 of the RHK is at the end of this stretch, just before the first lock. There is a fairly busy traffic of barges in the canal, but passage through the locks is quick and easy. The full length of the canal is likely to take some 9 hours to traverse.

The Rhein-Herne-Kanal is a *Bundeswasserstrasse* operated by WSD-West, and passage is free. The locks operate on weekdays for 24 hours a day, but starting at 0500 on Mondays. On Saturdays they work until 2100 and on Sundays their hours are 0500 to 1300.

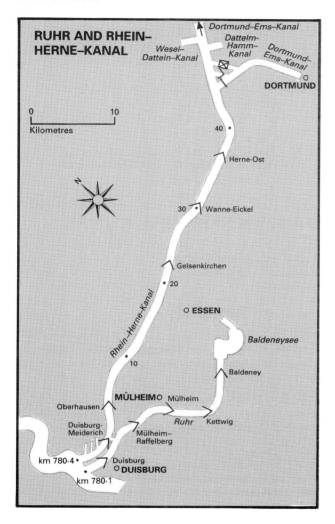

Schleuse Herne-Ost.

Km	
30·1	*Schleuse Wanne-Eickel* *Rise 8·1m.* *VHF* Ch 78.
37·0	*Schleuse Herne-Ost* *Rise 12·6m.* *VHF* Ch 22. Floating bollards on north side.
37·8	Yacht harbour on south bank.
38·2	Yacht harbour on north bank. Water, electricity, clubhouse.
45·6	Junction with Dortmund-Ems-Kanal Km 15·5.

WESEL-DATTELN-KANAL

Navigable distance 60·3km
Maximum draught 2·50m
Maximum height 4·50m
Current Nil
Locks 6
Speed limit 12km/h

Like the RHK, this canal carries a considerable traffic of barges, but it runs entirely through pleasant rural countryside. The locks are all easy to deal with and for planning purposes it is likely to take about 8 hours to travel from one end to the other. It is possible to tie up for the night above or below all the locks except Friedrichsfeld, but if entering from the Rhein it may be useful to note that the yacht harbour at Wesel, close to the entrance to the canal, is well equipped for an overnight stop.

The WDK is administered by WSD-West and there are no charges. None of the locks have floating bollards. Although the locks operate round the clock from 0500 on Mondays to 2100 on Saturdays (Sundays 0500 to 1300), in fact the barge traffic in practice ceases at night.

Km	
0·0	Junction with Rhein Km 813·2.
1·8	*Schleuse Friedrichsfeld* *Rise 8m. Depends on water level in Rhein.* *VHF* Ch 20.

Km
0·0   Start of Hafenkanal Duisburg. Junction with Rhein Km 780·4.
3·6/0·0 End of Hafenkanal Duisburg. Start of Rhein-Herne-Kanal.
0·7   *Schleuse Duisburg-Meiderich*
      Rise 5m (depends on water level in Rhein).
      VHF Ch 82.
1·8   Connecting link to Ruhr river.
5·5   *Schleuse Oberhausen*
      Rise 4·1m.
      VHF Ch 81.
13 to
20   **Essen.**
23·0 *Schleuse Gelsenkirchen*
      Rise 6·5m.
      VHF Ch 79.
      Floating bollards on south side.

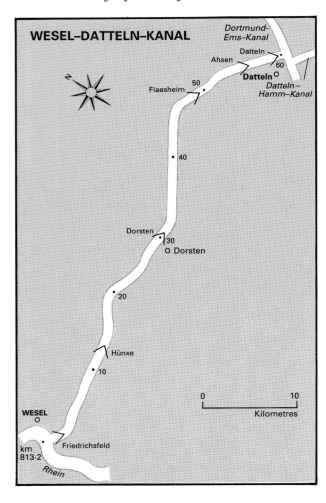

WESEL–DATTELN–KANAL

2·0	Work harbour on south bank. Mooring possible by negotiation.
13·2	*Schleuse Hünxe* Rise 5·5m. *VHF* Ch 78.
28·5	Yacht harbour on north bank. Water, electricity, showers, clubhouse.
30·5	*Schleuse Dorsten* Rise 9·0m. *VHF* Ch 79.
37·7	Commercial harbour on south bank. Possibility of mooring, with permission.
49·4	*Schleuse Flaesheim* Rise 4·0m. *VHF* Ch 81.
55·8	*Schleuse Ahsen* Rise 7·5m. *VHF* Ch 82.
59·3	Water authority harbour on south bank. Possibility of mooring, with permission.
59·5	*Schleuse Datteln* Rise 7·5m. *VHF* Ch 78.
60·3	Junction with Dortmund-Ems-Kanal Km 21·3. Bunker boats for diesel in DEK at Datteln.

DATTELN–HAMM–KANAL

Navigable distance 47·2km
Maximum draught 2·50m
Maximum height 4·0m
Current Nil
Locks 2
Hours 0500–2100 weekdays only
Speed limit 12km/h

The modernisation of German industry has improved the ambience of this canal, but it is not one of the most interesting of waterways. Its traffic is mostly commercial.

Km

0·0	Junction with Dortmund-Ems-Kanal Km 19·5.
1·9	Yacht harbour on south bank. Water, electricity, shops.
23·3	Yacht harbour on south bank.
27·0	Yacht club on south bank.
ca30	**Hamm**.
36·9	*Schleuse Hamm* Rise 1·7m. *VHF* Ch 18.
40·3	*Schleuse Werries* Rise 5·1m. *VHF* Ch 22.
47·2	End of canal.

One of the very straightforward locks on the Wesel-Datteln-Kanal.

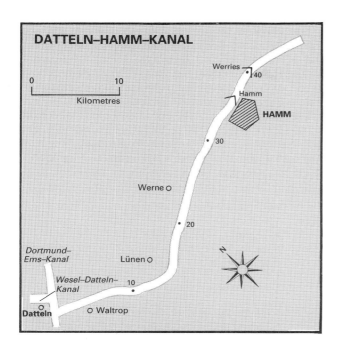

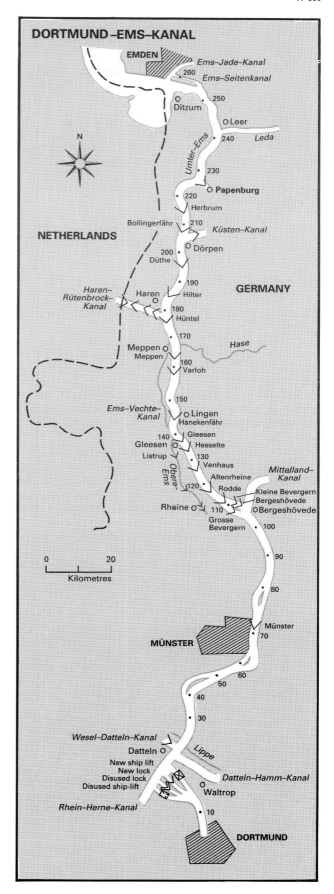

DORTMUND-EMS-KANAL

Navigable distance 225·8km (see note below)
Maximum draught 2·50m
Maximum height 4·25m
Current Nil
Locks 16
Speed limit 12km/h

The first 15km, from Dortmund to Henrichenburg/Waltrop, was once through an area of heavy industry, but most of the industrial debris has now been cleared away and the countryside is gradually becoming rural.

For those interested in canal engineering it is mandatory to stop for a few hours at Henrichenburg/Waltrop, at the junction of the Rhein-Herne-Kanal with the Dortmund-Ems-Kanal, to see the old *Schiffshebewerk* (ship lift), opened in 1899 and with a vertical lift of 13·5m. Alongside it is the original *Schachtschleuse* (shaft lock), built in 1914 to provide extra capacity. The two now form the basis of a very interesting canal museum; they have been replaced by the present ship lift, opened in 1962, and next to it the 1989 shaft lock. All are fascinating examples of canal engineering.

From the ship lifts, the DEK passes through Datteln, an important canal crossroads, and then northwards through Münster to join the Ems and pass into the North Sea. More importantly from the point of view of inland waterway navigation, it provides links to the Mittellandkanal, which traverses northern Germany from east to west, and to the Küstenkanal, which is a fast barge route to the lower Weser.

From Datteln northwards the route is almost entirely rural, passing through fertile farmlands and interesting small towns. Not surprisingly, being so close to the Dutch border, the more northerly stretches of the canal have a distinctly Dutch atmosphere, with fewer trees, grassy dykes, cattle grazing, herons fishing and a general air of neatness.

The ship-lift and *Schachtschleuse* at Henrichenburg from the southeast.

The university city of Münster, capital of the old kingdom of Westphalia, played an important part in the early history of Germany. Badly bombed in World War II, its rebuilt cathedral has at its entrance a stone from the equally badly damaged Coventry Cathedral as a symbol of mutual forgiveness.

There are numerous yacht clubs along the canal. In addition there are long stretches of canal bank with mooring bollards or rings where a pleasant overnight stay amongst pleasant rural scenery can be had after the barge traffic stops, around 2100 on weekdays.

The canal is controlled by WSD-West, and the locks work from 0500 to 2100 Monday to Saturday and 0900 to 1200 on Sundays. There are no fees. All the locks are equipped with VHF radio and have fixed bollards, except the new Henrichenburg shaft lock, which has floating bollards.

Technically, the DEK continues along the tidal Unter Ems beyond Km 225·8 and includes the Ems-Seitenkanal, terminating in Emden. North of Km 225·8 the waterway is administered by WSD-Nordwest. For the sake of simplicity, this book deals with the Unter Ems and the Ems-Seitenkanal as separate entities.

Km	
0·0	Dortmund south harbour.
15·0	*Schachtschleuse Henrichenburg* *Fall* 13·5m. *VHF* Ch 20. *Schiffshebewerk Henrichenburg* *Fall* 13·5m. *VHF* Ch 20.
15·3	Motorboot-Club Lüdenscheid below old shaft lock. Water, electricity, showers, shops, restaurants. Fuel nearby. Yachtclub Hebewerk Henrichenburg below old ship lift. Water, electricity, showers, shops, restaurants. Fuel nearby.
15·5	Junction with Rhein-Herne-Kanal Km 45·6.
19·5	Junction with Datteln-Hamm-Kanal Km 0·0.
20·5	Hafen Datteln on east bank. Commercial harbour, but possibility of overnight mooring if space allows.
21·2	Bunker boat for diesel on west side. Also repairs and supplies nearby.
21·3	Junction with Wesel-Datteln-Kanal Km 60·3.
30·0	Yachtclub Dortmund-Ems in old river on west bank. Water, electricity. Depth 2m.

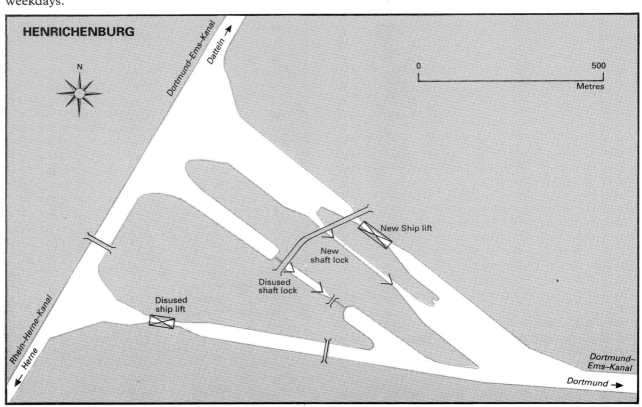

The ship-lift at Henrichenburg from the west.

34·6	Hafen Lüdinghausen on west bank. Water authority harbour, but overnight mooring a possibility.
39·6	Motor-Yacht-Club Datteln in southern entrance to old river on east bank. Water, electricity, showers, clubhouse. Depth 1·5–2·5m.
46·6	Yachtclub Kranecamp Senden in northern entrance to old river on east bank. Depth 1·2m. Water, electricity. Supermarket nearby.
50·3	Yachtclub Tomberge on east bank. Depth 1m. Water, electricity.
55·7	Yachtclub Münsterland in inlet on east bank. Depth 2m. Water, electricity, showers. Shops and restaurants 2km.
67 to 68	Commercial harbour on west bank. Mooring possible. No facilities.
70·5	Bunker station for diesel.
70·7	**Münster**. Monasteria Yacht-Club Münster in inlet on west bank. Depth 2m. Water, electricity, showers, slip. Supermarket nearby. Good base for exploring Münster.
71·5	*Schleuse Münster* *Fall 6·2m.* *VHF* Ch 22.
77·6	Boots-Center Münster on east bank. Depth 2m. Water, electricity, showers, slip, crane, repairs, fuel. Shops nearby, restaurants 10 mins.
79·7	Marina Alte-Fahrt Fuestrup in old canal on east side. Depth 2m. Water, electricity, showers, restaurant, slip, crane.
107·6	Bunker boat (for diesel) and grocery shop and chandlery on west bank. Restaurant nearby. Bunker boat for diesel on east bank. Extensive bank-side mooring places.
108·3	Junction with Mittellandkanal Km 0·0.
108·4	Channel divides. Eastern channel leads through two locks, Schleuse Bergeshövede and Kleine Schleuse Bevergern, whilst the western channel leads through a single lock, Grosse Schleuse Bevergern, before the two branches rejoin each other ca. Km 110. Pleasure craft normally lock through the two smaller locks.

Eastern branch

108·6	*Schleuse Bergeshövede* *Fall 4·1m.* *VHF* Ch 20.
109·7	*Kleine Schleuse Bevergern* *Fall 4·0m.* *VHF* Ch 20.

Western branch

109·3	*Grosse Schleuse Bevergern* *Fall 8·1m.* *VHF* Ch 20.
ca110	Channels reunite.
112·5	*Schleuse Rodde* *Fall 3·8m.* *VHF* Ch 18.
117·9	*Schleuse Altenrheine* *Fall 3·6m.* *VHF* Ch 82.
123·1	Hafen Spelle-Venhaus. Small commercial harbour without facilities, but suitable for overnight mooring if space can be found. Depth 3m.
126·6	*Schleuse Venhaus* *Fall 3·5m.* *VHF* Ch 81.
134·5	*Schleuse Hesselte* *Fall 3·4m.* *VHF* Ch 79. Shop and restaurant at lock.
137·9	*Schleuse Gleesen* *Fall 6·4m.* *VHF* Ch 78.
138·3	Junction with Obere Ems on west side. Navigable for 7–8km to Schleuse Listrup for vessels drawing up to 1m. Three more locks above Listrup, but for shallow-draught boats only. Yachtclub Lingen-Ems near Leschede, 6km from DEK. Water, electricity.
139·8	Entrance to Ems-Vechte-Kanal on west side. Yachtclub Lingen (Ems). Water, electricity.
141·0	*Flood lock Hanekenfähr.* *VHF* Ch 22.
141·6	Entrance to old canal. Two yacht clubs. Water, electricity, showers.
144·4	**Lingen** south harbour. No facilities.
145·9	Lingen old harbour. No facilities.
146·5	Lingen new harbour. No facilities.

Hafen Spelle-Venhaus at Km 123·1.

Moored above Schleuse Varloh for the night.

148·6   Small commercial harbour. Suitable for overnight mooring if space allows.

158·1   *Schleuse Varloh*
         Fall 3·7m.
         VHF Ch 20.
         Attractive mooring above and between locks. Pleasure craft usually use small lock.

163·9   *Schleuse Meppen*
         Fall 7·5m.
         VHF Ch 18.

166·9   Hafen Meppen. Uncomfortable. No facilities.

169·2   Old river entrance. Attractive stopping place. Yachtclub Hase-Ems. Water, electricity, showers, restaurant, repairs, slip, crane. Supplies nearby.

174·2   *Schleuse Hüntel*
         Fall 2·9m.
         VHF Ch 82.
         Shop at lock.

178·1   Junction with Haren-Rütenbrock-Kanal.

179·0   Hafen **Haren** on west bank. Water, electricity, fuel, slip. Convenient for Haren town centre.

Hafen Ditzum, on the west side of the Unter Ems.

186·0   *Schleuse Hilter*
         Fall 1·5m.
         VHF Ch 81.

195·0   *Schleuse Düthe*
         Fall 2·2m.
         VHF Ch 79.

197·0   Old river entrance. Navigable for 7km by vessels drawing up to 1m. Good overnight stop.

200·5   Small yacht harbour on east bank.

202·6   Junction with Küstenkanal Km 69·6.

205·8   *Schleuse Bollingerfähr*
         Fall 1·8m.
         VHF Ch 78.

212·5   *Schleuse Herbrum*
         Fall 0·2–1·8m (depends on tide).
         VHF Ch 22.
         River below lock is tidal. Minimum depth at LW ca. 1·5m. Soft bottom. Channel well marked with red/green and cardinal buoys.

218·5   Harbour of Wassersportclub Rhede on west side. Water, electricity, showers, fuel.

225·8   Entrance to basin below Schleuse Papenburg on east side. Possible overnight mooring.

UNTER EMS

Navigable distance 40·7km to Emden
Maximum draught 1·5m at LW
Maximum height Unlimited (2 opening bridges)
Current Tide 5–8km/h
Locks None

The Unter Ems north of Km 225·8 and the Ems-Seitenkanal are administratively considered to be a continuation of the DEK to Emden. The situation is slightly confused by the fact that the DEK kilometering continues beyond Km 225·8, but then changes to the Unter Ems markings. For the sake of simplicity this book treats the DEK, the Unter Ems and the Ems-Seiten as separate entities.

The tidal Ems winds its way northwards through mudflats, saltmarsh and sea banks. Redshanks, oystercatchers and other waders wheel around, fishermen manipulate drop nets and fishing boats ply to and fro. Estuary life has not changed much over the years.

The channel is well marked with red, green and cardinal marks, to such an extent that a detailed chart is not essential. The tide, however, runs strongly, and whether entering or leaving good timing is important.

The city of Emden, the small fishing village of Ditzum opposite and the attractive small town of Leer all make interesting overnight stops. It is also from this stretch that access is gained to the fascinating small northern waterways: the Leda, the Jümme and the Ems-Jade-Kanal.

Km

0·0   Junction with Dortmund-Ems-Kanal Km 225·8. Entrance to lock basin at **Papenburg**. Possible overnight stop.

6·9   Opening bridge. *VHF Ch 15.*

7·6   Weener. Yacht harbour on left bank. Fuel, restaurant.

14·3   Junction with Leda.
         Town moorings in **Leer** through sea lock, 1·7km upstream from mouth of Leda. Passage is free if

with commercial ships or at 1730 on Fridays, 0800, 1400 and 1730 on Saturdays and Sundays. Otherwise there is a fee of DM 5. *VHF* Ch 13.

15·1   Opening bridge. *VHF* Ch 15.

16·9   Marina Bingum on left bank. Fuel, shops.

21·3   Hafen Jemgum. Dries at LW.

30·3   **Oldersum**. Junction with Ems-Seitenkanal (DEK Km 256·4).

33·8   **Ditzum**. Small fishing harbour on left bank. Dries at LW but very soft mud. Major boatyard.

40·7   **Emden**. Sea lock on right bank. *VHF* Ch 13. Access to port, yacht harbour, Ems-Jade-Kanal and outer end of Ems-Seitenkanal. Bunker boat for diesel in Emden harbour. See plan page 56.

EMS-SEITENKANAL

Navigable distance 9·1km
Maximum draught 1·50–2·00m (varies)
Maximum height 2·80–3·20m (varies)
Current Negligible
Locks 2
Speed limit 7km/h if draught is less than 1·30m, 5km/h if draught is more than 1·30m.

Technically considered to be an extension of the Dortmund-Ems-Kanal, the Ems-Seitenkanal provides access for inland shipping to the port of Emden, minimising the amount of tidal navigation necessary. It also links to the Ems-Jade-Kanal.

Km
256·4   Start of canal. Junction with Unter Ems Km 30·3.

256·6   *Schleuse Oldersum*
         Rise 0·5–2·3m (depends on tide).
         VHF Ch 13.
         Hours Mon–Fri 0700–2000, Sat/Sun 0800–1100 and 1500–1800 (depends on tide).

265·1   Junction with connecting canal to Ems-Jade-Kanal.

265·4   *Schleuse Borssum*
         Rise 2·1m.
         Hours Mon–Fri 0700–1200 and 1230–1900, Sat/Sun 0800–1200 and 1230–1630.

265·5   End of canal in Emden port. Also connects to EJK.

HAREN-RÜTENBROCK-KANAL

Navigable distance 13·5km
Maximum draught 1·50
Maximum height 3·70
Locks 4
Speed limit 5km/h

Passing through flat and rural but nevertheless attractive countryside, the Haren-Rütenbrock-Kanal is a useful waterway link between Holland and Germany for pleasure boats up to 6m beam. There are 12 opening bridges, and the locks work on Mondays to Fridays 0700 to 1200 and 1300 to 1800. On Saturday mornings boats must travel in organised convoys, at 0900 from the DEK towards Holland and 1100 from the Dutch border towards the DEK. The canal is closed at other times during the weekend. A fee of DM 3·80 is payable.

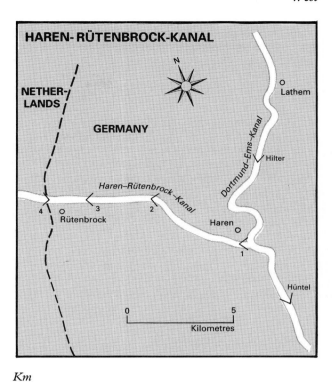

HAREN-RÜTENBROCK-KANAL

Km
0·0   Junction with Dortmund-Ems-Kanal Km 178·2.

0·1   *Schleuse 1 (Haren)*
       Rise 3·70m.

6·8   *Schleuse 2*
       Rise 1·60m.

10·9   *Schleuse 3*
        Rise 1·70m.

13·5   *Schleuse 4 (Rütenbrock)*. Permanently open. Junction with Dutch *Stadtskanaal* at border.

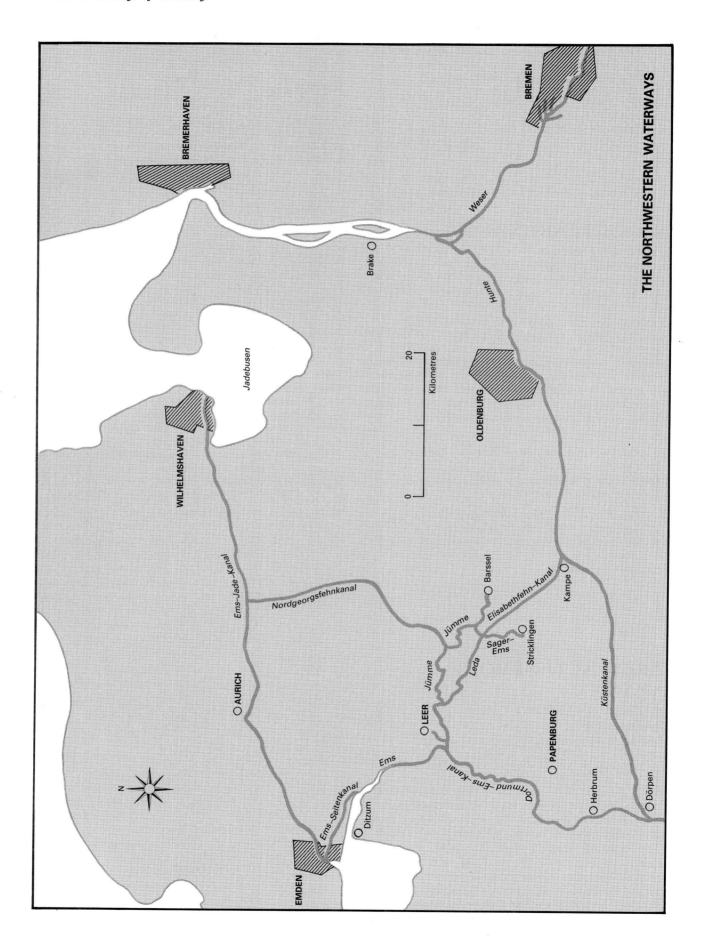

THE NORTHWESTERN WATERWAYS

BREMEN

BREMERHAVEN

Weser

Brake

Hunte

Jadebusen

20

Kilometres

OLDENBURG

0

WILHELMSHAVEN

Ems–Jade–Kanal

Nordgeorgsfehnkanal

Barssel

Elisabethfehn-Kanal

Jümme

Sager–
Ems

Stricklingen

Kampe

Küstenkanal

AURICH

Jümme

Leda

LEER

PAPENBURG

N

Ems

Dortmund–Ems–Kanal

Ems–Seitenkanal

Ditzum

Herbrum

Dörpen

EMDEN

Northwest

EMS-JADE-KANAL

Navigable distance 72·3km
Maximum draught 1·70m
Maximum height 3·80m
Locks 7
Speed limit 8km/h if draught is less than 1·00m,
    6km/h if draught is more than 1·00m.

This canal is not particularly scenic, but it passes through pleasant rural countryside with much wildlife in evidence. It is owned by several local authorities: from Km 0·0 to Km 61·9 it is owned by the *Land* of Niedersachsen, from Km 61·9 to Km 67·4 it is state-owned, and from Km 67·4 to its end in Wilhelmshaven it is owned by the town of Wilhelmshaven. The *Seeschleuse* at Wilhelmshaven is owned and operated by the navy. There are no charges.

In dry summers the minimum depth in the summit reach can be less than the amount indicated, and it is best to make enquiries about the situation when entering the canal. There are many opening bridges, and it is necessary to give advance warning of one's arrival by sounding a foghorn.

The Kesselschleuse at Emden is a very interesting example of canal engineering: it is a 'crossroads' with four gates (see below), built in 1886. The Ems-Jade route is the one which is normally kept open.

In summer the locks work every day from 0800 to 1700, although there may be slight variation from lock to lock. All locks, however, cease operation for an hour at lunch time.

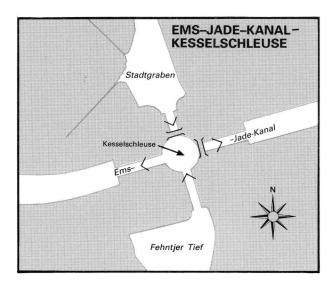

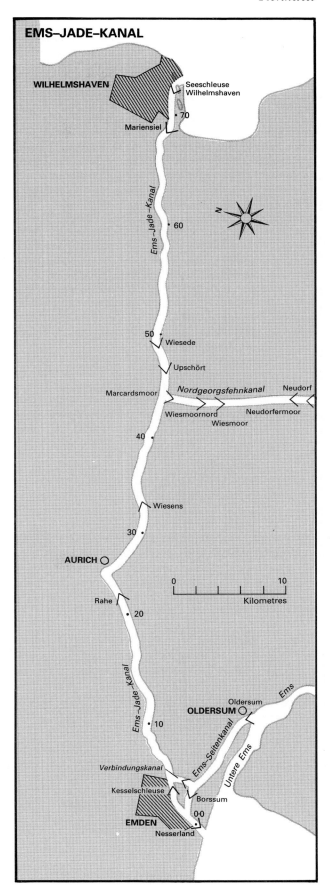

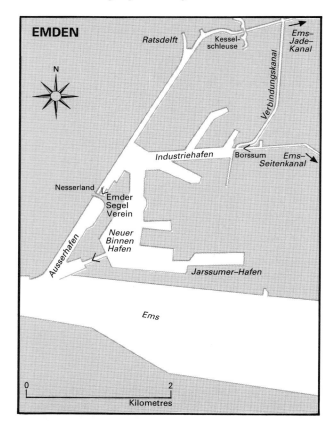

EMDEN

Ratsdelft

Kessel-
schleuse

Ems–
Jade–
Kanal

Verbindungskanal

Industriehafen

Borssum

Ems–
Seitenkanal

Nesserland

Emder
Segel
Verein

Neuer
Binnen
Hafen

Ausserhafen

Jarssumer–Hafen

Ems

0   2
Kilometres

Km

0·0   **Emden**. Emder Segel-Verein.
Sea lock Emden.
VHF Ch 13.
Good moorings outside lock close to centre of
town, fuel and supplies. Also in Jarssumer-Hafen.

2·5   Ratsdelft. Good moorings in front of Rathaus.
No facilities.

3·3   *Kesselschleuse Emden*
Rise Nil.

4·2   2·1km connecting canal to Ems-Seitenkanal
(DEK).

22·8   *Schleuse Rahe*
Rise 1·90m.

25·0   **Aurich**. Commercial harbour, but mooring
possible. Supplies nearby.

32·6   *Schleuse Wiesens*
Rise 2·60m.

42·4   Junction with Nordgeorgsfehnkanal.

44·0   *Schleuse Upschört*
Fall 2·90m.

45·9   *Schleuse Wiesede*
Fall 1·40m.
Mooring below lock.

60·0   Dykhausen. Mooring place and supplies in
village.

67·3   *Schleuse Mariensiel*
Fall 0·30m.

71·1   Jade Wassersport Club. Repairs, chandlery. Bus
to town.

71·5   **Wilhelmshaven**. Hochsee Yacht Club.
Customs, police, bus to town.

72·3   *Seeschleuse Wilhelmshaven*
Fall Depends on tide level.
VHF Ch 13.
Mooring possible in Grosser Hafen, Nordhafen
and Nassauhafen. Avoid military areas.

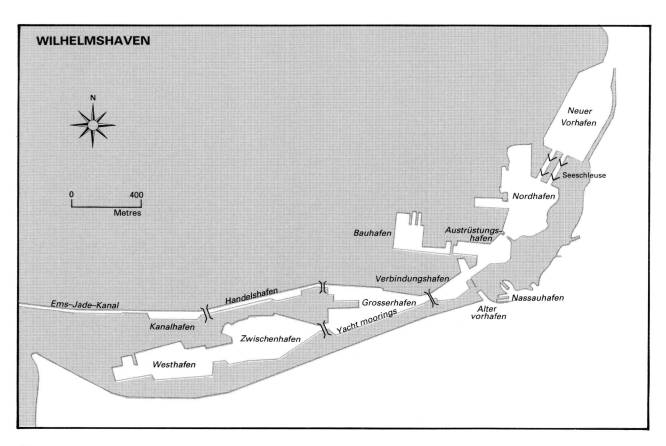

WILHELMSHAVEN

N

0   400
Metres

Neuer
Vorhafen

Seeschleuse

Nordhafen

Bauhafen

Austrüstungs-
hafen

Verbindungshafen

Ems–Jade–Kanal

Handelshafen

Grosserhafen

Nassauhafen

Alter
vorhafen

Kanalhafen

Yacht moorings

Zwischenhafen

Westhafen

NORDGEORGSFEHNKANAL

Navigable distance 31·8km
Maximum draught 1·40m
Maximum height 1·50m (soon to be 3·50m)
Current Nil
Locks 8
Speed limit 6km/h

A quiet, little-used canal linking the Ems-Jade to the Jümme, and running through low-lying agricultural land. Administered by the *Land* of Niedersachsen, it is open only by arrangement. It is necessary to contact *Staatliches Amt für Wasser und Abfall*, in Aurich – ☎ 04948 219, 04956 3339 or 04941 2392. A small fee is payable. It is also possible to go from the EJK at Marcardsmoor southwards to Wiesmoor and back by hiring a key which allows the Marcardsmoor (if not standing open), Wiesmoor Nord and Wiesmoor locks to be operated by the boat crew. A fee of DM 2 is payable for this, together with a deposit of DM 20.

The depth can reduce to below 1·40m during especially dry summers. There is a fixed bridge between Wiesmoor and Neudorfermoor locks, with a clearance of only 1·50. One more fixed bridge, further south, with headroom of 1·70m.

Km	
0·0	Junction with Jümme Km 9·8.
5·7	*Schleuse Nordgeorgsfehn I* Rise 2·20m.
9·5	*Schleuse Nordgeorgsfehn II* Rise 1·70m.
12·0	*Schleuse Remels III* Rise 1·10m.
18·5	*Schleuse Neudorf IV* Rise 2·20m.
19·9	*Schleuse Neudorfermoor V* Rise 1·50m.
27·1	*Schleuse Wiesmoor VI* Fall 1·70m.
28·1	*Schleuse Wiesmoor-Nord VII* Fall 1·40m.
31·5	*Schleuse Marcardsmoor VIII* Fall Nil (normally stands open).
31·8	Junction with Ems-Jade-Kanal Km 42·4.

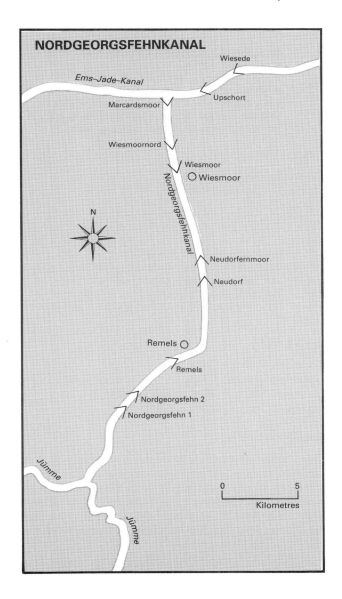

Windmill at Remels.

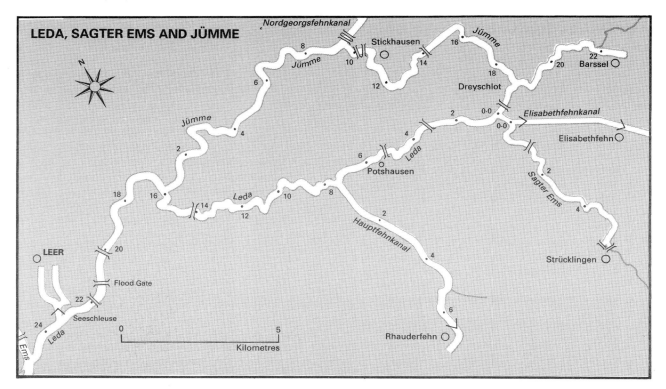

LEDA AND SAGTER EMS

The tidal Leda forms a link from the Unter Ems to the Jümme, the Sagter Ems and the Elisabethfehn-kanal. The surrounding terrain is flat, fertile and agricultural, but not without charm. The area abounds in wildlife and is especially good for the bird-watcher.

The Sagter Ems is the continuation of the Leda to Strücklingen. It is a quiet backwater which meanders gently through agricultural land and is the home of two sailing clubs. Towards Strücklingen the depth dwindles to 0·6m.

1. LEDA

Navigable distance 24·7km
Maximum draught 1·20m at LW, 2·50m at HW.
Maximum height 6·10m at LW, 4·80m at HW.
Current Tidal. Strong at times.
Locks None
Speed limit 7km/h against the tide,
    10km/h with the tide.

Km
24·7   Junction with Untere Ems Km 14·3.
23·0   *Seeschleuse Leer*, leading into Leer town harbour. Passage through the sea lock is free if with commercial ships or at 1730 on Fridays, 0800, 1400 and 1730 on Saturdays and Sundays. Otherwise there is a fee of DM 5. *VHF* Ch 13.
22·6   Sailing club with staging on right bank.
21·1   Flood barrier. 5 openings, each 14m wide. Use centre opening.
18·4   Sailing club on right bank. Water, electricity available.
16·9   Sailing club on left bank. Water, electricity available.
16·0   Junction with Jümme Km 0·0.

7·5   Junction with Hauptfehnkanal on left bank.
5·3   Potshausen. Lift bridge. Will open 0830–1000, 1300–1400 and 1700–2000 in summer.
0·0   Entrance to Dreyschlot on right bank, giving second connection with Jümme (and access to Barssel). Length 1·1km. Depth 1·40m at LW. River continues upstream as Sagter Ems.

2. SAGTER EMS

Navigable distance 5·9km
Maximum draught 1·40m
Current Tidal
Locks None

Km
0·0   Junction with Leda Km 0·0.
0·3   Junction with Elisabethfehnkanal on right bank.
1·2   Lift bridge. Advance notice required.
1·9   Sailing club on right bank.
5·9   Strücklingen. Sailing club. End of navigation.

JÜMME

Navigable distance 22·3km
Maximum draught 1·40m at LW, 2·90m at HW.
Maximum height 1·30m at HW, 2·80m at LW.
Current Tidal
Locks None
Speed limit 6km/h

The Jümme is a tributary of the Leda, joining it at Km 16. It is also connected to the Leda further upstream at the point where it becomes the Sagter Ems. The 1km linking canal is known as the Dreyschlot. There is a low fixed bridge at Km 14·8 and vessels heading for Barssel should proceed via the Leda and the Dreyschlot.

The beautiful river Lahn.

Barge skippers are usually very tolerant towards small boats.

Work boat on the Elbe-Havel-Kanal.

The south arm of the Donau at Regensburg.

Schleuse Regensburg, on the north arm of the Donau.

The town hall at Bamberg.

The German waterways are alive: there is a sense of purpose.

Heidelberg: the first of many essential stopping places on the Neckar.

Km

0·0	Junction with Leda Km 16.
0·1	Sailing club on right bank. Water, electricity available.
9·5	Small yacht harbour at junction with Nord-georgsfehnkanal on right bank.
10·8	Lift bridge. When closed height 1·75m.
14·8	Fixed bridge 1·95m. Restaurant and moorings.
20·3	Junction with Dreyschlot on left bank. Connects to Leda Km 0·0.
25·8	Bootshafen Barssel. Large yacht harbour with good facilities in centre of village.

ELISABETHFEHNKANAL

Navigable distance 14·9km
Maximum draught 0·90m
Maximum height 4·00m
Maximum beam 4·5m
Current None
Locks 4
Speed limit 7km/h if draught is less than 1·30m.
  5km/h if draught is more than 1·30m.

The Elisabethfehnkanal provides a link for shallow-draught boats from Kampe on the Küstenkanal to the Leda. It is fairly straight, passing through low-lying agricultural land, but is very peaceful and pleasant.

It is administered by WSD. Passage through the canal, which takes 3–4 hours, can be made only between May and September inclusive, and is organised in convoys. The collecting points are at the first bridge (Kamperfehn) when coming from the Küstenkanal and downstream of Osterhausen lock when coming from the Leda. There is only one lock-master, who travels from lock to lock by bicycle, operating the locks and the 8 opening bridges.

It is necessary to give advance notice of an intention to use the canal. This must be done by 1500 the day before the passage (Fridays for Sundays and Mondays), by informing the lock-master (☎ 04405 49852 or 04405 7437). Alternatively, notice can be given to the lock-masters at either Oldenburg or Dörpen on the Küstenkanal.

Km

0·0	Junction with Küstenkanal Km 29·3.
5·3	*Schleuse Reekenfeld* *Fall* 1·40m.
7·7	*Schleuse Brandreeken* *Fall* 1·00m.
11·3	*Schleuse Elisabethfehn* *Fall* 1·35m.
11·5	**Elisabethfehn.** Attractive mooring in village. Fuel available.
14·4	*Schleuse Osterhausen* *Fall* 0·3–0·8m.
14·8	Junction with Sagter Ems Km 0·3.

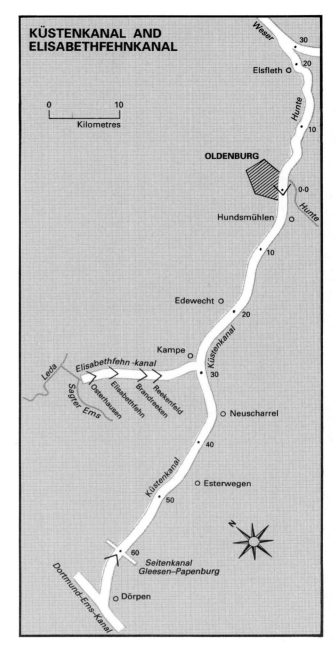

KÜSTENKANAL AND ELISABETHFEHNKANAL

KÜSTENKANAL AND UNTERE HUNTE

The Küstenkanal is straight, fairly heavily used by commercial shipping and not particularly interesting from the scenic point of view, but it is nevertheless a quick and convenient through route between the Dortmund-Ems-Kanal and the Weser. After the lock at Oldenburg the Küstenkanal becomes the tidal Untere Hunte, which flows into the Unterweser at Elsfleth.

The two locks work from 0500 to 2100 Mondays to Saturdays and 0900 to 1200 on Sundays. There are no real overnight stopping places, but it is usually possible to find an out-of-the-way spot at one of the barge overnight moorings if need be.

To the west of Km 8·1 the canal is administered by WSD-West. To the east it is under the control of WSD-Nordwest. The Untere Hunte is operated by WSD-Nordwest. There are no charges in any section, but there is strict enforcement of the 10km/h speed limit on the Untere Hunte.

The Untere Hunte, from Oldenburg to the Weser, is a wide tidal river, bordered by sea walls and mudflats. It is an excellent area for sea birds and waders, but is otherwise somewhat featureless. However, if the tide is judged correctly the 25km will be covered in a very short time. Navigation at night is forbidden in the direction from Oldenburg to Elsfleth.

1. KÜSTENKANAL

Navigable length 69·6km
Maximum draught 2·50m
Maximum height 4·50m
Current None
Locks 2
Speed limit 12km/h

Km
69·6   Junction with Dortmund-Ems-Kanal Km 202·6.
64·8   *Schleuse Dörpen*
        Rise 1·2m.
        VHF Ch 82.
64·0   Junction with Seitenkanal Gleesen-Papenburg. Water-sports club with deep-water moorings. Water, electricity, showers.
55·0   Yachtclub Surwold on north bank. Water, electricity, showers, fuel, repairs.
47·8   Esterwegen. Barge overnight stopping place.
38·4   Neuscharrel. Barge turning place. Possible mooring.
29·3   Junction with Elisabethfehnkanal Km 0·0.
28·8   Kampe. Barge overnight stop.
19·7   Edewechterdamm. Possible overnight stop.
5·5   Hundsmühlen. Possible overnight stop.
5·2   Flood barrier. Open at all normal times.
2·6   Bunker boat for diesel. Repairs.
1·9   *Schleuse Oldenburg*
        Fall 2·8–5·6m.
        VHF Ch 20.
0·8   Lift bridge. Make sound signal to open.

0·0   **Oldenburg** town harbour. North side no facilities. South side Yacht-Club Oldenburg. Water, electricity, showers, repairs, shops.
        Junction with Untere Hunte Km 0·0.

2. UNTERE HUNTE

Navigable length 25·1km
Maximum draught 2·30m at LW (tidal range approx 3m)
Maximum height 4·50m at mean HW
Current Strong tide
Locks None
Speed limit 10km/h

Km
0·0   Junction with Küstenkanal Km 0·0.
        Hafen Oldenburg. Commercial harbour.
0·5   Opening railway bridge. Call on Ch 73.
18·4   Huntebrücke. Call *Hunte Bridge* on Ch 73.
20·7   Opening railway bridge Elsfleth-Ohrt. Call *Elsfleth Bridge* on Ch 73.
21·7   Old branch of river (Westergate) on right bank. Shallow.
22·6   Hafen Elsfleth. Possibility of mooring. Bunker boat.
24·1   Flood barrier. Normally open.
25·1   Junction with Unterweser Km 32·0.

Huntebrücke, at Km 18·4 on the Untere Hunte.

Middle

FULDA

Navigable distance 29·0km
Maximum draught 1·20m
Maximum height 3·40m
Current Slight
Locks 5
Speed limit 12km/h upstream, 18km/h downstream.

Once the industrial surroundings of Kassel are left behind, the Fulda flows through attractive hilly countryside to its confluence with the Werra, which, like the Fulda upstream of Kassel, is unnavigable except by very shallow-draught boats.

With no commercial traffic, this is an extremely pleasant area in which to cruise, but it should be done in the earlier part of the summer, when water levels are less likely to be depleted. The beautiful old town of Hannoversch-Münden, standing at the junction of the Fulda and the Werra, should not be missed.

The river is controlled by WSD-Mitte, and no fees are payable. The locks, which are not equipped with VHF, operate from 0800 to 2000 daily during the summer months. The new Wahnhausen lock, with a rise of 8·5m, replaces four older locks.

Km

79·8	Motor-Yacht-Club **Kassel**. Water, electricity, showers, clubhouse, repairs, slip. Shops and restaurants nearby.
81·1	Nautic-Club Kassel. Water, electricity, showers, clubhouse, repairs, slip. Shops and restaurants nearby.
81·3	*Schleuse Kassel* Fall 2·8m.
82·2	Hafen Kassel. Yacht harbour with water, electricity, clubhouse. Shops and restaurants nearby.
85·4	Motor-Yacht-Club Sandershausen.
90·4	Yacht harbour on left bank.
93·5	*Schleuse Wahnhausen* Fall 8·5m.
101·0	Motor-Yacht-Club Wilhelmshausen.
101·4	*Schleuse Wilhelmshausen* Fall 2·4m.
105·3	*Schleuse Bonaforth* Fall 2·4m.
108·3	*Schleuse Hannoversch-Münden* Fall 2·9m.
108·8	Junction with Werra and Weser Km 0·0.

WESER

The Weser is formed by the Fulda joining forces with the Werra at Hannoversch-Münden. From here to Minden, where it crosses underneath the Mittellandkanal, it is known as the Oberweser. From Minden to Bremen it is the Mittelweser, and the tidal part below Bremen is the Unterweser.

The Oberweser is very attractive and there is no commercial shipping above Hameln, but it suffers from a shortage of water in the middle-to-late summer in most years. The Mittelweser is a commercial

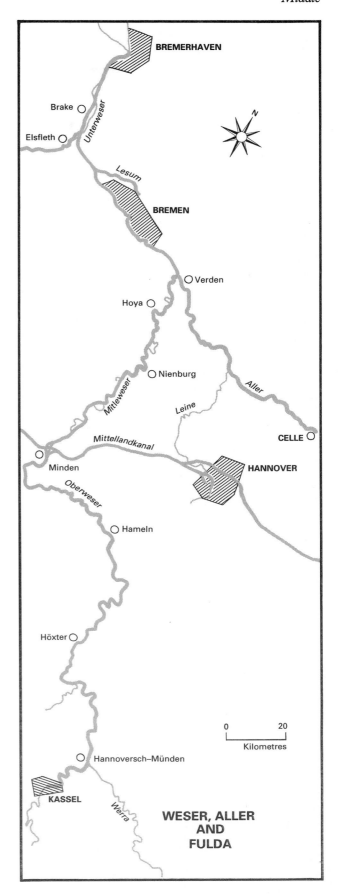

WESER, ALLER AND FULDA

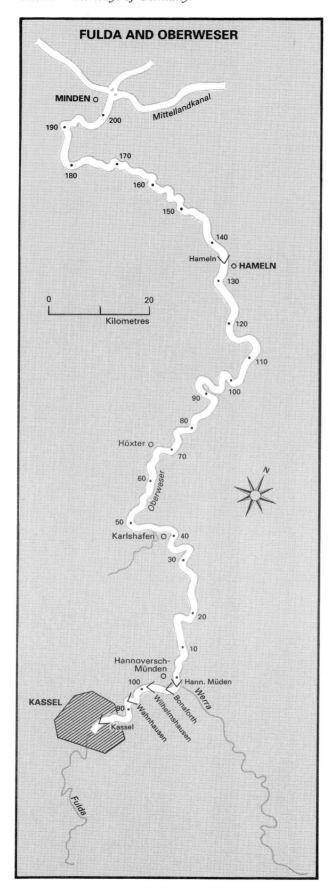

FULDA AND OBERWESER

shipping route and flows through pleasant rolling farmland. The tidal section below Bremen unfolds to become a typical low-lying estuary with salt-marsh, mudflats and sea walls.

Hannoversch-Münden, Hameln (of Pied Piper fame) and Minden are interesting historic towns, as is the old part of Bremen. However, away from the *Altstadt*, Bremen suffers somewhat from the same problems which beset most large industrial cities in our present age.

1. OBERWESER: HANNOVERSCH-MÜNDEN TO MINDEN
Km 0·0–Km 204·9

Navigable distance 204·9km
Maximum draught See table below.
Maximum height 4·30m
Current 2–5km/h at normal water levels
Locks 1
Speed limit 12km/h upstream, 18km/h downstream.

The depth of the Oberweser varies between 0·8m and 4·2m according to the volume of water in the river, and the current can attain speeds of 10kn in places in times of flood. It is necessary to check the level of water at the appropriate *Pegel* to establish the depth of water at any specific time. The highest and lowest levels shown in the table below demonstrate the variation in water levels.

Depths

Pegel	☎	*Min*	*Mid*	*Max*
Hann. Münden	05541 19429	1·00	1·90	5·10
Karlshafen	05672 19429	0·90	1·90	4·20
Hameln Wehrbergen	05151 19429	0·80	1·90	5·70

The one lock, at Hameln, works from 0630 to 1800 on weekdays and Saturdays and 0800 to 1100 on Sundays.

Km

0·0	Junction with Fulda and Werra.
44·0	Motorsportclub Weser-Diemel on left bank. Water, electricity, showers, clubhouse, slip. Shops and restaurants nearby.
50·5	Yacht club. Difficult to enter when water level is low.
69·9	Höxter. Water authority harbour which also houses a yacht club.
80·2	Holzminden. Yacht harbour on right bank. Depth uncertain.
111·9	Hafen Kemnade. Motorbootclub Bodenwerder. Water, electricity, clubhouse, crane.
132·3	Yacht harbour on right bank. Motorboot-Club Hameln. Water, electricity, showers, clubhouse, slip, restaurant.
134·5	Hafen **Hameln**. Less than ideal for pleasure boats, but repairs available at boatyard.
134·8	*Schleuse Hameln* *Fall* 2·60m. *VHF* Ch 20.
134·9	Yacht moorings near centre of town.
163·6	Rinteln. Tripper-boat quay near centre of town.
166·4	Entrance to Doktorsee on left bank. Entrance marked by red and green buoys. Water, electricity, showers, clubhouse, slip, crane. Shops and restaurants nearby.
173·1	Entrance to yacht harbour on left bank. Water, electricity, clubhouse.

175·6 Yacht harbour on left bank. Westfälischer Motor-yachtclub. Water, electricity, clubhouse, slip. Depth uncertain.

177·7 Yacht harbour on right bank. Water, electricity, clubhouse, slip, crane. Shops and restaurants nearby.

204·5 Junction with Verbindungskanal Süd, Minden. 2 locks to Mittellandkanal.
VHF Ch 22.

204·6 Motorboot-Club Minden on left bank. Water, electricity. Shops and restaurants nearby.

204·9 Mittellandkanal viaduct.
Bunker boats in Mittellandkanal near entrance to *Schachtschleuse*.

2. MITTELWESER: MINDEN TO BREMEN
Km 204·9–Km 366·7

Navigable distance 140·0km
Maximum draught 2·30m
Maximum height 4·50m
Current Slight
Locks 7
Speed limit 35km/h in river, 12km/h in lock canals.

Water levels in the Mittelweser are closely controlled and the waterway has a least depth of 2·50m. It is used by commercial shipping, but it is a fine river set in a very pleasant landscape.

The locks are all fitted with VHF, but not with floating bollards. All except the Weserschleuse at Bremen operate from 0600 to 2200 Mondays to Saturdays and from 0800 to 1100 on Sundays. Langwedel also operates from 1700 to 1800 on Sundays during the summer. The operating hours of the Bremer Weserschleuse are given in the route description.

Km
204·9 Mittellandkanal viaduct.
206·2 Junction with Verbindungskanal Nord. *Schacht-schleuse Minden*
VHF Ch 22.
213·5 Junction with Schleusenkanal Petershagen Km 0·0.
213·6 Motor-Yacht-Club Lahde. Water, electricity, clubhouse, slip.
214·0 Weir.

Schleusenkanal Petershagen
0·0 Junction with Weser Km 213·5.
6·7 Possible mooring place on left bank.
7·0 *Schleuse Petershagen*
Fall 6·0m.
VHF Ch 20.
7·3 Possible mooring place on left bank.
8·3 Junction with Weser Km 224·1

Mittelweser (continued)
224·1 Junction with Schleusenkanal Petershagen.
231·4 Junction with Schleusenkanal Schlüsselburg.
236·6 Weir.

Schleusenkanal Schlüsselburg
0·0 Junction with Weser Km 231·4.
2·5 Possible mooring place on left bank.
2·8 *Schleuse Schlüsselburg*
Fall 4·5m.
VHF Ch 18.
3·1 Possible mooring place on left bank.
3·6 Junction with Weser Km 238·8.

Mittelweser (continued) ·
238·8 Junction with Schleusenkanal Schlüsselburg.
243·5 Hafen Stolzenau on left bank. No facilities, but overnight mooring permitted.
250·9 Junction with Schleusenkanal Landesbergen.
252·0 Weir.

Schleusenkanal Landesbergen
0·0 Junction with Weser Km 250·9.
1·3 Possible mooring place on left bank.
1·5 *Schleuse Landesbergen*
Fall 5·5m.
VHF Ch 22.
1·8 Possible mooring place on left bank.
2·2 Junction with Weser Km 252·5.

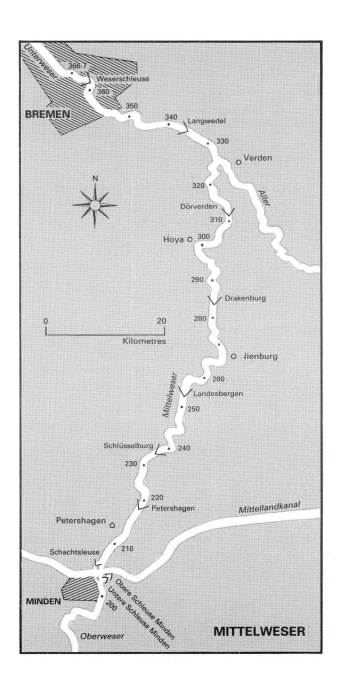

The Mittelweser near Nienburg.

Mittelweser (continued)
268·5	**Nienburg**. Water authority harbour and yacht harbour on right bank. Close to town centre.
269·4	Boatyard. Repairs.
274·2	Marina Mehlbergen on left bank. Water, electricity, repairs, slip.
275·6	Junction with Schleusenkanal Drakenburg.
277·7	Weir.

Schleusenkanal Drakenburg
0·0	Junction with Weser Km 275·6.
2·9	Possible mooring place on left bank.
3·2	*Schleuse Drakenburg*
	Fall 6·4m.
	VHF Ch 20.
3·5	Possible mooring place on left bank.
4·4	Junction with Weser Km 286·3.

Mittelweser (continued)
286·3	Junction with Schleusenkanal Drakenburg.
298·3	Yacht harbour on left bank. Water, electricity, showers, clubhouse, repairs. Shops and restaurants nearby.
308·4	Junction with Schleusenkanal Dörverden.
308·8	Weir.

The Unterweser estuary.

Schleusenkanal Dörverden
0·0	Junction with Weser Km 308·4.
1·7	Possible mooring place on left bank.
2·0	*Schleuse Dörverden*
	Fall 4·6m.
	VHF Ch 18.
2·2	Possible mooring place on left bank.
2·7	Junction with Weser Km 314·4.

Mittelweser (continued)
314·4	Junction with Schleusenkanal Dörverden.
323·2	Bunker boat and shipyard.
326·4	Junction with Aller Km 117·2.
327·7	Junction with Schleusenkanal Langwedel.
329·4	Weir.

Schleusenkanal Langwedel
0·0	Junction with Weser Km 327·7.
5·3	Possible mooring place on left bank.
5·6	*Schleuse Langwedel*
	Fall 5·50m.
	VHF Ch 22.
5·8	Possible mooring place on left bank.
8·5	Junction with Weser Km 338·9.

Mittelweser (continued)
338·9	Junction with Schleusenkanal Langwedel.
340·9	Mooring place at ferry on left bank.
341·0	Entrance to gravel pit on right bank. Overnight mooring with permission.
350 to 366·7	**Bremen**.
355·2	Marina Wieltsee on left bank. Water, diesel.
359·1	Marina Oberweser on right bank. Bremer Motor-Yacht-Club. Water, electricity, showers, fuel, repairs, slip, crane. Shops and restaurants nearby.
359·5	Yacht harbour on left bank. Water, electricity, slip.
360·4	Yacht harbour on right bank. Water, electricity, clubhouse, slip, crane.
360·8	Yacht harbour on left bank. Water, electricity, clubhouse.
362·0	*Bremer Weserschleuse (Hemelingen)*
	Fall 2·00–6·00m according to tide.
	VHF Ch 20.
	Operates Mon–Sat 0500–2100. Sundays during summer: 0800–1400 and 1730–1930.
363·0	Waiting place for pleasure craft on right bank.
364·6	Yacht harbour on right bank. Bremer Yacht Club. Dries at LW.
366·7	Wilhelm-Kaisen-Brücke. End of Mittelweser and start of Unterweser.

3. UNTERWESER: BREMEN TO BREMERHAVEN
Km 0·0–Km 66·0

Navigable distance 66·0km
Maximum draught No practical limit
Maximum height 5·20 above MHW
Current Tidal
Locks None

The tidal part of the Weser carries a considerable amount of traffic, and both Bremen and Bremerhaven are major ports. There are numerous commercial docks and port facilities along the Unterweser, but no attempt has been made to give details of them, as it is unlikely that they will be relevant to pleasure craft.

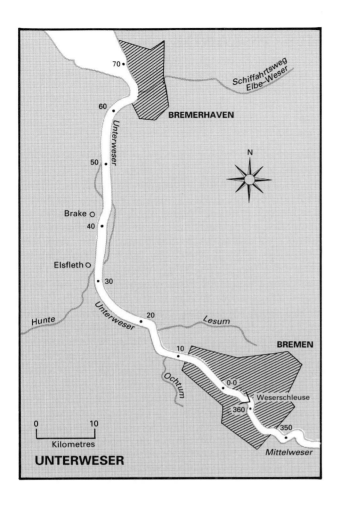

UNTERWESER

ALLER

Navigable distance 117·1km
Maximum draught 2·20m (water level varies)
Maximum height 2·30m (water level varies)
Current 3–5km/h
Locks 4
Speed limit 12km/h upstream, 18km/h downstream.

The Aller attracts many pleasure craft in summer. It carries no commercial traffic and flows through very pleasant farmland and woods. There are attractive overnight stopping places. Celle, the town at the head of navigation, has 700 years of history on display, with numerous beautiful old buildings in the *Altstadt*.

Possible problems are that the depth can reduce to as little as 1m during the latter half of a dry summer and that there is one bridge, at Km 50·6, with a clearance of only 2·3m at HW. However, as the water level varies by about 3m, by careful judgement it may be possible to pass. It is possible to assess the current state of the water levels by telephoning *Pegel* Celle, ☎ 05141 19429.

The river is administered by WSD-Mitte and there are no charges. In the summer months the locks operate from 0900 to 1200 and 1400 to 1600 on weekdays and from 0800 to 1200 and 1300 to

Km	
0·0	Junction with Mittelweser Km 366·7.
0·0 to	
10·0	**Bremen**.
11·5	Sporthafen Hasenbüren on left bank.
12·8	Junction with Ochtum on left bank.
17·2	Yacht harbour of Weser-Yacht-Club on left bank.
17·5	Junction with Lesum on right bank. Fuelling berth inside. Several yacht clubs and boatyards.
25·6	Yachthafen Juliusplate on left bank.
32·6	Junction with Untere Hunte. Entrance to Hunte and Küstenkanal.
32·8	Yacht harbour with lock in the old mouth of the Hunte.
40·6	Brake. Sea lock into commercial harbour. Good mooring place inside.
49·9	Yacht-Club Absen on left bank. Available 2 hours either side of HW.
50·4	Yacht harbour Strohausersiel on left bank. Available 3 hours either side of HW.
51·6	Entrance to Marina Rodenkirchen on right bank.
56·0	Grossensiel. Yacht harbour on left bank.
65·6	Junction with Geeste. Entrance to Hadelner Kanal (Schiffahrtsweg Elbe-Weser) and via lock into fishing harbour on right bank.
66·0	**Bremerhaven**. Four mooring places for yachts inside main harbour. Perhaps the most convenient in the Haupt-Kanal (immediately to port after the *Fischereihafenschleuse*).

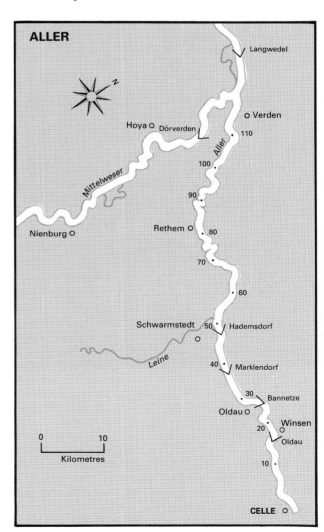

1700 on Saturdays and Sundays. Oldau in addition works from 1600 to 1800 on Tuesdays, Thursdays, Saturdays and Sundays.

Km	
0·0	Head of navigation.
0·9	Hafen Celle. Yacht-Club Celle. Water, electricity, showers, clubhouse, repairs, slip, crane. Shops and restaurants nearby.
ca2	**Celle.**
14·4	Oldauer Bootsclub. Restaurants and shops nearby.
14·6	Overnight mooring possible (with permission) above lock.
14·7	*Schleuse Oldau* *Fall* 3·4m.
14·8	**Oldau.**
16·8	Good overnight mooring on right bank.
21·0	Restaurant with mooring place on left bank.
26·7	*Schleuse Bannetze* *Fall* 2·2m.
38·3	*Schleuse Marklendorf* *Fall* 3·2m.
49·8	*Schleuse Hademsdorf* *Fall* 1·2m.
50·0	Junction with Leine.
66·4	Restaurant with mooring place on left bank.
78·0	Overnight mooring at camp site on left bank.
112·7	**Verden.**
113·4	Water authority harbour on right bank. Mooring possible with permission.
114·9	Yacht harbour on right bank. Water, electricity, showers, slip.
117·1	Junction with Mittelweser Km 326·4.

The Aller near Verden.

MITTELLANDKANAL

Navigable distance 325·1km
Maximum draught 2·10m (2·00m east of Km 258·7)
Maximum height 4·00m
Current Nil
Locks 3
Speed limit 12km/h (10km/h east of Km 258·7)

This canal is a major axis of the German waterway system: it is the East–West trunk route. Through the Mittellandkanal it is possible to travel from Holland, France or Switzerland to eastern Germany, the Czech Republic, Poland or the eastern Baltic.

It is not particularly scenic, as it traverses mainly flat agricultural and wooded terrain. The canal and its surroundings do, however, create a good habitat for a wide range of wildlife, including otters, kites, herons and ducks of various breeds. Its main asset for cruising people is that it is a fast and easy route to and from interesting cruising grounds in other parts of the new Europe. It has only two locks and a ship-lift, and there is a variety of comfortable overnight stopping places, both at established yacht clubs and in inlets specially reserved for pleasure boats. It is best to allow 6–7 days to travel from the DEK to the Elbe, or vice versa, plus whatever time is required for exploration en route, perhaps in Osnabrück, Minden, Hannover, Hildesheim or Braunschweig, all of which are places of considerable historical interest.

For canal engineering enthusiasts, there are several installations worthy of inspection. The 375m-long eight-arch Minden viaduct, constructed in 1914 in ferroconcrete, was a major achievement at the time. Nearby, the Minden *Schachtschleuse*, completed in 1912, and linking the MLK with the Weser, was an important example of sophisticated lock technology. The 1939-built Rothensee ship-lift at Magdeburg is yet another interesting piece of canal engineering history.

All the locks (and the ship-lift) work from 0600 to 2200 Mondays to Saturdays. On Sundays Schleuse Anderten operates from 0700 to 1230, Sülfeld from 0800 to 1730 and Rothensee from 0800 to 2000.

There is a fairly steady traffic of barges and push-tows, but this presents little difficulty for a pleasure boat travelling at 5–6kn through the water. The only serious problem is that during the latter part of a dry summer the water levels in the Elbe tend to be very low, and it may be that during such conditions only vessels drawing less than 1·20m will be able to use the 10km stretch of Elbe between the eastern end of the MLK and the start of the Elbe-Havel-Kanal. The route description for the Elbe provides more information on this topic.

For many years there has been a plan to link the Mittellandkanal to the Elbe-Havel-Kanal, removing the need to use this short section of the Elbe, and indeed work was started before World War II. The bases of the pillars of the aqueduct over the Elbe were put in place, but work was stopped at the beginning of World War II and has so far not been resumed. However, the project ('Project 17') seems

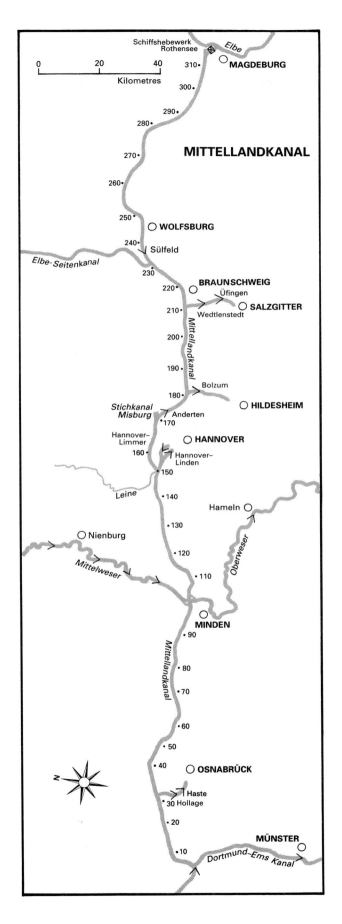

now to be restarting and there is hope that it will be brought to fruition in the near future (see pages 83 and 84).

Km

0·0   Junction with Dortmund-Ems-Kanal Km 108·4.

4·4   Entrance to old channel on south bank. Possible mooring.

7·5   Mooring place for pleasure craft on both banks.

30·0   Mooring place for pleasure craft on north bank.

30·4   Junction with Stichkanal Osnabrück on south bank.

Stichkanal Osnabrück

Navigable distance 14·5km

Maximum draught 2·10m

Maximum height 4·00m

Current Nil

Locks 2

Hours Mon–Fri 0600–2000, Sat 0600–1600, Sun closed.

Speed limit 12km/h

This short canal links the town of Osnabrück to the Mittellandkanal.

Km

0·0   Junction with Mittellandkanal Km 30·4.

5·7   Yacht harbour on east bank. Depth 2m. Water, electricity, showers, clubhouse, slip, crane.

7·2   *Schleuse Hollage*
        Rise 4·8m.
        VHF Ch 78.

12·7   *Schleuse Haste*
        Rise 4·8m.
        VHF Ch 78.

14·0   Hafen **Osnabrück**. Depth 3m. Commercial harbour, but it may be possible to find a place to moor. 20 mins from town centre.

Mittellandkanal (continued)

33·2   Mooring place for pleasure craft on north bank.

33·8   Mooring place for pleasure craft on north bank.

46·9   Mooring place for pleasure craft on south bank.

47·5   Inlet with moorings for pleasure craft on north bank.

53·9   Mooring place for pleasure craft on north bank.

62·1   Yacht harbour in quiet basin on north bank. Motoryachtclub Mittelland Bad Essen. Depth 1·7m in entrance. Water, electricity, showers, clubhouse, fuel, repairs, slip, crane. Shops 1·5km.

70·6   Yacht harbour in small bay on south bank. Depth 1m. Water, electricity, showers, clubhouse, repairs. Shops nearby.

71·3   Mooring place for pleasure craft on north bank. Shallows at eastern end.

80·4   Sportboothafen Lübbecke. Motor-Yacht-Club Lübbecke in small basin on south bank. Depth 1·5m. Water, electricity, showers, clubhouse, fuel, slip, crane. Shops 3km.

89·0   Possible moorings on south bank.

100·6   Bunker boat for diesel on south bank.

101·6   Junction with Nordabstieg zur Weser (northern connecting canal to Weser). Good bank-side mooring without facilities in entrance to lock.

Nordabstieg zur Weser (Verbindungskanal Nord)

Navigable distance 1·2km
Maximum draught 2·10m
Maximum height 4·00m
Current Nil
Locks 1

At the old town of Minden, the Mittellandkanal crosses the Weser by means of a high viaduct. Ships can transfer from the canal to the river via either of two *Verbindungskanäle* (connecting canals). (See plan below.) The Nordabstieg has one lock, Schachtschleuse Minden, which is an interesting piece of engineering, having been one of the first locks to have its water inlets in the bottom of the chamber. This creates considerably less turbulence when the lock is filling than the normal method of filling by means of sluices in the upper gates. The turbulence is so slight that the local advice to skippers is that there is no need to moor the boat in the lock. It is perhaps questionable, however, whether many owners of pleasure boats will take this advice.

The *Schachtschleuse* operates 0500 to 2100 Mondays to Saturdays and 0800 to 1100 on Sundays.

Km
0·0   Junction with Mittellandkanal Km 101·6.
0·1   Pleasant mooring to bank on west side above lock.
0·5   *Schachtschleuse Minden*
       Fall 13·2m.
       VHF Ch 22.
1·0   Mooring place below lock.
1·2   Junction with Weser Km 206·2.

Mittellandkanal (continued)

102·4   Aqueduct over the Weser river, width of channel 24m. Straight north of it a new aqueduct is under construction, width of channel 40m.
102·9   Junction with *Südabstieg zur Weser* (southern connecting canal to Weser).

Südabstieg zur Weser (Verbindungskanal Süd)

Navigable distance 1·4km
Maximum draught 1·90m
Maximum height 3·8m
Current Nil
Locks 2

As an alternative to the *Schachtschleuse*, traffic transferring from the MLK to the Weser or vice versa can use the Verbindungskanal Süd, with two conventional locks. It also provides access to Minden commercial harbour.

Both locks work from 0730 to 1600 on weekdays and from 0800 to 1200 on Saturdays. They do not operate on Sundays.

Km
0·0   Junction with Mittellandkanal Km 102·9.
0·2   *Obere Schleuse*
       Fall 6·3m.
       VHF Ch 22.
0·5   Hafen **Minden**. Commercial harbour.
1·0   *Untere Schleuse*
       Fall 7·0m.
       VHF Ch 22.
1·4   Junction with Weser Km 204·5.

Mittellandkanal (continued)

111·5   Mooring place for pleasure craft on north bank.
123·3   Mooring place (piled) for barges and pleasure craft on south bank. Village nearby.
135·2   Major marina on north bank. Depth 2m. Water, electricity, showers, clubhouse, fuel, repairs, slip, crane. Shops 1km.
149·4   Bunker boat for diesel on south bank.
149·7   Junction with Stichkanal Hannover-Linden.

Stichkanal Hannover-Linden

Navigable distance 11·2km
Maximum draught 1·90m
Maximum height 4·00m
Current Nil
Locks 1
Hours Mon–Fri 0900–1900, Sat 0600–1200, Sun closed.

Connecting canal between Hannover and the Mittellandkanal. Also links to a short navigable stretch of the Leine, chiefly to transport fuel to the power station situated there.

Km
0·0   Junction with Mittellandkanal Km 149·7.
2·4   Motorboot-Sportclub Seelze. Depth 2m. Water, electricity, showers, fuel, repairs, slip, crane. Shops and restaurants 10 mins.
8·5   Niedersächsischer Motor-Boot-Club. Depth 1·5m. Water, electricity, showers, crane. Shops and restaurants Limmer, 25mins. Trams to Hannover from Limmer.
       Junction with *Abstiegskanal zur Leine* (linking canal to Leine).

Abstiegskanal zur Leine

Navigable distance 1·8km
Maximum draught 1·50m
Maximum height 4·00m
Locks 1
Hours Mon–Fri 0700–1430 (by advance notice only)

This short canal connects the Stichkanal Hannover-Linden and the short navigable stretch of the Leine. Its main purpose is to serve the nearby power station.

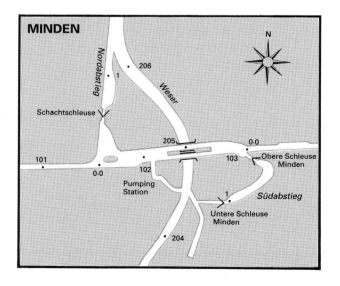

Km
0·0   Junction with Stichkanal Hannover-Linden.
0·6   *Schleuse Hannover-Limmer*
        Fall 2·0m.
        VHF Ch 20.
1·8   Junction with Leine.

Stichkanal Hannover-Linden (continued)
9·5   *Hafenschleuse Hannover-Linden*
        Rise 7·8m.
        VHF Ch 20.
11·2   Linden commercial harbour. End of canal.

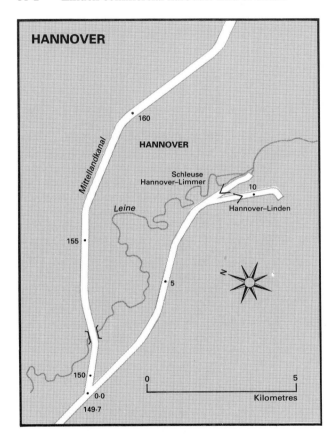

Close quarters on the Mittellandkanal near Hannover.

Fixed bollards. Pleasure boats must lock with commercial vessels.
174·9   Inlet on south bank below lock. Suitable for waiting for the lock and a possible overnight mooring.
183·2   Junction with Stichkanal Hildesheim.

Stichkanal Hildesheim
Navigable distance 15·1km
Maximum draught 2·10m
Maximum height 4·00m
Locks 1
Speed limit 12km/h

Links the historic city of Hildesheim to the Mittellandkanal. There are no yacht clubs or harbours, but it is possible to lie alongside the quay at the end of the main harbour. No facilities. Shops and restaurants in the vicinity.

The Bolzum lock works from 0600 to 2000 on weekdays and on Saturdays from 0600 to 1600. Pleasure boats must lock with commercial vessels.

Km
0·0   Junction with Mittellandkanal Km 183·2.
0·6   *Schleuse Bolzum*
        Rise 8·0m.
        VHF Ch 78.
0·7   Possible mooring above lock.
14·6 to
15·1   Hafen **Hildesheim**. Mooring at end of main harbour.

Mittellandkanal (continued)
184·6   Small yacht harbour on north bank. Depth 1·3m. Water, electricity, showers, slip, crane.
192·9   Inlet on north bank. Possible overnight mooring.
200·4   Inlet on south bank. Possible overnight mooring.
201·1   Water-sports club on north bank. Depth 1·5m. Water, electricity, showers, clubhouse, crane.
210·9   Overnight mooring place with café on north bank.
ca213   Piled quay along north bank for pleasure craft.
213·5   Junction with Stichkanal Salzgitter.

Mittellandkanal (continued)
163·5   Yacht harbour on south bank. Depth 2m. Water, electricity, showers, clubhouse, diesel, repairs. 15 minutes to **Hannover** by bus.
171·2   Junction with Stichkanal Misburg.

Stichkanal Misburg
Navigable distance 3·5km
Maximum draught 1·90m
Maximum height 4·00m
Locks None

This is a short canal leading past an oil terminal into quiet and rural surroundings. Beyond lies more industry.

Km
0·0   Junction with Mittellandkanal Km 171·2.
ca1   Possible mooring on north bank.
3·5   End of canal.

Mittellandkanal (continued)
174·2   *Schleuse Anderten*
        Rise 14·7m.
        VHF Ch 18.

Stichkanal Salzgitter
Navigable distance 18·0km
Maximum draught 2·20m
Maximum height 3·80m
Locks 2
Hours Mon–Sat 0600–2200, Sun closed.
Speed limit 12km/h

This canal is heavily industrial, although the Heidanger yacht harbour is very pleasant. If pleasure craft venture further along the canal they should use the eastern chamber at each lock and must lock with commercial vessels.

Km
0·0   Junction with Mittellandkanal Km 213·5.
3·6   Heidanger yacht harbour on east bank. Depth 2m. Water, electricity, showers, clubhouse, repairs, slip, crane. Shops 1km. Restaurant in the harbour.
4·6   *Schleuse Wedtlenstedt*
        Rise 9·3m.
        VHF Ch 79.
10·7   *Schleuse Üfingen*
        Rise 9·0m.
        VHF Ch 79.
14·8   Bunker boat for diesel.
18·0   **Salzgitter**. End of canal.

Mittellandkanal (continued)
217·5   Small yacht basin on north bank. Depth 1·5m. Water, electricity, showers, clubhouse, diesel, repairs, crane.
219·6   Bunker boat for diesel on south bank.
ca220·0   **Braunschweig**. Possible mooring place on north bank.
222·4   Mooring place for pleasure craft on south bank.
225·5   Mooring place for pleasure craft on south bank.
227·3   Small yacht harbour on south bank. Depth 2·5m. Water, electricity, showers, clubhouse, fuel, repairs.
233·7   Junction with Elbe-Seitenkanal Km 0·0.
235·2   Yacht basin on south bank. Water, electricity, showers, slip. Shops 15 mins.
236·9   *Schleuse Sülfeld*
        Fall 9·0m.
        VHF Ch 20.
        Pleasure boats must lock with commercial vessels.
235·2   Possible mooring place on north bank.
239·7   Possible mooring place on south bank.
ca245   **Wolfsburg**. Volkswagen car plant.
246·9   Moorings on south bank.
ca255   Possible mooring place on north bank.
268·7   Moorings on north bank.
283·1   Moorings on south bank.
294·7   Moorings on north bank.
299·0   Moorings on north bank.
301·0   Haldensleben. Mooring for commercial vessels on north bank.
319·9   Start of the *Abstiegskanal*, the continuation of the MLK through the Rothensee ship-lift and into the Elbe.
320·4   *Schiffshebewerk Rothensee*.
        Fall 11–18m (depends on level in Elbe).
        VHF Ch 79.
        Elbe depth displayed daily.
325·1   **Magdeburg**. Junction with Elbe Km 333·6.

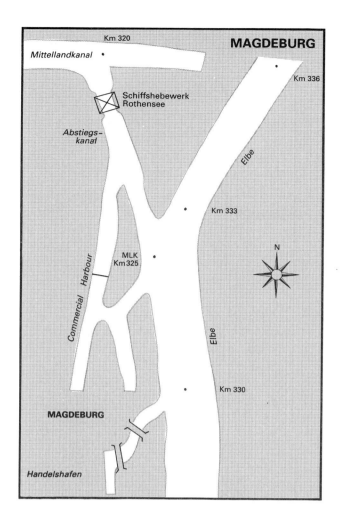

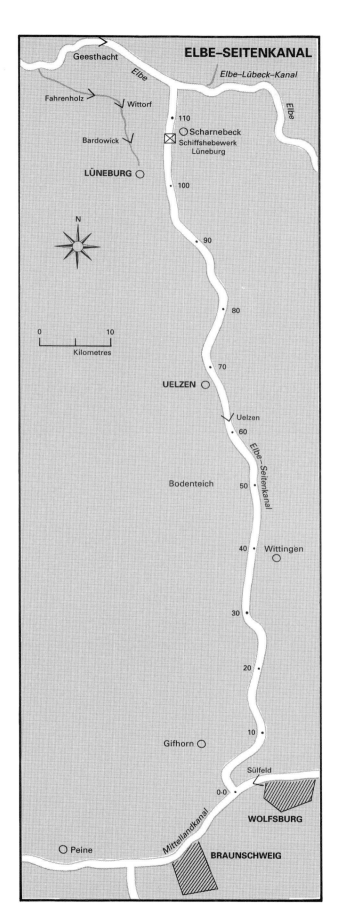

ELBE-SEITENKANAL

Navigable distance 115·2km
Maximum draught 2·50m
Maximum height 5·25m
Current Nil
Locks 2
Hours Mon–Sat 0600–2200, Sun 0800–1730.
Speed limit 12km/h

The Elbe-Seitenkanal, opened in 1976, was built to provide a link between Hamburg and the Mittellandkanal without passing through East Germany. It is straight and is flanked by banks just too tall to see over, which makes for a boring, albeit fast, journey. It is best to time one's journey to enable an overnight stop to be made at Uelzen, a pleasant, well equipped yacht harbour at a convenient point on the canal.

The difference in level of 61m between the MLK and the Elbe is accomplished with only two installations: the huge Lüneburg twin ship-lifts and a 23m-deep lock at Uelzen, both of which are exceedingly impressive engineering accomplishments. The experience of using them easily makes up for an otherwise boring journey. The layout of the ship-lift installation is shown on page 72.

The canal is operated by WSD-Mitte and use of it is free. The Uelzen lock has floating bollards.

Km
0·0   Junction with Mittellandkanal Km 233·7.
10·0   Osloss. Mooring for commercial vessels on east bank.
24·2   Siedlung Weisses Moor. Mooring for commercial vessels on east bank.
38·6   Hafen **Wittingen**. Commercial harbour on east side.
39·6   Possible mooring place on east bank.
50·0   Bodenteich. Overnight moorings on east bank.
60·6   *Schleuse Uelzen*
       Fall 23·0m.
       VHF Ch 18.

The Elbe-Seitenkanal is straight and boring – but fast.

Lüneburg ship-lift.

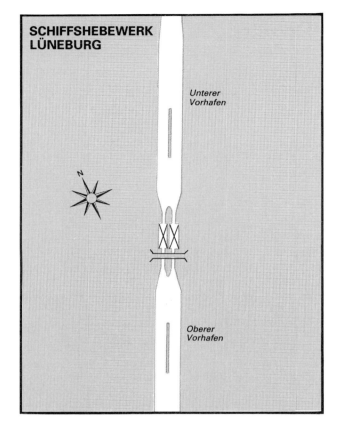

65·9   **Uelzen**. Yacht harbour on east bank. Yachtclub Uelzen. Water, electricity, showers, clubhouse. Shop nearby.

71·1   Hafen Uelzen. Commercial harbour on west side.

79·6   Bad Bevensen. Overnight yacht moorings on west bank.

92·0   Wulfstorf. Overnight yacht moorings on east bank.

100·2   Hafen **Lüneburg**. Commercial harbour on west side.

106·1   *Schiffshebewerk Lüneburg.*
Fall 38·0m.
VHF Ch 20.
Twin ship-lifts. Moor to piled walls above and below lift whilst waiting.

115·2   Junction with Elbe Km 573·0.

North

SCHIFFAHRTSWEG ELBE-WESER

Navigable distance 61·5km
Maximum draught 1·50m
Maximum height 2·60m
Current Negligible
Locks 3
Speed limit 8km/h

Originally built in the late 19th century, the delightful little Schiffahrtsweg Elbe-Weser (Elbe-Weser shipping route) was reopened in 1962, linking the tidal Elbe with the tidal Weser. It comprises several waterways: the Medem, the Hadelner Kanal, the Aue, the Bederkesa-Geeste-Kanal and the Geeste.

Between the picturesque and historic villages of Otterndorf and Bederkesa the route passes through fertile agricultural land. At Bederkesa it skirts the See von Bederkesa (Sea of Bederkesa) and continues towards Bremerhaven through a relatively marshy area, rich in wildlife. The waterway is quite narrow, and is suitable only for vessels under 33·5m long, 5m beam and 1·50m draught. At normal water levels the maximum permitted height of vessel is 2·60m. There is little commercial traffic, but meeting a barge can be a little hair-raising. Fortunately, the barge skippers are usually extremely helpful. Westbound vessels take priority over eastbound vessels when they meet.

At Otterndorf access from the Elbe is via the mouth of the Medem, then via a lock through to the Hadelner Kanal. Timing a passage through this is a matter of judgement, as at HW there is insufficient headroom, whilst at LW the tidal part of the Medem dries. However, as the bottom of the tidal

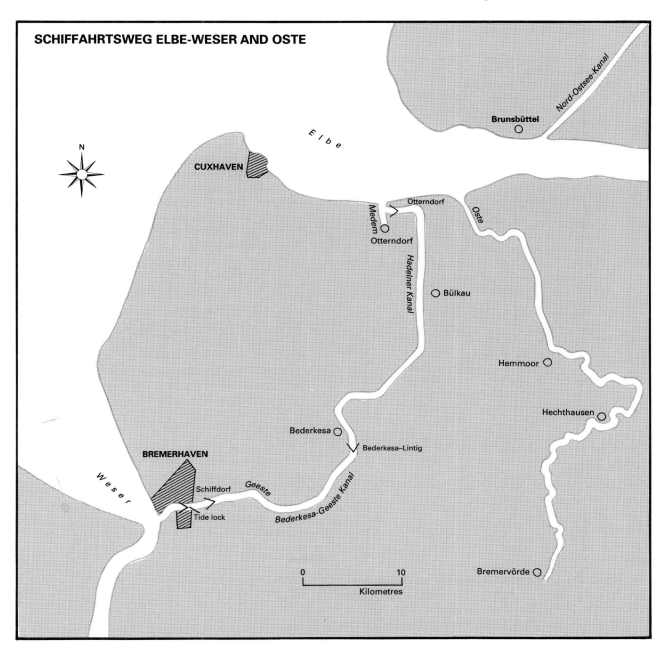

SCHIFFAHRTSWEG ELBE-WESER AND OSTE

harbour is so soft that deep-keeled yachts sit upright, running aground is unlikely to be disastrous. The harbourmaster will advise, and if necessary arrange access to the crane for removing or replacing masts.

At Bremerhaven the entrance to the Geeste is at Km 65·5 on the Unterweser, between a pair of light towers on the ends of the short moles guarding the entrance. Just inside, it is possible to lock into the fishing harbour, where there are good facilities for yachts. Alternatively, a vessel may proceed into the Geeste to the tide lock.

The waterway is not operated by WSD, but by the *Land* of Niedersachsen (Lower Saxony), and a charge of DM 6 is levied for using the canal, together with DM 3–5 per lock. There is a strict speed limit of 8km/h on the waterway, and a vessel's speed is checked from the timed lock tickets. The lock operating times are given in the route description.

Boats with a beam greater than 3·00m are required to fly flag N of the International Code of Signals on the bow.

Km	
0·0	Junction with Elbe Km 712·5.
1·2	*Schleuse Otterndorf*
	Rise Depends on tide in Elbe.
	Hours 0730–1730 4 hours around HW.
1·3	Possible mooring above lock on left bank.
1·4	Quiet mooring on left bank.
8·2	Railway bridge. Height 2·60m.
22·0	Possible overnight mooring.
ca31	**Bederkesa**. Pleasant overnight mooring. Water, electricity, showers. Shops and restaurants nearby.
34·0	*Schleuse Bederkesa-Lintig*
	Rise Very small.
	Hours Mon–Sat 0730–1730, Sun 1000–1200 and 1500–1700.
	Overnight mooring. Fuel.
52·2	Former *Schleuse Schiffdorf*. Permanently open. Restaurant, mooring possible.
55·5	Yacht club. Water, electricity.
56·0	*Tidesperrwerk.*
	Fall Depends on tide in Weser.
	Hours 0700–1830.
60·4	Flood barrier under bridge.
61·2	Tidal mooring place. Water, electricity, chandlery. Shops and restaurants nearby.
61·4	Entry to fishing harbour on left side via lock. Marina. Water, electricity, showers, restaurant.
61·5	Junction with Unterweser Km 65·5.

NORD-OSTSEE-KANAL (KIEL CANAL)

Navigable distance 98·2km
Maximum draught 9·50m
Maximum height 40m
Current None
Locks 2
Speed limit 15km/h

The Nord-Ostsee-Kanal is a heavily used commercial shipping route carrying the world's shipping between the North Sea and the Baltic. Throughout the day and night there is a constant stream of large seagoing vessels passing through it. Pleasure craft without pilots may not transit the canal at night or in fog.

Negotiating the canal in a small boat is very easy. Approaching either lock, all that is necessary is to hover in view of the control tower (but out of the way of commercial shipping) outside the lock until the white lights flash. There is no need to speak to the lock-keepers on VHF, although this is of course possible in case of difficulty. The fees for using the canal are as follows:

Length	Fee
Up to 10m	DM 21
10–12m	DM 32
12–16m	DM 60
16–20m	DM 73
Over 20m	DM 80 + DM 1 for every extra metre

The appropriate fee is payable at the Holtenau end of the canal (during locking) whichever direction the transit is made in. A ticket should be bought from the news stand on the north side of the old (north) lock at Kiel-Holtenau and taken to the lock-keepers in the control tower to be stamped. It is possible, however, that the system may soon be changed so that the ticket is actually bought from the lock-keeper. Mooring in the locks is to wooden pontoons floating low in the water. Fenders are required at water level.

It goes without saying that a small boat should stay close to the starboard bank, well clear of the heavy traffic of large seagoing ships. Sailing is theoretically not permitted in the canal, but as it is acceptable to motor-sail it is difficult to see how the authorities are to tell whether or not the engine is running. Anchoring in the canal is forbidden, and stopping is restricted to the places listed below in the route description.

The canal authorities can be contacted during transit by calling *Kiel Canal 2* on VHF Ch 2 for the stretch from Brunsbüttel to Breiholz (Km 50) or *Kiel Canal 3* on VHF Ch 3 for the stretch from Breiholz to Kiel-Holtenau.

It may be useful to know that British, German and Scandinavian charts and navigational books can be bought at the Kiel-Holtenau lock from Kapitän Stegmann, whose shop is on the small industrial estate immediately south of the new lock.

The transit, which can be accomplished in one day in most cruising boats, is on the whole lacking in interest, except for the wonderful old transporter bridge at Rendsburg – and of course the world's ships, which pass in a continuous stream.

Km	
0·0	Junction with Elbe Km 696·4.
1·5	*Neue Schleuse und Alte Schleuse Brunsbüttel*
	Rise Depends on tide in Elbe.
	VHF Ch 13 (call *Kiel Canal 1*).
	Two old locks and two new locks.

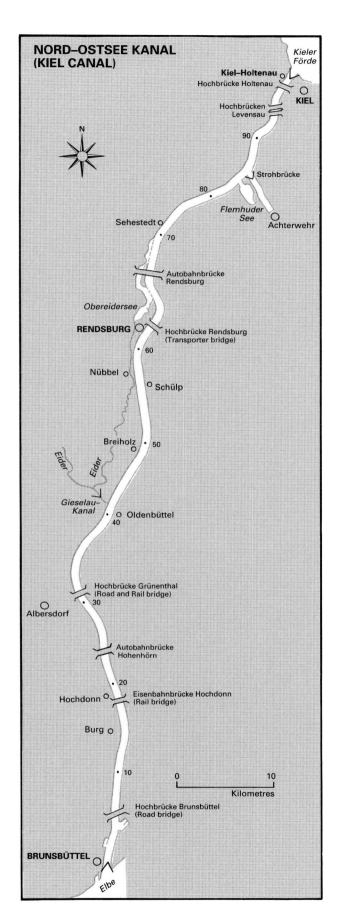

NORD–OSTSEE KANAL
(KIEL CANAL)

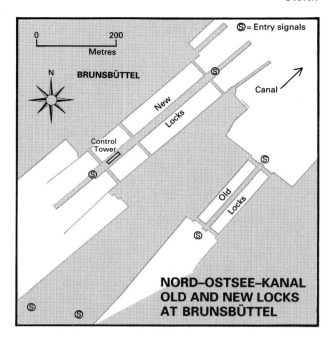

NORD–OSTSEE-KANAL
OLD AND NEW LOCKS
AT BRUNSBÜTTEL

1·8   Yachthafen **Brunsbüttel** on north bank.
2·7   Additional yacht moorings on north side of canal.
20·6   Possible overnight mooring on north side.
40·7   Junction with Gieselaukanal, linking to Eider. Mooring permitted before lock.
62·7   **Rendsburg**. Transporter bridge for cars. Trains cross at high level.
66·1   Entrance to Obereidersee (old Eider). Yacht harbour. Diesel.
70·0   Borgstedter Enge. Floating moorings on north side.
85·5   Entrance to the Flemhuder See. Pleasant tree-lined anchorage on south bank.
85·6   Entrance to Achterwehrer Schiffahrtskanal via *Schleuse Strohbrücke*. Maximum draught 2m. Speed limit 8km/h.
98·0   *Neue Schleuse und Alte Schleuse Kiel-Holtenau*
Fall Very small: probably 20cm.
VHF Ch 12 (call *Kiel Canal 4*).
Two old locks and two new locks.
98·5   **Kiel-Holtenau**. Yacht harbour on north side outside lock.
98·6   Junction with Kieler Förde (Kiel Fiord).

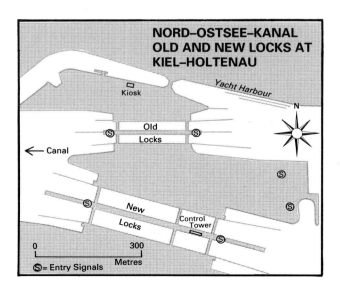

NORD–OSTSEE-KANAL
OLD AND NEW LOCKS AT
KIEL-HOLTENAU

EIDER AND GIESELAUKANAL

For a boat heading for the Baltic via the Nord-Ost-see-Kanal (Kiel Canal), it is well worth considering the more leisurely route via the Eider as an alternative to braving the tides of the Elbe estuary and then slogging along the first part of the NOK. The home of the ubiquitous eider duck, the Eider is a little-used but quite delightful river, meandering in huge loops through pastoral countryside with cattle standing knee-deep at the banks, buzzards wheeling overhead, an abundance of herons and – of course – eider ducks by the thousand.

1. EIDER: NORTH SEA TO GIESELAU-KANAL
Km 110·0–Km 22·8

Navigable distance 87·2km
Maximum draught 2·50m, 2m in tidal section at LW
Maximum height Unlimited
Current Tidal to Nordfeld, then 2–3km/h
Locks 3
Speed limit 15km/h upstream of Friedrichstadt

From the off-lying Eider buoy there is a clearly buoyed channel to the flood barrier with a two-way tide lock on the north side of the barrier. From there to Tönning, 11km from the flood barrier, the route crosses a wild salt-water mere before narrowing to a river which continues to the Nordfeld lock. The channel is tidal but well marked with buoys and withies and has a minimum depth of 2m. Nevertheless it is advisable to carry out this passage on a rising tide.

At Friedrichstadt, between Tönning and Nordfeld, it is possible to go through the Friedrichstadt

lock into the Treene. There is a good yacht club for an overnight stay at Friedrichstadt, a picturesque mediaeval town.

Shortly after the Lexfähre lock the river swings to port towards Rendsburg, but the route to the NOK goes to starboard into the short Giselaukanal.

Each lock has its own operating times. These are shown in the route description below. Only the lock at the flood barrier is equipped with VHF radio. A fee is levied for using the locks.

Km
110·0   *Eider flood barrier with lock*
      Rise Depends on tide.
      Hours Always available.
      VHF Ch 14.
100·2   Hafen Tönning. Dries at LW. Soft mud.
99·0   Opening road bridge. Closed height 5·60m above mean HW. Operates 0700–1900 daily during summer. On Sundays advance notice is required (☎ 04861 5690).
85·0   Opening railway bridge. Closed height 3·95m above mean HW. Operates Mon–Sat 0430–2300 and Sun 0600–2300.
83·7   **Friedrichstadt**. Junction with Treene via *Schleuse Friedrichstadt*. Approach to lock 1m deep at LW. Operating hours (in summer): Mon–Sat 0700– 1900, Sun 0900–1000 and 1700–1800. Yacht harbour 1km into Treene.
83·0   Opening road bridge. Closed height 5·60m above mean HW. Operates 0700–1900 daily, but on Sundays advance notice is required (☎ 04881 260).
78·0   *Schleuse Nordfeld*
      Rise 0·20–1·60m.
      Hours Mon–Sat 0600–1900, Sun 0600–1000 and 1600–1800.

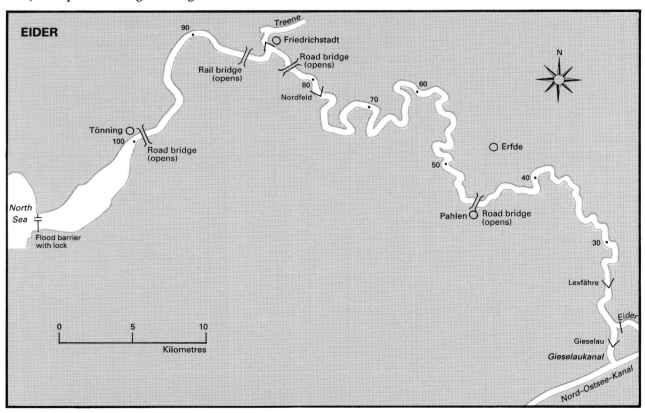

46·0	Opening road bridge. Closed height 3·50m above mean HW. Operates 0700–1900 daily, but on Sundays advance notice is required (☎ 04803 211).
26·0	*Schleuse Lexfähre* with opening bridge. *Rise* 0·10–0·20m. *Hours* Mon–Sat 0800–1900, Sun 0800–1000 and 1600–1800.
23·0	Junction with Gieselaukanal. Eider continues to Obereidersee, but through passage is not possible.

2. GIESELAUKANAL: EIDER TO NORD-OSTSEE-KANAL
Km 2·9–Km 0·0

Navigable distance 2·9km
Maximum draught 2·70m
Maximum height 21m
Current Nil
Locks 1
Speed limit 10km/h

The stretch of the Gieselaukanal between the lock and the Nord-Ostsee-Kanal is a convenient and peaceful overnight stop for small vessels passing through the Nord-Ostsee-Kanal.

Fees are DM 5·50 for a boat up to 12m and DM 8 for boats longer than this. Navigation at night is forbidden.

Km

2·9	Junction with Eider Km 23·0
1·3	*Schleuse Gieselau* *Rise* 0·20–1·60m. *Hours* Mon–Sat 0800–1300 and 1400–1800, Sun 0800–1000 and 1600–1800.
ca1	Mooring at bank.
0·0	Junction with Nord-Ostsee-Kanal Km 40·7.

ELBE-LÜBECK-KANAL AND TRAVE

Navigable distance 88·6km
Maximum draught 2·00m
Maximum height 4·20m
Current Negligible
Locks 7
Speed limit 10km/h on ELK, 12km/h on Trave downstream from Km 5·6.

The Elbe-Lübeck-Kanal links the Elbe to the Baltic at Travemünde. The section from the Elbe at Lauenburg to the beautiful seven-spired Hanseatic city of Lübeck is amongst lush countryside, partly wooded and partly agricultural, the home of herons, grebes and goldeneye. The canal joins the Trave near Lübeck, and from here onwards to the sea the river banks are mostly wooded until the busy ferry port of Travemünde is reached.

There is very little commercial traffic. The journey from Lauenburg to Lübeck normally takes about 12 hours, which makes an overnight stop desirable. The complex of old gravel pits at Güster, known as the Prüss-See and now converted into a leisure area, is a pleasant stopping-place. Alternatively, there are a number of places where it is possible to moor at the bank-side.

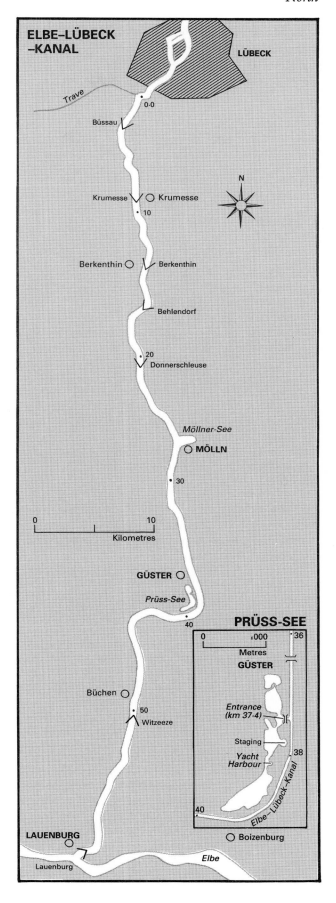

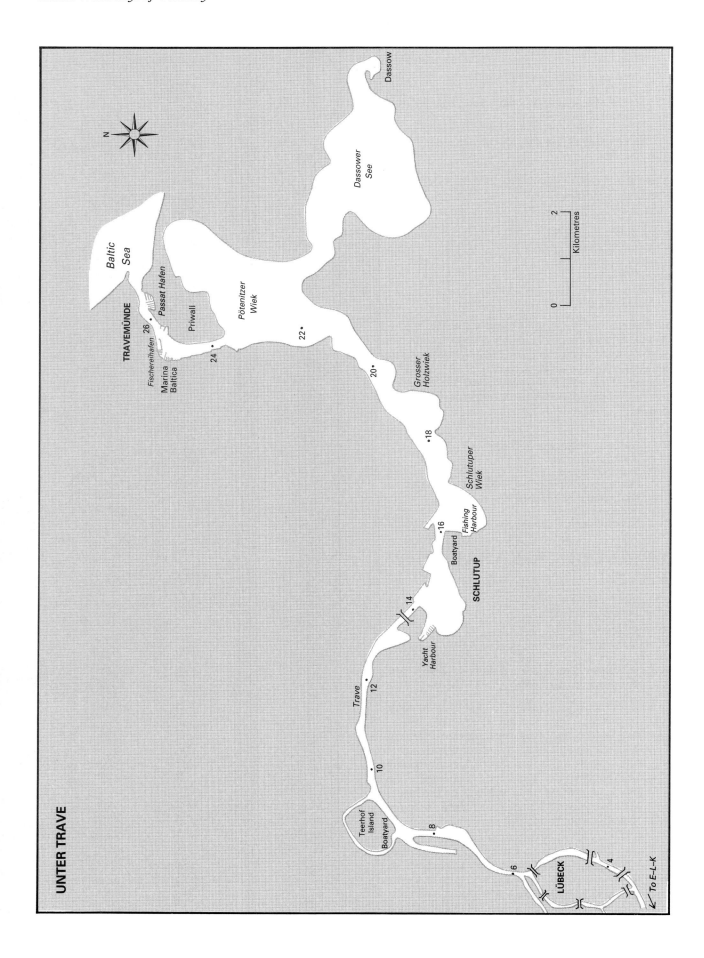

UNTER TRAVE

Baltic
Sea

Dassow

*Dassower
See*

TRAVEMÜNDE

Passat Hafen

Priwall

*Pötenitzer
Wiek*

•26

Fischereihafen

Marina
Baltica

•24

•22

•20

*Grosser
Holzwiek*

•18

*Schlutuper
Wiek*

•16

Boatyard

*Fishing
Harbour*

SCHLUTUP

•14

Yacht
Harbour

Trave

•12

•10

Teerhof
Island

Boatyard

•8

•6

LÜBECK

•4

To E–L–K

2

Kilometres

0

The locks operate in summer from 0600 to 2100 on weekdays, 0600 to 1800 on Saturdays and 0700 to 1200 on Sundays. The canal is controlled by WSD-Ost, the Trave by WSD-Nord.

There is strict enforcement of the 10km/h speed limit on the canal. The lock-keepers check the running times between locks.

1. ELBE-LÜBECK-KANAL

Km

61·6	Junction with Elbe Km 569·2.
60·0	Hafen Lauenburg. Busy yacht harbour at staging on west side.
59·9	*Schleuse Lauenburg* *Rise 4·8m.* *VHF Ch 22.*
50·4	*Schleuse Witzeeze* *Rise 3·3m.* *VHF Ch 79.*
37·4	Entrance to Prüss-See. Privately owned leisure area, based on converted gravel pits. Yacht harbour and other mooring places. Camp site, restaurant, showers, shop. Depth in main parts varies 1·50–2·00m.
26·5	**Mölln**. Fuel and short-term mooring at town quay on Möllner-See on east side of canal. Depth 1·50m. 3 yacht clubs. Water, electricity, showers, clubhouse. Shops and restaurants nearby.
20·7	*Schleuse Donnerschleuse* *Fall 4·2m.* *VHF Ch 79.*
16·5	*Schleuse Behlendorf* *Fall 1·7m.*
13·3	*Schleuse Berkenthin* *Fall 1·8m.*
8·5	*Schleuse Krummesse* *Fall 2·8m.*
3·4	*Schleuse Büssau* *Fall 1·5m.* *VHF Ch 78.*
0·0	Junction with Trave. Keep right into Trave for easiest through route.

2. TRAVE

0·0	Junction with Elbe-Lübeck-Kanal.
2·6	Yacht club on west side. Water, electricity, clubhouse. 2km from centre of Lübeck.
ca5	**Lübeck**. Historic ships' harbour in Holstenhafen. close to city centre, but permission needed for mooring. Commercial *Hansahafen* beyond opening bridge. No facilities at either.
9·8	Yacht harbour on west side.
12·3	Yacht harbour on east side.
15·9	Fishing harbour, yacht harbour and boatyard on east side.
22 to 27	**Travemünde**.
24·4	Scandinavian ferry quay on west side.
25·2	Marina Baltica on west side. All facilities.
25·4	Fuelling berth on west side.
25·8	Fuelling berth on east bank.
26·6	Passathafen on east side behind square-rigger *Passat*. All facilities, including crane for mast stepping and unstepping. Frequent ferry to town centre on west side of harbour.
27·0	Mouth of Trave. Access to Baltic Sea.

A busy lock on the Elbe-Lübeck-Kanal.

Junction of the Elbe-Lübeck-Kanal with the Elbe.

Historic ships at Lübeck, including Nansen's supply ship, the *Fridthjof*.

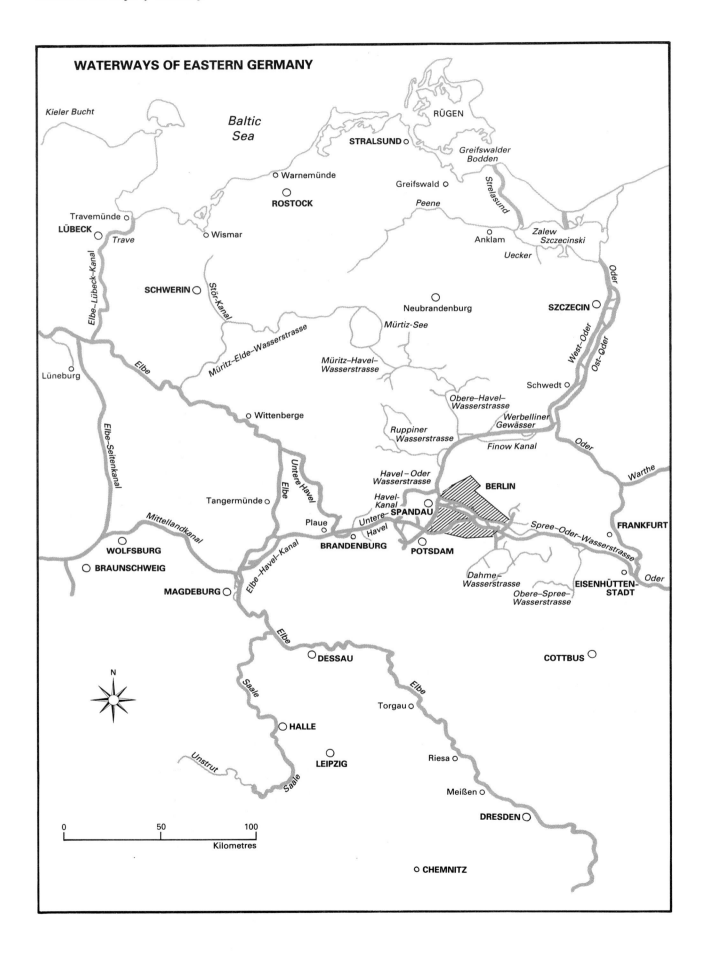

WATERWAYS OF EASTERN GERMANY

Kieler Bucht

*Baltic
Sea*

RÜGEN

STRALSUND ○

*Greifswalder
Bodden*

○ Warnemünde

Greifswald ○

Peene

ROSTOCK

Strelasund

Travemünde ○

○ Wismar

*Zalew
Szczecinski*

LÜBECK ○

Trave

Anklam ○

Uecker

SCHWERIN ○

Stör-Kanal

Neubrandenburg ○

Oder

SZCZECIN ○

Müritz-See

Müritz-Elde-Wasserstrasse

West-Oder

Ost-Oder

*Müritz–Havel–
Wasserstrasse*

Elbe

Schwedt ○

Elbe–Lübeck–Kanal

Lüneburg ○

*Obere–Havel–
Wasserstrasse*

*Werbelliner
Gewässer*

○ Wittenberge

*Ruppiner
Wasserstrasse*

Finow Kanal

Oder

Elbe-Seitenkanal

*Havel–Oder
Wasserstrasse*

BERLIN

Warthe

Untere Havel

*Havel-
Kanal*

Tangermünde ○

Elbe

SPANDAU ○

Mittellandkanal

Plaue ○

Untere

Havel

Spree–Oder–Wasserstrasse

FRANKFURT ○

WOLFSBURG ○

BRANDENBURG

POTSDAM ○

○ **BRAUNSCHWEIG**

Elbe–Havel–Kanal

*Dahme–
Wasserstrasse*

Oder

**EISENHÜTTEN-
STADT**

MAGDEBURG ○

*Obere–Spree–
Wasserstrasse*

Elbe

COTTBUS ○

○ **DESSAU**

Saale

Elbe

HALLE ○

Torgau ○

N

Unstrut

LEIPZIG ○

Riesa ○

Saale

Meißen ○

0   50   100

DRESDEN ○

Kilometres

○ **CHEMNITZ**

East

ELBE

The Elbe starts life as the Labe in the northern part of the Czech Republic. It is navigable for commercial shipping from Chvaletice, about 70km to the east of Prague. There are 15 locks from here to Melnik, where the Vltava (Moldau) joins the Labe from Prague. From Melnik to the border, where it flows into Germany as the Elbe, there are 6 locks. There are no locks in Germany except at Geesthacht, near Hamburg, where the river becomes tidal. The kilometering system in Germany is not contiguous with that within the Czech Republic, starting again with Km 0·0 at the border.

The river can be used by cruising boats from its mouth near Cuxhaven through to the interior of the Czech Republic, either to Prague and beyond on the Vltava or to Chvaletice (and possibly beyond) on the Labe. This gives a total cruising distance of some 950km, through scenery ranging from the wildness of the estuary to the towering sandstone cliffs of *die Bastei* in Sächsische Schweiz (Saxon Switzerland), the national park near the Czech border which embraces perhaps the most dramatic scenery in Germany.

Hydrology

Both the depth of the river and the strength of the current can vary widely. In normal conditions the minimum depth is in the range 1·50m to 3·00m and the strongest current is around 4 to 5km/h. However, when the river is in flood the current can become as much as 8 to 10km/h, whilst in dry seasons the depth can be as little as 0·70m in certain places. The trouble spots so far as depth is concerned are Torgau (Km 153·6–Km 154·8), Wittenberg (ca Km 217), Barby (Km 293·4–Km 312·1) and Magdeburg (Km 324·7–Km 333·6). The large hotel ships, drawing 1·15m, which operate between Prague, Hamburg and Szczecin (via the Havel-Oder-Wasserstrasse) are seldom unable to get through the whole length of the Elbe. The table below, based on ten years' statistics, shows the monthly variations in minimum depth of water which might typically be expected in the Elbe between Lauenburg and the Czech border. As can be seen, the best time of the year for cruising on the Elbe is normally during May and June, when the probability of shoal depths is relatively low.

ELBE. MINIMUM DEPTHS (Recorded depths over 10 years)			
	Days under 1·00m	*Days 1·00 to 1·50m*	*Days 1·50 to 2·00m*	*Days over 2·00m*
May	0	3	5	23
June	0	6	11	13
July	3	15	9	4
August	4	13	6	8
September	1	14	12	3
October	1	14	9	7

For convenience in publishing depth information, the river is considered as 9 *Strecken* (stretches):

Elbe-Strecke 1. Schöna to Dresden
Elbe-Strecke 2. Dresden to Riesa
Elbe-Strecke 3. Riesa to mouth of the Elster
Elbe-Strecke 4. Mouth of the Elster to Barby
Elbe-Strecke 5. Barby to Magdeburg
Elbe-Strecke 6. Magdeburg to Niegripp
Elbe-Strecke 7. Niegripp to Havelberg
Elbe-Strecke 8. Havelberg to Dömitz
Elbe-Strecke 9. Dömitz to Lauenburg

With the exception of *Strecke* 6, the transit from the Mittelland-Kanal to the Elbe-Havel-Kanal, the *Tauchtiefe* (maximum permissible draught) for each *Strecke* is announced daily at 0755 and 1255 on Radio Aktuel (FM 89·0, 89·2 and 89·4MHz). For *Strecke* 6, the channel depth is announced, and ship captains are left to decide the weight of cargo which they can safely carry. *Tauchtiefen* can also be obtained over VHF from Geesthacht (Ch 22), Hitzacker (Ch 18) and Lauenburg (Ch 22). It is also possible to ask for the latest figures from WSA offices by VHF or by telephoning the following numbers:

Hamburg	☎ 040 44 11 03 30
Lauenburg	☎ 04153 59 40 or 04159 43 48
Magdeburg	☎ 0391 33631
Dresden	☎ 0351 5022611

Below Lauenburg there are no depth restrictions so far as cruising boats are concerned.

VHF radio

VHF frequencies are allocated as follows:

Ch	Purpose
10	Calling and safety channel (including police)
11	Ship to ship
12	Ship to land (including traffic control)
13	Ship to lock
14	Ship to land (including traffic control)
69	Tripper-boat channel
71	Ship to ship (including on-board communication)
73	WSA offices

The procedure is generally to use Ch 10 to establish the call, then to ask for the appropriate working channel. However, it may be found in many instances that direct calling on the working channel is usual.

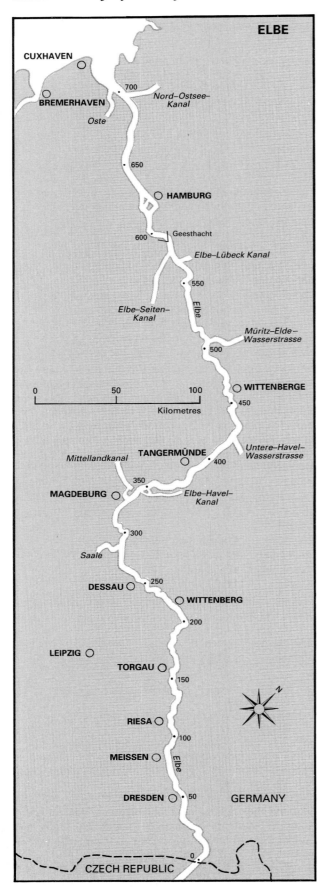

ELBE

Fuel

The only diesel bunker stations on the Elbe above Geesthacht are at Wittenberge (Km 454·9), Magdeburg (Km 327·3 and Km 332·8) and Borschütz (Km 124·7). In general, therefore, it is necessary to buy fuel in cans from street filling stations, of which there are many within reasonable striking distance of mooring places.

Buoyage and markings

Buoyage along the whole length of the river is conventional: greens to the left and reds to the right heading downstream. Where the channel crosses from one side of the river to the other, it is marked by yellow crosses on the bank. Otherwise, internationally standard warning signs are placed as appropriate on banks and bridges (see Appendix VI). Kilometre marks are on the right bank.

1. CZECH BORDER TO GEESTHACHT
Km 0–Km 585·8

Navigable length 585·8km
Maximum draught See table
Maximum height 4·50m
Current 2–10km/h
Locks 1

The first stretch of the river is dramatic. From the frontier town of Schmilka, the river flows through the Sächsische Schweiz (Saxon Switzerland), an area of breathtaking beauty, past interesting old towns and villages such as Bad Schandau, Königstein (with its spectacular mediaeval fortress hanging high above the river), Rathen and Wehlen, to the haunting city of Dresden.

For centuries Dresden was a major centre of culture and full of art treasures. It was a city of immense cultural importance and entirely without military significance, yet it was the scene of one of the worst atrocities of World War II. On the night of 13 February 1945 the British sent a force of 800 bombers to destroy it. Dresden was wiped out. 50,000 people, mostly women, children and the elderly, were massacred. For an Englishman, walking in the streets of Dresden is – to say the least – a thought-provoking experience. Unfortunately, the city has more recently become the centre of extreme nationalist activities, chiefly directed against foreign immigrant workers. It remains, however, a great Baroque city. The famous Zwinger palace has been beautifully reconstructed, as have Semper's magnificent opera house, the Catholic Hofkirche and the public buildings along the waterfront. It is a most interesting and attractive city.

Below Dresden the scenery loses much of its drama, but nevertheless the river runs through many interesting places. The old city of Meissen, for example, where the cathedral and the castle stand joined together high above the river, is famous the world over for its porcelain. Wittenberg, Luther's town and the birthplace of the Reformation and the Protestant world, still has the austere feel of Luther's day. Dessau, where the famous Bauhaus school of art originated, is fascinating, even though it too was largely destroyed by Allied bombing in World War II.

Magdeburg, although in times past an important religious and scholastic centre, is badly scarred by some of the worst architectural atrocities of the Communist era, but further downstream Tangermünde, the old Hanseatic town on the left bank of the river, is something of a jewel of mediaeval buildings. From here onwards the river meanders through low-lying agricultural land as far as Geesthacht, where a lock marks the beginning of the tidal part of the Elbe.

The Elbe above Magdeburg is an extremely interesting area in which to cruise, but the higher reaches of the river do perhaps present a number of practical problems. Depths can be a serious problem in a dry season during July, August and September, and the currents, although normally in the region of 4–5kn, can vary widely according to the volume of water coming down the river. Recognised overnight mooring places are also somewhat few and far between, and finding a quiet place to tie up for the night may sometimes call for the exercise of some degree of ingenuity.

The depth of the river at Magdeburg has always been a problem for east/west shipping passing from the Mittellandkanal to the Elbe-Havel-Kanal, and most people had given up all hope that the viaduct to carry the MLK over the Elbe, on which work was abandoned at the outbreak of World War II, would ever come to fruition. However, the project has now been re-established, and there is every hope that in the not too distant future shipping will bypass the Rothensee lift and continue over the top of the Elbe to a new lock, Doppelschleuse Hohenwarthe, which will have a rise of 18·5m and provide a direct connection to the EHK behind Schleuse Niegripp. The new layout is shown on page 84.

Km

0·0	Border with Czech Republic on left bank.
2·7	Customs post on right bank.
3·4	Border with Czech Republic on right bank.
3·9	Schmilka.
8·0	Mooring place on right bank. Water, toilets. Provisions and restaurants 2km.
9·0	Shipyard on right bank.
11·0	Bad Schandau. Quay near railway station.
13·2	Hafen Prossen on right bank. Water authority harbour. Mooring not normally allowed.
15·5	Filling station near to left bank.
17·2	Königstein. Public harbour. No facilities. Possible depth problems when water levels low.
17·5	Festung Königstein on left bank.
22·7	Rathen. Possibility of mooring at ferry landing on right bank.
23·5	Bastei. Towering sandstone cliffs on right bank.
26·0	Wehlen. Possibility of mooring at ferry landing.
33·5	Hafen Copitz. Shallow: 1·00m when *Pegel* Dresden reads 190. Access to Pirna. Showers. Shops and restaurants nearby.
45·6	Possible mooring place on left bank.
42·0 to	
43·0	Nature reserve on Pillnitzer island. Mooring place behind island, but enter only from downstream.
43·0	Schloss Pillnitz on right bank.

47·2	Sailing club on right bank. Clubhouse. Shops and restaurants nearby.
48·5	Possible mooring at staging on left bank.
50·5	Hafen Dresden-Loschwitz. City centre 5km. Enter carefully – possibly subject to silting. Water, electricity, showers, clubhouse, slip. Shops and restaurants nearby. Filling station 1km.
55·0	**Dresden**. Possibility of mooring amongst passenger ships on left bank close to city centre.
57·3	Hafen Dresden-Neustadt. Harbour for passenger ships on right bank. Sport boats prohibited.
58·5	Hafen Pieschen on right bank. Water, clubhouse, provisions, fuel nearby. City centre 2km. Shallow-draught boats only.
60·5	Hafen Dresden-Friedrichstadt. Commercial harbour.
68·1	Yachthafen Kötzschenbroda (Radebeul) on right bank. Showers, provisions, clubhouse, repairs.
72·9	Yachthafen Coswig on right bank. Water, electricity, showers, clubhouse, provisions 1km.
73·9	Schloss Gauernitz on left bank.
74·3	Entrance to backwater on right bank. Possible mooring, but depth uncertain.
80·5	Yacht moorings at staging on right bank. Showers, clubhouse. Shops and restaurants nearby. Filling station 150m. Meissen centre 2km.
82·5	**Meissen**. Albrechtsburg palace/cathedral/castle on left bank. Busy passenger quay.
83·3	Winterhafen Meissen on right bank. Filling station nearby, but no other facilities.
89·7	Possible mooring at ferry landing.
96·2	Schloss Hirschstein on left bank.
102·0	Possible mooring on right bank above mill.
103·8	Possible mooring in small harbour on right bank at entrance to Grödel-Elsterwerdaer Flosskanal.
107·1	Entrance to Promnitzer Lache on right bank. Possible mooring, but depth uncertain.
107·6	**Riesa**. Commercial quay on left bank.
109·4	Gröba. Entrance to commercial harbour (Hafen Riesa) on left side.
116·0	Hafen Lorenzkirch. Possible mooring.
124·7	Entrance to Baggersee Borschütz on right bank. Working gravel pit. Anchorage possible, but noisy day and night. Diesel bunker station.
127·1	Hafen Mühlberg. Water authority harbour on right bank. Possible mooring, with permission. Clubhouse of rowing club, with showers. Shops and restaurants nearby.

The castle and cathedral at Meissen.

139·6	Hafen Belgern on left bank. Possible mooring.
140·5	Belgern.
150 to 165	Navigation difficult due to narrow channel and protruding groynes. Do not go outside channel markers.
154·1	Hafen Torgau. Access forbidden to private pleasure craft.
154·6	Torgau road bridge. When *Pegel* Torgau is 315 or less, all traffic must use the left (west) arch.
154·7	Schloss Hartenfels.
155·2	Mooring to left bank. No facilities.
155·5	**Torgau** railway bridge. Upstream traffic must use right (east) arch and downstream traffic must use left (west) arch.
184·8	Possible mooring below ferry on left bank. Restaurant nearby.
185·0	Schloss Pretzsch.
198·6	Junction with Schwarze Elster. Possible anchorage if depth allows.
200·2	Elster. Possible mooring on right bank above ferry. Shops and restaurants.
213·0	**Wittenberg**. Mooring at staging on right bank. No facilities.
216·5	Hafen Wittenberg. Commercial harbour. Possible mooring.
236·6	Yachthafen Coswig on right bank. No facilities, but shops and restaurants nearby.
257·9	Rosslau. Possible mooring on right bank. Filling station 300m.
261·5	**Dessau**. Entrance to Leopoldhafen near 'Regatta Tower' on left bank. Two yacht clubs. Water, electricity, showers, slip, clubhouse. Shops and restaurants nearby.
264·2	Hafen Rodleben. Commercial harbour on right bank.
274·8	Hornhafen Aken. Commercial harbour on left bank.
276·0	Aken. Mooring on left bank at staging.
276·6	Mooring at sailing club on left bank. Showers, slip, repairs. Provisions and restaurants in town.
277·3	Verkehrshafen Aken. Commercial harbour on left bank. Possible mooring at rowing club at end of harbour.
290·7	Junction with Saale.
291·5	Ronney. Possible mooring near ferry on left bank.
293·5	Barby.
294·1	Barby railway bridge. Choice of arch depends on water level at *Pegel* Barby. When *Pegel* Barby reads less than 140 only one vessel is permitted to pass through the bridge at any one time.
295·5	Hafen Barby. Commercial harbour. Mooring, but no facilities.
309·8	Schönebeck. Yacht harbour on left bank. Showers. Shops and restaurants nearby.
311·8	Schönebeck road bridge. When *Pegel* Barby shows less than 200 only left (west) arch is used.
312·0	Possible mooring on left bank.
314·6	Hafen Schönebeck-Frohse. Commercial harbour on left bank. Yacht moorings in harbour. Clubhouse, showers, shops, crane.
317 to 333	**Magdeburg**.
317 to 318	Stony shallow patch stretches from left bank almost to centre of stream.
318·0	Possible mooring on left bank near ferry.
322·0	Yacht harbour Magdeburg-Südost on left bank. Water, electricity, clubhouse, showers, slip, repairs. City centre 5km. Shops and restaurants within 1km.
322·8	Yacht clubs in old (east) branch of Elbe. Useable only when water level adequate: depth 0·50m when *Pegel* Magdeburg-Strombrücke reads 120. No facilities.
324·1	Sülzehafen. Commercial harbour on left bank. Possible mooring place.
324·8 to 329·9	Stromstrecke Magdeburg. Special regulations and control system for commercial shipping only. Vessels under 33m in length are not subject to control.
325·1	Signal station on left bank. Traffic control point for passage through Domfelsen.
325·7	Domfelsen. Strong current and shallow patch stretching from left bank almost to centre of river.
327·2	Signal station on right bank. Traffic control point for passage through Domfelsen.
327·3	Zollhafen. Marina Magdeburg on right bank. Convenient for city centre. Water, electricity, clubhouse, showers, fuel, repairs. Shopping centre nearby.
328 to 343	Channel zigzags due to shallows. Course indicated by yellow crosses on both banks. Current normally 3–4km/h, but can vary considerably according to volume of water. See plan.
329·9	Handelshafen. Commercial harbour on left bank. Mooring, but no facilities. Shops nearby. Close to city centre.
332·8	Industriehafen. Commercial and water authorities harbours. Two bunker boats for diesel, but no facilities for yachts.
333·6	Junction with Mittellandkanal (via Abstiegskanal Rothensee and ship-lift) on left bank.
339·7	Unfinished canal crossing from Mittellandkanal to Elbe-Havel-Kanal. Work abandoned during World War II.

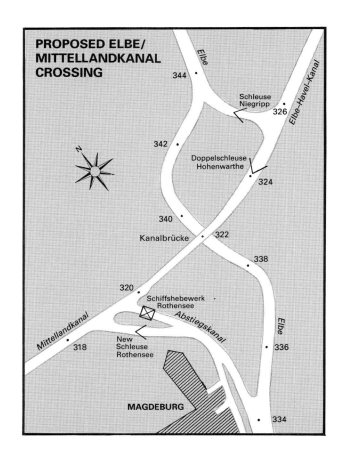

PROPOSED ELBE/ MITTELLANDKANAL CROSSING

343·7	Junction with Elbe-Havel-Kanal (via Niegripper Verbindungskanal and *Schleuse Niegripp*) on right bank.
346·1	Entrance to Hafen Niegripp on right bank. No facilities.
350·6	Rogätz. Possible mooring at staging on left bank near ferry. No facilities, but shops and restaurants nearby.
354·2	Entrance to gravel pit on left bank. Good anchorage in rural surroundings, but no facilities of any sort.
365·5	Gravel quay on right bank. No facilities.
371·5	Junction with Pareyer Verbindungskanal, linking with Elbe-Havel-Kanal Km 351·4.
374·3	Ship repair yard on right bank in entrance to Baggerelbe. No facilities.
388·2	Hafen **Tangermünde** on left bank. Commercial harbour with yacht harbour. Clubhouse, showers. Shops and restaurants in town. Filling station 800m.
403·6	Water authority harbour on left bank. No mooring.
422·8	Havelberg. Junction with Untere Havel-Wasserstasse Km 148·5.
438·1	Junction with Gnevsdorfer Vorfluter on right bank. Link to Untere Havel-Wasserstrasse via *Schleuse Gnevsdorf* and *Schleuse Quitzöbel*. Depth 1m. Information from lock-masters at Gnevsdorf (☎ 038791 2098) or Quitzöbel (☎ 039387 391).
454·9	Hafen **Wittenberge**. Two yacht harbours and commercial harbour. Water, showers, shops, restaurants. Diesel bunker station in commercial harbour.
469·5	Moorings in former frontier-control harbour on right bank. No facilities.
474·6	Hafen Schnackenburg on left bank. Mooring possible in commercial harbour. Water, electricity, shops.
484·6	Hafen Lenzen. Harbour for commercial ships on right bank. No facilities for yachts.
493·0	Gorlebener Haken on left bank. Water authority harbour. No facilities for sport boats.
504·1	Junction with Müritz-Elde-Wasserstrasse on right bank. Hafen Dömitz at entrance. No facilities. Shops and restaurants nearby.
509·0	Staging on left bank suitable for small boats. No facilities.
509 to 569	Dömitz to Lauenburg depth normally 2–4m, but in dry periods can reduce to 0·90m.
522·8	Sportboothafen Hitzacker on left bank. Motor-Yacht-Club Oberelbe Hitzacker. Water, electricity, slip. Filling station, shops and restaurants nearby in town.
528·1	Tiessau. Harbour on left bank for tankers. No entry except in emergency.
536·5	Neu Darchau. Yacht harbour in town centre. Water, electricity, showers, slip, shops, restaurants.
543·3	Alt Garge. Yacht harbour at end of backwater on left bank. Water, electricity, slip.
550·0	Hafen Bleckede on left bank. Commercial harbour with yacht moorings. Water, slip. Filling station, shops and restaurant nearby.
559·5	Hafen Boizenburg on right bank. Commercial harbour with yacht moorings. No facilities, but filling station, shops and restaurants close by.

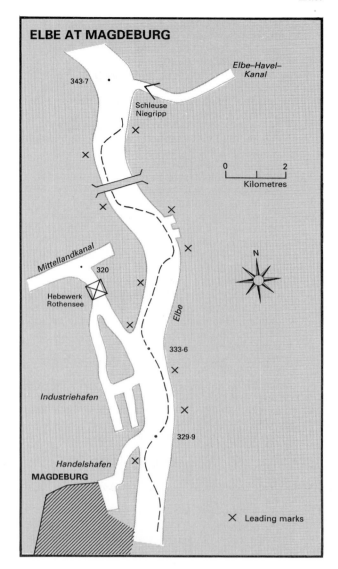

The waterfront at Tangermünde.

569·2   Staging on left bank.
         Junction with Elbe-Lübeck-Kanal Km 61·6.
         Yacht harbour 1·5km inside canal at Lauenburg.
         Good facilities. See Elbe-Lübeck-Kanal.
569·2 to
585·8   Underwater obstructions outside channel mark-
         ers. Stay inside channel. Minimum depth in
         channel 3·60m.
573·0   Junction with Elbe-Seitenkanal Km 115·2.
574·5   Artlenburg. Yacht harbour on left bank. Entrance
         subject to silting. Deepest water on starboard
         side of entrance. Artlenburger Boots Club.
         Water, electricity, showers, slip, repairs. Filling
         station, shops and restaurants nearby.
579·0   Tesperhude. Possible mooring on right bank.
584·5   Yacht moorings in old harbour on right bank.
         Motor-Yacht-Club Geesthacht. No facilities.
585·8   *Schleuse Geesthacht*
         Fall 4·50m at LW.
         VHF Ch 22.
         Hours 0500–2200.
         Note Water inlets at both ends of chambers:
         avoid last 20m either end. N wall of N chamber
         is piled. Other side of N chamber and both sides
         of S chamber are smooth. No floating bollards.
         Level of water below lock can be higher than
         level above lock under certain tidal conditions.

Schleuse Geesthacht.

2. GEESTHACHT TO CUXHAVEN
Km 585·8–Km 724·9

Navigable length 139·1km
Maximum draught 3·20m at mid-tide
Current Tidal
Locks None

The tidal part of the river, the Unterelbe, from
Geesthacht to Cuxhaven and beyond to the North
Sea, carries a considerable traffic of shipping, has
strong tidal streams and can become dangerously
rough in bad weather. It would be inadvisable to
attempt to navigate this part of the river without
detailed charts and a vessel suitable for sea passages.

Hamburg, 35km below Geesthacht, is Germany's
biggest port and one of the ten most important

container ports in the world. It is a maze of harbour
basins and connecting waterways covering 100
square kilometres. The port provides employment
for 100,000 people.

Apart from the many attractions of this major city,
be they historical, maritime, cultural, sporting,
gastronomic or social, it may be useful to know that
two of the best maritime book shops in the world
are situated in Hamburg: Eckardt and Messtorff at
Rödingsmarkt 16, and Bade and Hornig at Herrengraben 31.

In the port area the Elbe splits into the Norderelbe and the Süderelbe (part of which is known as
the Köhlbrand), which come together again on the
seaward side of the port as the Unterelbe. Below
Hamburg the low-lying banks become once again
rural, and the tidal mudflats and sandbanks of the
estuary have a wildness which is in complete contrast to the bustle of the busy city. Cuxhaven, a
pleasant resort and fishing harbour, provides an
excellent staging point when working the tides into
or out of the estuary.

Km
590·0   Elbstorf. Mooring on left bank. Shops and
         restaurants nearby.
599·0   Junction with Ilmenau Km 28·6. Marina 300m
         into Ilmenau. Water, electricity, showers, slip,
         provisions nearby.
         Note The Ilmenau is navigable for 28km to
         Lüneburg for vessels drawing less than 0·90m.
         There are three locks: *Fahrenholz*, *Wittorf* and
         Bardowick.
601·8   Staging on left bank. Water, electricity, restau-
         rant.
607·2   Mooring possible in commercial harbour on right
         bank. Boatyard.
608·5   River divides into Süderelbe/Köhlbrand and
         Norderelbe.

Süderelbe/Köhlbrand
612·0   Wilhelmsburger Motor Boot Club.
615·0   Yacht harbour and boatyard.
615·6   Lock on left bank leading to Binnenhafen.
         Mooring possible for private craft by permission
         from harbourmaster.
         Entrance via *Ernst-August-Schleuse* to Motor-
         Yacht-Club Dove-Elbe Wilhelmsburg on right
         bank. Water, electricity, slip. Locking Mon–Sat
         0800–1600. Bridge clearance 3·70m.
621·5   Süderelbe becomes Köhlbrand.
624·6   Köhlbrand rejoins Norderelbe and becomes
         Unterelbe.

Norderelbe
615·0   Junction with Dove-Elbe.
         The Dove-Elbe is 14km in length and has two
         locks, *Tatenberg* at Km 1·6 and *Krapphof* at Km
         12·5. Between the two locks there are two boat-
         yards and three yacht clubs, including the Ham-
         burger Yacht-Club with its attractive harbour,
         good facilities and bus links to the city centre.
         The channel can be used by vessels drawing up
         to 1·80m and with a maximum height above the
         water of 4·15m. *Schleuse Tatenberg* operates
         Mon–Fri 0630–2000 and weekends 0630–2100.
         A small locking fee is payable. Speed limit 8km/h.

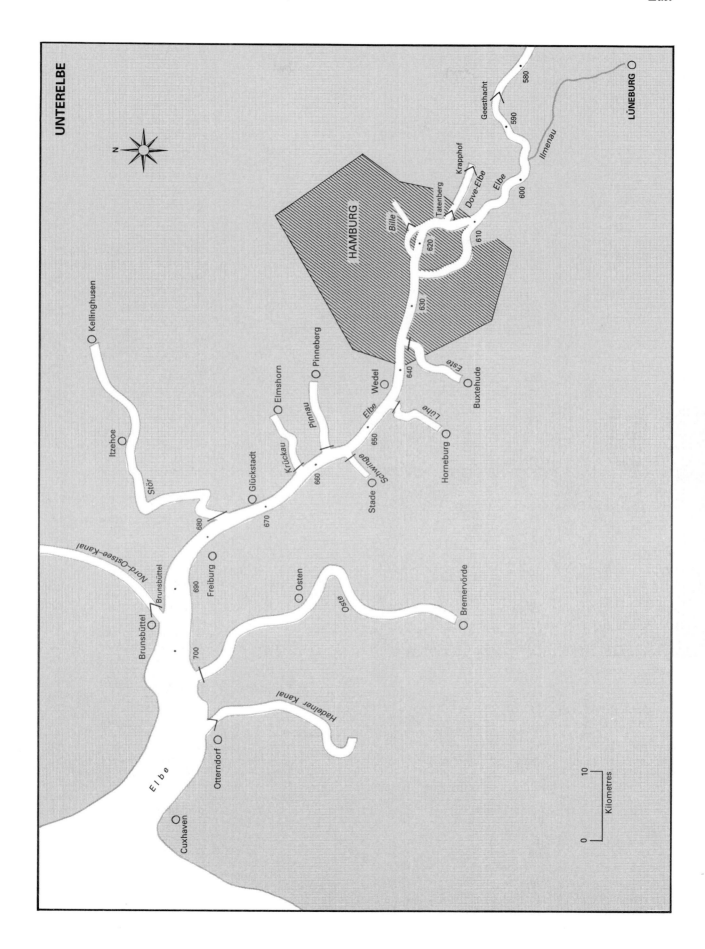

UNTERELBE

N

HAMBURG

Bille
Tatenberg
Krapphof
Dove-Elbe
Elbe
Geesthacht

580
590
600
610
620
630

Ilmenau

LÜNEBURG

Kellinghusen

Itzehoe

Elmshorn
Pinneberg

Stör

Pinnau
Krückau

Wedel
Elbe
Lühe
Este
Buxtehude

640

Horneburg

650

Glückstadt

Schwinge
Stade

660

670

Freiburg

680

690

Nord-Ostsee-Kanal

Brunsbüttel
Brunsbüttel

Osten

Oste

Bremervörde

700

Hadelner Kanal

Otterndorf

Elbe

Cuxhaven

0   10
Kilometres

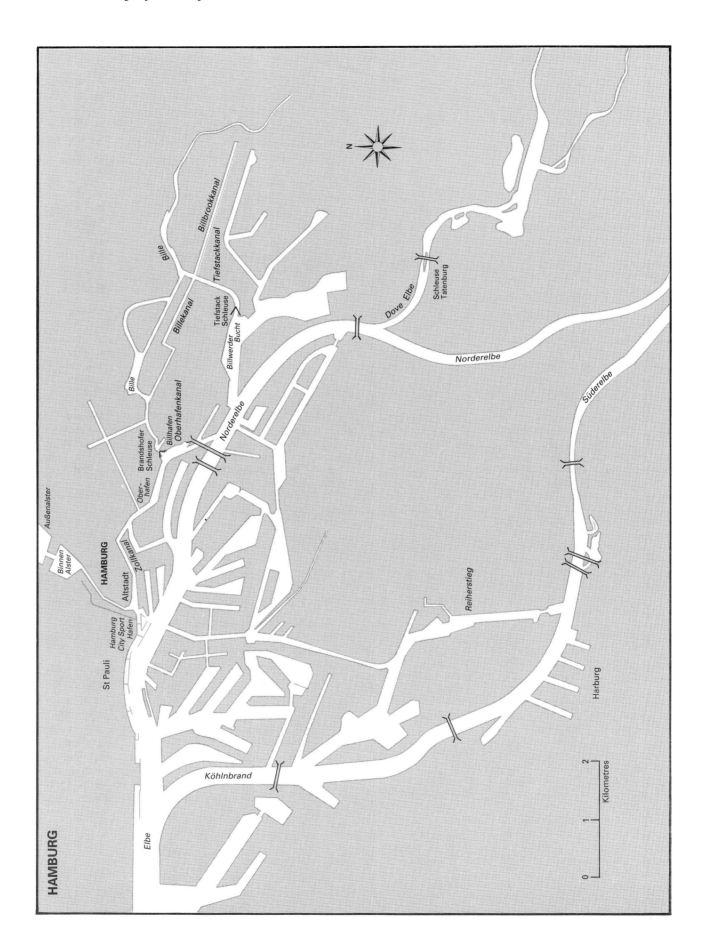

HAMBURG

618·0 Entrance on right hand to Billwerder Bucht and *Tiefstackschleuse*, leading into the Bille, which has three well equipped yacht clubs. Depth 2m. Good bus and U-Bahn connections to city centre. Diesel bunker boat near entrance.

618·9 Entrance on right hand to Binnenhafen via the Oberhafenkanal, Oberhafen and Zollkanal, emerging again in the Norderelbe at Km 622·2. This route passes the Motor-Yacht-Club von Deutschland Hamburg, right in the city centre. Junction with Bille via *Brandshofer Schleuse* in Oberhafenkanal.

622·2 Entrance to Hamburg City-Sporthafen (for short-term visitors) and Binnenhafen on right side. Junction with Alster just beyond yacht haven through Schaartor and Rathaus locks.

623·0 St Pauli landing stages. Passenger ferries to England and other destinations. Close to main shopping centre. Floating bunker station for diesel.

625·7 Norderelbe converges with Köhlbrand to form the Unterelbe Km 624·6.

Unterelbe

625·7 to
642·5 Three yacht harbours on south side and four on north side.

641·3 Schulau yacht harbour on right bank. Dries at LW.

642·5 Hamburger Yachthafen at Wedel on right bank. All facilities, including fuel, but very busy.

643·2 Buoyed channel to Este on left bank. Navigable 12km to Buxtehude. Minimum depth 1·00m. No locks but 2 flood barriers (VHF Ch 10). Yacht harbour.

644·0 Entrance to Hahnöfer Nebenelbe. Small yacht harbour. Depth 1·5m.

645·5 Junction with Lühe on left bank. Navigable 12km to Horneburg using the tide.

654·7 Diesel bunker station on left bank.

654·8 Junction with Schwinge. Navigable for 5km to Stade. Minimum depth 1·50m. Motor- und Yachtclub Stade in town centre. Water, electricity, showers, slip, crane, repairs.

657·8 to
666·3 Pagensand island on right bank. The stream running east of the island, the Pagensander Nebenelbe, has a drying harbour and entrances to the rivers Pinnau and Krückau. The Pinnau is navigable for 19km, and at low water has a minimum depth of 0·80m. The Krückau is navigable for 11·6km, but effectively dries at low water. However, at high water it is possible to reach the harbour at Elmshorn, the head of navigation.

669·8 Junction with Glückstadter Nebenelbe on right bank. Rejoins Elbe at Km 678. Entrance to Aussenhafen and Binnenhafen Glückstadt.

670·0 Junction with Ruthenstrom on left bank. Mooring place with water and electricity.

679·3 Junction with Stör (Km 50·6) on right bank. Buoyed channel. The Stör is tidal, but it is possible to reach Itzehoe (Km 23·6) at any state of tide. To reach Kellinghusen, the head of navigation (Km 0·0), it is necessary to use the tide, but entry from the Elbe can be at any time.

695·7 **Brunsbüttel**. Junction with Nord-Ostsee-Kanal on right bank.

696·9 Hafen Brunsbüttel on right bank.

707·0 Junction with Oste. The Oste is navigable for 74·6km to Bremervörde, passing through flat green agricultural land. Craft drawing not more

Yachts near St Pauli landing stage, in the port of Hamburg.

than 1·70m can reach Bremervörde, but deeper-draught vessels can easily reach Osten, some 20km from the Elbe, where the mid-tide depth is around 4m. The flood barrier at the junction with the Elbe is closed only for high tides in the Elbe. There are two opening bridges.

The Oste was once connected to the Hamme, which is a tributary of the Weser, by the Hamme-Oste-Kanal, but there is no longer any connection.

712·5 Junction with Medem and Hadelner Kanal on left bank.

724·5 Cuxhaven Alter Hafen. New marina under construction.

724·9 **Cuxhaven** yacht harbour. All facilities.

SAALE

Navigable length 160·6km
Maximum draught 1·40m (but see note below)
Maximum height 3·20m
Current 2–5km/h
Locks 17
Speed limit 12km/h

The Saale, especially in its higher reaches, is a very attractive river, flowing in beautiful countryside and through picturesque and interesting old towns and villages where very little has changed over the years. Heading upstream for the last 30km (from Bad Dürrenberg to Naumburg) the river runs along an idyllic wooded valley full of wildlife and providing from time to time dramatic glimpses of castles perched high on the hill tops. Apart from tripper boats, which are fairly numerous in the summer months, commercial shipping has no reason to go above Halle, leaving the upper stretches of the river to pleasure craft. Unfortunately, the lower reaches have not yet recovered from the pollution which was allowed to develop during the years of Communism.

The largest town on the river is Halle, the birthplace of Handel. Although a major industrial centre, Halle is one of Germany's oldest towns. It escaped damage during World War II, and in spite of suffering somewhat from neglect whilst under Communist control, most of its cobbled streets and gabled houses still survive. An important collection of German paintings is housed in Moritzburg Castle, near the cathedral.

Merseburg, a little further upstream, suffers from having two large chemical works on its outskirts and was also badly damaged in the war. Nevertheless it possesses a number of historic buildings, including a splendid Renaissance castle and an 11th-century cathedral.

Unfortunately, the depth of the water limits the size of vessel which can enjoy the delightful scenery of the river above Merseburg. Early in the summer months it is possible for craft drawing 1·40m to reach Naumburg, but later, especially in dry years, no vessel drawing more than 1·00m can reach this far upstream, let alone venture beyond this point into the lovely but shallow River Unstrut, which is navigable for small boats with a draught of 0·80m to Karsdorf.

Official information on depths is made available daily over Radio Aktuel, on VHF and by telephone, along with the data provided for the Elbe. For the purposes of these announcements, the lower part of the river is divided into two stretches: *Strecke* 1 from Trotha to Calbe and *Strecke* 2 from Calbe to the junction with the Elbe. When water levels are low, special care should be taken in the lock cut below Schleuse Trotha and also that below Schleuse Meuschau. If in doubt consult one of the lock-keepers.

From the mouth to Merseburg (Km 124·2) the river is administered by WSD-Ost, and no fees are demanded for using it. Above Merseburg, for many years there was disagreement over which body should be responsible, WSD-Ost or the *Land*. It has now been decided, however, that the upper Saale should become a *Landeswasserstrasse*, although as yet no fees are being demanded.

Above Merseburg there are several ferries which use a rope across the river a metre or so above the water. These are indicated in the route description, but a good lookout needs to be kept as they are not easy to see. A blast on the ship's horn will usually bring the ferryman out to remove the line, provided of course the ferry is not about to cross.

The locks are not equipped with VHF. Lock working times are as follows:

Schleuse Calbe to Schleuse Wettin Mon–Sat 0700–1700; Sun 0700–1500

Schleuse Trotha to Schleuse Rischmühle Mon–Tue closed; Wed–Thu 0800–1200, 1245–1600; Fri–Sun 0800–1200, 1245–1845

Schleuse Bad Dürrenberg to Schleuse Oeblitz Mon–Tue closed; Wed–Sun 0800–1200, 1300–1800

Km
0·0   Junction with Elbe Km 290·8.
0·4   Possible mooring on right bank.
0·5   Junction with old river on right bank. Possible anchorage for shallow-draught boats.
15 to
17   Channel very narrow. Observe signs.
19·5   Junction with weir stream on left bank. Possible mooring place for shallow-draught boats.

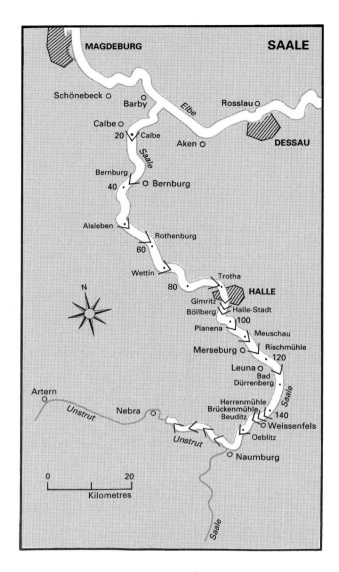

20·0   *Schleuse Calbe*
       Rise 3·4m.
20·9   Junction with weir stream on left bank. Possible mooring place for shallow-draught boats.
21·5   **Calbe**.
22·0   Junction with old river on right bank. Possible anchorage, but depth uncertain.
27·2   Nienburg. Possible mooring on left bank.
27·6   Junction with Bode on left bank. Possible mooring place.
34·6   Possible mooring place on left bank.
36·0   **Bernburg**. Possible mooring on left bank. Filling station in street.
36·1   *Schleuse Bernburg*
       Rise 3·2m.
36·4   Weir on left bank. Beware strong undertow.
37·0   Possible mooring at staging on right bank.
41·0   Gröna. Possible mooring on right bank.
50·3   *Schleuse Alsleben*
       Rise 3·5m.
50·8   Weir stream on left bank. Possible mooring at quay.
51·1   Alsleben. Possible mooring on right bank.
58·4   Entrance to weir stream on right bank. Possible anchorage for shallow-draught boats.
58·7   *Schleuse Rothenburg*
       Rise 2·5m.
60·0   Rothenburg.

Schleuse Hollerich: an idyllic setting on the Lahn.

The Lahn near Nassau.

The square-rigger *Rickmer Rickmers* at Hamburg.

The Nordgeorgsfehnkanal.

Castles perched on hill tops.

The transporter bridge at Rendsburg on the Nord-Ostsee-Kanal.

The Hanseatic city of Lübeck.

70·4	*Schleuse Wettin* Rise 2·3m.
70·9	Entrance to upper part of weir stream on right bank. Possible mooring.
71·1	Wettin. Possible mooring on right bank.
71·6	Possible mooring on right bank near ferry.
78·5	Salzmünde. Possible mooring on left bank.
86·5	Entrance to Hafen Halle-Trotha on right bank. Commercial harbour. Possible mooring.
88·7	*Fangschleuse Trotha* on left side. Used when water levels are low to avoid shallows below main lock. If in doubt, telephone Schleuse Trotha (☎ 0345 25588) before reaching this point.
89·1	Signal for upstream traffic.
89·2	*Schleuse Trotha* Rise 2·5m.
89·3	Trotha.
89·4	Signal for downstream traffic.
90·4	Sailing club on left bank. Clubhouse. Provisions nearby in Halle. Filling station in street.
92·6	*Schleuse Gimritz* Rise 0·8m.
92·9	Sophienhafen on left bank. Possible mooring.
93·5	**Halle**. Old town on right, new town on left.
93·6	*Schleuse Halle-Stadt* Rise 1·0m.
95·9	*Schleuse Böllberg* Rise 1·0m.
96·0	Beware weir at entrance to lock cut above lock.
96·2	Wörmlitz. Yacht club on right bank. Clubhouse, water, electricity. Shops and restaurants nearby.
97·2	Possible mooring at camp site on right bank.
104·5	*Schleuse Planena* Rise 2·0m.
104·7	Possible mooring place in weir stream above lock.
113·5	*Schleuse Meuschau* Rise 2·5m.
114·0	**Merseburg**.
115·2	*Schleuse Rischmühle* Rise 1·2m.
120·0	Ferry with rope across river. Beware!
124·2	End of *Bundeswasserstrasse* and start of *Landeswasserstrasse*.
126·2	*Schleuse Bad Dürrenberg* Rise 1·5m.
126·4	Bad Dürrenberg.
132·5	Possible mooring at staging on right bank.
132·6	Ferry with rope across river. Beware!
141·0	*Schleuse Herrenmühle* Rise 3·0m.
142·5	*Schleuse Brückenmühle* Rise 1·0m. Beware sloping walls.
142·6	Beware undertow at weir above lock.
143·2	*Schleuse Beuditz* Rise 1·0m. Beware sloping wall.
143·3	Beware undertow at weir above lock.
147·9	Ferry with rope across river. Beware! Possible mooring on right bank near ferry.
150·6	*Schleuse Oeblitz* Rise 1·4m. Beware sloping walls.
156·9	**Naumburg**. Possible mooring on right bank.
160·5	Ferry with rope across river. Beware!
160·6	Junction with Unstrut. Navigation by small boats is possible for a further 25km, with 4 locks to Karsdorf.

ELBE-HAVEL-KANAL
Niegripp Km 1·8 to Plauersee Km 382·0

Navigable length 57·8km
Maximum draught 2·00m
Maximum height 4·30m
Current Nil
Locks 3
Speed limit 9km/h

The Elbe-Havel-Kanal is a key east-west link in the European water transport system. It is in effect a continuation of the Mittellandkanal, and its kilometre numbering reflects this. As discussed elsewhere, the plans for a direct connection between the two canals, cutting out the problematic short stretch of the Elbe, have been revived, and there is now optimism that this long-awaited link will become a reality.

The Elbe-Havel-Kanal carries a considerable traffic of barges, but represents no problems for the cruising boat. Its course is entirely in attractive rural countryside, bustling with wildlife such as deer, kites, golden orioles and of course swans and ducks. There are a number of pleasant overnight stopping places.

For the most part the canal has a depth of 3m, but between Niegripp and Zerben the level is tied to the level of the Elbe, as Schleuse Niegripp normally stands open when the level of the Elbe at *Pegel* Magdeburg is less than 140cm. Because of this, the water level at Niegripp can fall to 2·00m, or even as little as 1·50m in exceptionally dry seasons in August and September.

Strictly speaking, the last 1·8km at the western end is the Niegripper Verbindungskanal, but for convenience this short section is considered here to be part of the Elbe-Havel-Kanal.

The waterway is of course a *Bundeswasserstrasse*, administered by WSD-Ost, and there are no dues payable for using it. All three locks have VHF and operate from 0600 to 2000 Mondays to Saturdays and 0700 to 1900 on Sundays. Schleuse Niegripp

Schleuse Brandenburg, on the main shipping route.

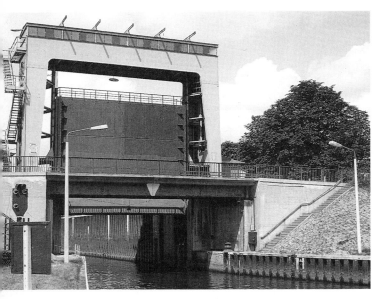

Schleuse Niegripp.

has piled walls without inset bollards. Zerben and
Wusterwitz have stepped bollards in their walls.

Km

1·8	Junction with Elbe Km 343·7.
0·7	*Schleuse Niegripp* *Fall 0–5·1m.* *VHF Ch 22.* See note above. Passage controlled by light signals.
326·0	Possible mooring in pleasant surroundings in barge waiting bay on east side.
329·7	**Niegripp**. Entrance to old gravel pit (Kiesgrube Niegripp) on west side. Depth 1·20–2·00m. Anchorage and staging. Shops and restaurants in Niegripp.
331·3	Entrance to Niegripper Altkanal on west side. Possible mooring places. Depth 1·20m.
332 to *333*	Possible mooring place on east bank.
334·0	**Burg**. Yacht harbour on west side. Depth 1m. Mooring between posts. Clubhouse. Shops and restaurants 10 minutes.
345·4	*Schleuse Zerben* *Fall 5·2m.* *VHF Ch 20.* Elbe *Pegel* information displayed at lock side.
351·4	Junction with 3·5km-long Pareyer Verbindungskanal on west side. Alternative exit to Elbe. Maximum draught 1·85m. Speed limit 6km/h. Depth after lock depends on level in Elbe. Possible mooring under bridge on south side approximately 1km into canal.
0·8	*Schleuse Parey* *Rise 1–5m.* *VHF Ch 78.*
350·0	**Parey**.
351·5	Pleasant mooring place on south bank. No facilities.
358 to *360*	Moorings along tree-lined south bank.

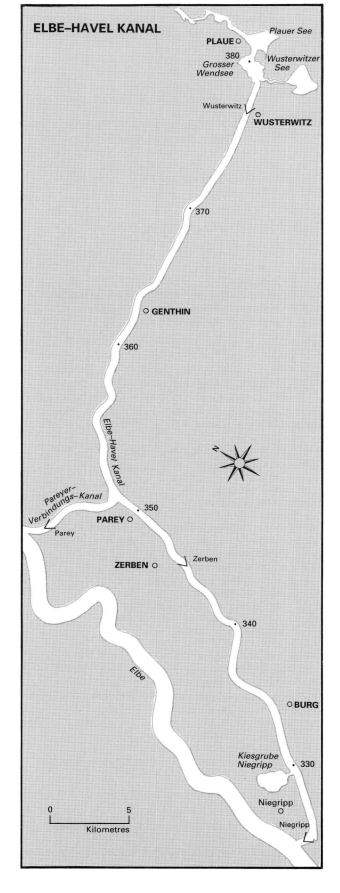

362·1 **Genthin**. Mooring to low quay on north bank. No facilities, but good access to supermarket over bridge.

376·7 *Schleuse Wusterwitz*
Fall 4·1m.
VHF Ch 18.
Mooring possible on north bank above lock. No facilities.

379·0 Entrance to Grosser Wendsee. Channel swings NE across lake. Access southwards to Wusterwitzer See. Good anchorages, but beware fishing posts.

382·0 **Plaue**. Junction with Untere Havel-Wasserstrasse Km 66·7.

UNTERE HAVEL-WASSER-STRASSE

The Havel, at first the Obere Havel, begins life about 100km to the northeast of Berlin in the beautiful Mecklenburg lake district. It flows southwards to join the Havel-Oder-Wasserstrasse, whence it turns south to Spandau on the northwestern outskirts of Berlin. Here it becomes the Untere Havel, with kilometering starting from zero at the point where the Havel-Oder, the Spree and the Untere Havel all meet.

South of Spandau the river widens into an enormous and beautiful lake, largely surrounded by woods. On a hot summer day it is covered with boats of all kinds. At Potsdam the waterway splits into the Potsdamer Havel and the Sacrow-Paretzer-Kanal. The former goes through Potsdam and continues through a very attractive area with wooded banks, pleasant anchorages and friendly yacht clubs. The latter bypasses Potsdam and provides a shorter, more rural and arguably less interesting route towards the west. In the Göttin See, near Ketzin, the two routes, together with the Havelkanal (a somewhat boring but very convenient route bypassing the whole Berlin area for boats intent on getting to or from Poland quickly), come back together. Once again as the Untere-Havel, the waterway continues westwards towards the old Hanseatic town of Brandenburg.

At Brandenburg barges use the larger Silokanal, which bypasses the town, and the Vorstadtschleuse, a standard big-ship lock. Small boats are required to go through the centre of the town on the smaller and older Stadtkanal. This is no hardship, as the historic town of Brandenburg is both charming and interesting. The little Stadtschleuse, overhung with trees, is quite delightful.

Both before and after Brandenburg the route crosses a number of meres or lakes (not unlike the Norfolk Broads) which abound with bird life: reed warblers, marsh harriers, bitterns, storks, cranes and herons can all be seen by the determined birdwatcher.

West of Brandenburg, at Plaue, the Elbe-Havel-Kanal branches off to the west and the Untere Havel turns northeast, winding through flat but pleasant agricultural land to Havelberg, where it joins the Elbe.

Genthin, on the Elbe-Havel-Kanal.

Schleuse Wusterwitz, on the Elbe-Havel-Kanal.

Berlin is of course a city of enormous interest from so many points of view, and to arrive here by water – and perhaps to move around on the labyrinth of waterways – is a fascinating experience. A few of the waterways of Berlin are industrial, but most are attractive tree-lined canals and rivers which provide a superb mini cruising ground. Well equipped yacht clubs are too numerous to list in detail (although a number have been included as being of special interest to cruising boats seeking convenient places for overnight stops). There is good access to the public transport system and facilities for fuelling, provisioning and repairs. Boats needing facilities for a short stay to explore the city will probably find Spandau, Potsdam or the Grosser Wannsee most convenient, but there is so much variety to choose from that it is difficult to recommend any one place.

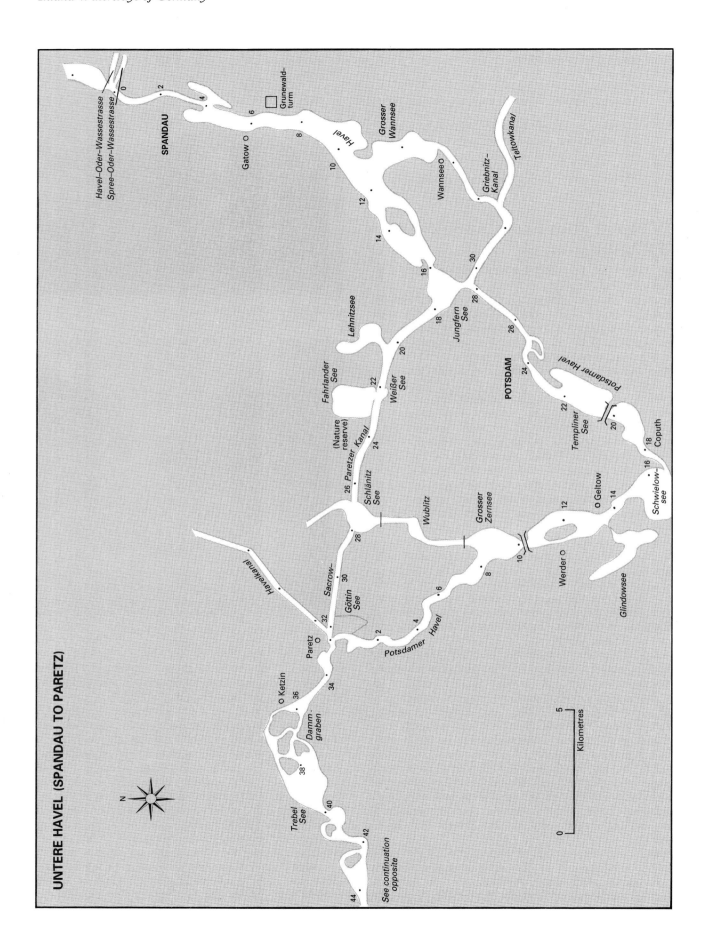

UNTERE HAVEL (SPANDAU TO PARETZ)

Havel–Oder–Wasserstrasse
Spree–Oder–Wasserstrasse

0

2

SPANDAU

4

Gatow O

6

8

10

Havel

Havel

12

Grunewald–turm

Grosser Wannsee

WannseeO

Griebnitz–Kanal

Taltowkanal

14

16

30

28

26

24

22

20

18

Lehnitzsee

Fahrlander See

(Nature reserve)

Weißer See

POTSDAM

Potsdamer Havel

Templiner See

Coputh

18

16

14

O Geltow

12

Schwielow–see

Jungfern See

Paretzer Kanal

Schlänitz See

Wublitz

Grosser Zernsee

Werder O

Glindowsee

28

26

24

22

20

Sacrow–

Göttin See

30

32

Paretz O

O Ketzin

34

36

Damm–graben

38

Havelkanal

10

8

6

4

2

40

Trebel See

42

See continuation opposite

44

N

0

5

Kilometres

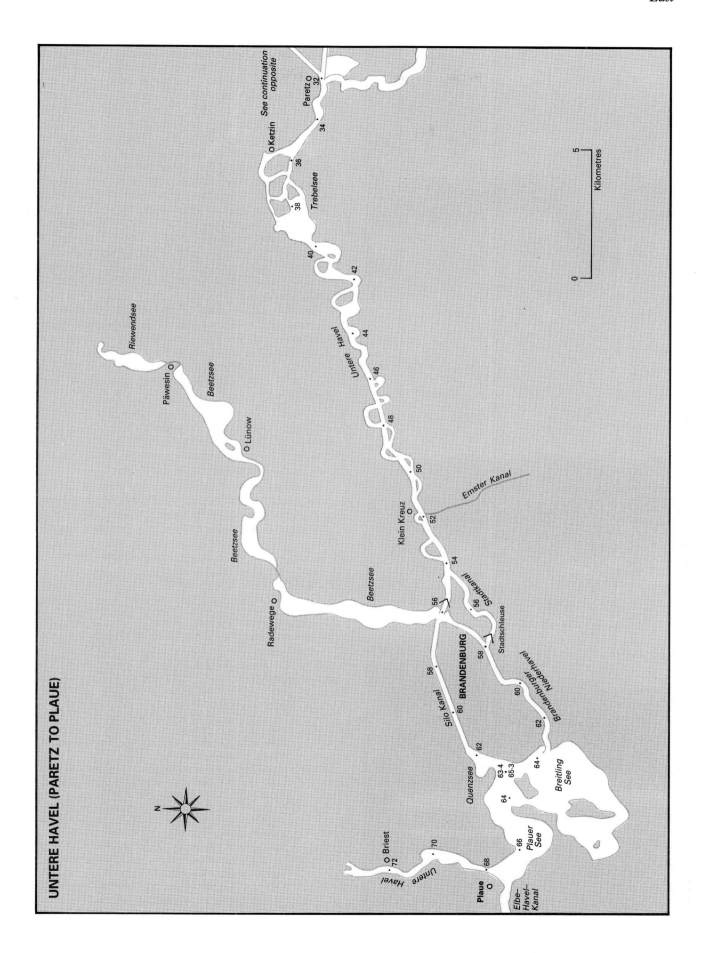

UNTERE HAVEL (PARETZ TO PLAUE)

Paretz O
32
34
O Ketzin
36
Trebelsee
38
40
42
Untere Havel
44
46
48
50
Klein Kreuz O
52
Emster Kanal
54
56
56
Stadtkanal
Stadtschleuse
58
58
Niederhavel
Brandenburger
60
60
BRANDENBURG
62
62
Quenzsee
63.4
65.3
64
64
64
Breitling See
Plauer See
66
70
O Briest
72
68
Plaue O
Untere Havel
Elbe-Havel-Kanal

Riewendsee
Päwesin O
Beetzsee
O Lünow
Beetzsee
Radewege O
Beetzsee
Silo Kanal

See continuation opposite

5

Kilometres

0

N

Schleuse Spandau.

The Grunewaldturm, overlooking the Havel in Berlin.

Moby Dick: the ubiquitous floating restaurant of Berlin.

Spandau is one of the oldest parts of Berlin, but has an excellent modern shopping centre. Potsdam is worthy of a stay of several days: the Cecilienhof is famous as the place where Churchill, Truman and Stalin met in 1945 to divide up Europe (the room where they met has been preserved and is open to the public); Frederick the Great's elegant Sanssouci palace is an amazing example of rococo architecture and is also open to the public. Much of the route of the waterway is across quite large lakes, but where it crosses open water the channel is well marked with buoys, red to starboard and green to port (heading downstream). The whole waterway system is run by WSD-Ost, and there are no fees.

The Vorstadtschleuse (in the Silokanal) at Brandenburg operates 0600 to 2000 Mon–Sat and 0700 to 1900 on Sundays. The other main locks (Bahnitz, Rathenow, Grütz, Garz and Havelberg) all operate 0600 to 1900 Mon–Sat and 0700 to 1800 Sunday.

As with other rivers of variable depth in eastern Germany, the Untere Havel is notionally divided into stretches, and the *Tauchtiefe* for each stretch is made available daily via signs at the sides of locks, over VHF radio and through broadcasts on Radio Aktuel. The *Strecke* used for this are set out in the table below:

Strecke 1   Havelberg to Rathenow
Strecke 2   Rathenow to Bahnitz
Strecke 3   Bahnitz to Plaue
Strecke 4   Plaue to Brandenburg
Strecke 5   Brandenburg to Spandau

It should be noted that there is a ship, the *Heimatland*, based at Spandau, which specialises in transporting yachts as deck cargo, should this become desirable as a result of low water levels in the Elbe. It can often be seen lying on the east bank in the vicinity of the Schulenburgbrücke (Km 1·5).

1. SPANDAU TO PLAUE
Km 0·0–Km 66·7

Navigable length 66·7km
Maximum draught 2·20m (may be slightly lower in dry seasons)
Maximum height 4·10m
Current Slight
Locks 1
Speed limit 9km/h

Km
0·0   **Spandau**. Junction with Spree (Km 0·0) and the Havel-Oder-Wasserstrasse (Km 0·0).
0 to 1   Convenient mooring to piled river bank on west side. No facilities, but supermarkets, restaurants, banks and the main post office nearby.
4·5   Several yacht clubs on right bank, immediately after the point where the Untere Havel-Wasserstrasse widens out into a lake to the south of Spandau. All facilities, including fuel. Convenient for major shopping centre in Spandau and for access to central Berlin by U-Bahn.
7·4   Grunewaldturm. Prominent red-brick tower high amongst trees on left bank.
9·0   Yacht club on right bank amongst trees.

10·0	Entrance to Grosser Wannsee on left side. Entrance shallow: observe buoyage. Speed limit 12km/h. At SW corner is the Potsdamer Yacht-Club, well equipped and convenient for the S-Bahn. Speed limit on lake 12km/h.
14·0	Pfaueninsel on left side. Wooded island with castle.
16·3	Route divides: Potsdamer Havel to left and Sacrow-Paretzer-Kanal to right. Kilometre markings follow Sacrow-Paretzer-Kanal.

Sacrow-Paretzer-Kanal (right branch)

17·8	Remains of old pontoon bridge, lookout tower and section of Berlin Wall.
17 to	
32	No overnight mooring places.
20·0	Entrance to Lehnitzsee. Speed limit 12km/h on lake.
22·5	Entrance to Fahrlander See. Nature reserve.
32·6	Junction with Havelkanal Km 34·9 on north side.
33·0	Junction with Potsdamer Havel Km 0·0 on south side.

Potsdamer Havel (left branch)

The Potsdamer Havel is a very attractive waterway. It has many places of interest and good facilities for visiting boats. The minimum depth at normal water levels is 1·90m. There is a speed limit of 12km/h throughout this waterway, including the lakes.

28·6	Glienicker Brücke.
28·4	Junction with Teltowkanal on east side.
24·3	Yacht harbour on right bank. Motorboot-Club Potsdam on island amongst trees. Depth 1·50–2·00m. Water, electricity, clubhouse. Shops and restaurants close by. Good centre for Sanssouci and a short walk to Potsdam Stadt railway station for trains to centre of Berlin.
23·9	Bunker station on right bank.
21·0	Rail bridge (6·6m headroom).
20·8	Yacht harbour on right bank immediately after railway bridge. Good facilities. Shops, restaurants and railway station near at hand.
18·2 to	
16·8	Narrow channel linking Templiner See and Schwielowsee. On exit into Schwielowsee, channel swings sharply northwards and is well buoyed. The remainder of the Schwielowsee is navigable, but there are many shoals outside the buoyed channel. It is possible to moor at Ferch, at the southwestern end of the lake.
18·0	Boatyards on each side of river. Repairs. Facilities for overnight mooring.
14·7	Narrow channel under road bridge into Zernsee.
13·5	Entrance to Glintowsee.
11·5	Mooring at staging on left side at Inselstadt Werder. MC Werder. Usually very busy. Possible also to anchor in vicinity.
10·3	Motorbootclub Werder on left bank. Attractive setting. Water, electricity, showers. Shops and restaurants nearby.
7·1	Boatyard on right bank just before *autobahn* bridge. Repairs. Facilities for overnight mooring.
4·2	Phöben. Mooring at staging on left bank.
0·0	Junction with Sacrow-Paretzer-Kanal Km 33·0.

Untere Havel-Wasserstrasse (continued)

33·1	**Paretz.** Possible mooring on right bank.
35·8	Entrance to Ketziner Havel on right bank. Depth 2m. Mooring possible at Ketzin. Ketziner Havel rejoins Untere Havel-Wasserstrasse at Km 36·8.
38 to	
40	Trebelsee. Follow buoyage.

Potsdamer Yacht-Club, on the Grosser Wannsee.

ca40	Garbage mountain and processing plant on left bank.
ca50	Harbour for small boats at camp site on right bank.
51·7	Junction with Emster-Kanal on left bank. Navigable for 15km to Lehnin for boats drawing less than 1m.
54·3	Channel divides. Right for Silokanal (for commercial ships and larger pleasure craft) and left for Brandenburger Stadtkanal (for pleasure craft drawing under 2·00m and with height 2·70m maximum), which links into Niederhavel below Stadtschleuse (Bootschleuse) Brandenburg.

Silokanal (right branch)

55·6	*Vorstadtschleuse Brandenburg* *Fall 1·0m.* *VHF Ch 20.*
56·2	Junction with Brandenburger Niederhavel (south). Junction with Beetzsee (north). The Beetzsee is navigable for 18km to Päwesin for boats drawing 1·70m. It has several possible mooring places and anchorages. Speed limit 6km/h. On the connecting Riewendsee motorboats are forbidden.
61·6	Mooring on right bank. Filling station.
63·4	Junction with Brandenburger Niederhavel (south).

Brandenburger Stadtkanal (left branch)

Pleasure boats with a height above water level of 2·70m or less must use this route in preference to the Silokanal. Speed limit 6km/h.

54 to	
56	Winding channel (depth 1·70m), not well marked. Care required (but bottom soft).
57·0	Possible mooring against wall on left bank. Easy access to town centre, but no facilities.
57·4	Stone bridge. Height 2·75m.
57·5	*Stadtschleuse Brandenburg* *Fall 1·0m.* Operates Mon–Sat 0700–1900, Sun 0700–2000.
58·0	Junction with Brandenburger Niederhavel.

The delightful Stadtschleuse on the Brandenburger Havel.

Brandenburger Niederhavel

56 to
65   Depth 1·80m. Passes through the town centre, then through woodlands and pastures to Plauer See. Speed limit 6km/h.

56·8   Yacht club on left bank. Clubhouse. Shops and restaurants in town.

58·0   Junction with Brandenburger Stadtkanal.

65·3   Junction with Untere Havel-Wasserstrasse Km 63·4.

Untere Havel-Wasserstrasse (continued)

63 to
66   Plauer See. Follow buoyage.

66·7   Plaue. Junction with Elbe-Havel-Kanal Km 382·0.

Stadtschleuse Rathenow.

2. PLAUE TO HAVELBERG
Km 66·7–Km 148·5

Navigable length 81·8km
Maximum draught 1·80m (see below)
Maximum height 4·70m
Current Slight
Locks 5
Speed limit 9km/h

This stretch of the Havel is far less heavily used than the Berlin–Brandenburg section. On average only about 20 barges pass through it in a day, and during the late summer months in a dry year this number may be even further reduced because of water levels as low as 1·20m.

Km
66·7   **Plaue**.

68·1   Yacht harbour on right bank.

68·4   Boatyard on left bank. Facilities for mooring.

78·6   Entrance to Pritzerber See on right side under road/rail bridge. Navigable for 3km. Depth 1·30m.

78·7   Possible mooring on right bank. No facilities, but near village.

81·5   Start of lock cut. Small boat lock in weir stream.

81·9   *Schleuse Bahnitz*
        Fall 0·30m.
        VHF Ch 78.
        Beware sloping wall.

83·8   End of lock cut.

86·9   Hafen Döberitz on right bank. Commercial harbour. No facilities for pleasure craft.

90·8   **Premnitz**. Yacht harbour on right bank. Depth uncertain. No facilities. Restaurant in floating clubhouse. Provisioning in village.

92·7   Yacht harbour on right bank. Clubhouse. Few facilities.

92·8   Boatyard on left bank. Attractive mooring. Shops and restaurants nearby.

102·8   **Rathenow**. River divides. Left to Hauptschleuse Rathenow, right to Stadtschleuse Rathenow (Stadtkanal).

Left branch

103·3   *Hauptschleuse Rathenow*
        Fall 1·0m.
        VHF Ch 79.
        Beware sloping wall. Pleasure craft drawing 1m or less forbidden when Stadtschleuse in operation.

104·2   Junction with right branch.

Right branch

104·0   Mooring on left side.

104·2   Mooring in Stadthafen above Stadtschleuse.

104·3   *Stadtschleuse Rathenow*
        Fall 1·0m.
        Mandatory for sport boats drawing under 1m and under 2·3m high. Operates 1 July to 31 August. Mon–Sat 0700–1100 and 1400–1800, Sun 0800–1200 and 1400–1800.

ca105   Stadtkanal depth possibly only 1m.

105·5   Jederitzer Brücke. Height 2·3m.

106·0   Junction with left branch.

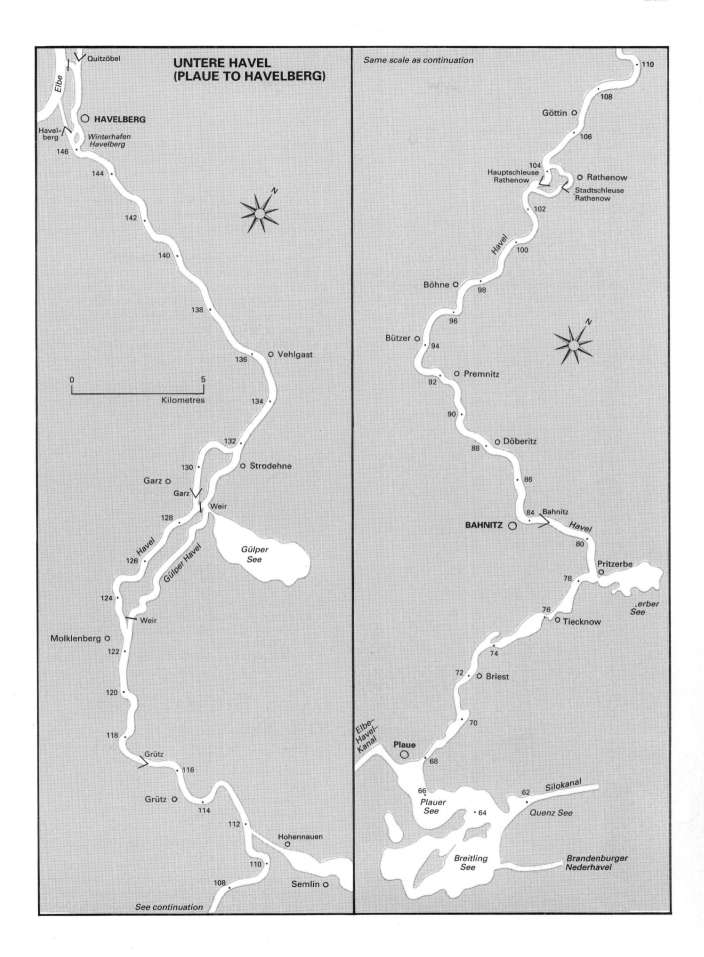

**UNTERE HAVEL
(PLAUE TO HAVELBERG)**

Same scale as continuation

Quitzöbel

Elbe

O **HAVELBERG**

Havel-
berg

*Winterhafen
Havelberg*

146

144

142

140

138

Vehlgast ○

136

0   5

Kilometres

134

132

130

Strodehne ○

Garz ○

Garz

Weir

128

Havel

Gülper Havel

*Gülper
See*

126

124

Weir

Molklenberg ○

122

120

118

Grütz

116

Grütz ○

114

112

Hohennauen ○

110

108

Semlin ○

See continuation

110

108

Göttin ○

106

104

Hauptschleuse
Rathenow

Rathenow ○

Stadtschleuse
Rathenow

102

Havel

100

Böhne ○

98

96

Bützer ○

94

Premnitz ○

92

90

Döberitz ○

88

86

84   Bahnitz

BAHNITZ ○

Havel

80

Pritzerbe ○

78

...erber
See

76

Tiecknow ○

74

72   Briest ○

70

Elbe–
Havel–
Kanal

Plaue ○

68

66

62   *Silokanal*

*Plauer
See*

64

Quenz See

*Breitling
See*

*Brandenburger
Nederhavel*

Untere Havel-Wasserstrasse (continued)

111·9 Junction with the beautiful Hohennauener Kanal on right bank. Navigable 10km to Ferchesar. Depth normally 1·70, but may reduce considerably during dry periods. Berthing bows to on north side at Hohennauen. Mooring also at Semlin on south side of Hohennauener See.

115·0 Grütz.

116·5 Start of lock cut. Small-boat lock (maximum beam 2·4m) in weir.

117·0 *Schleuse Grütz*
Fall 0·5m.
VHF Ch 22.
Beware sloping wall.

117·5 End of lock cut. Weir stream rejoins.

122·4 Junction with Gülper Havel on right bank. Depth 1·30m at normal levels. Two small-boat locks (in very bad condition), maximum beam 2·00m. Gülper Havel reunites with Untere Havel-Wasserstrasse at Km 129·0 below weir at Garz.

122·5 Hafen Molkenberg on left bank. Mooring to quay. No facilities.

129·0 *Schleuse Garz*
Fall 0·6m.
VHF Ch 20.
Beware sloping wall.

131·4 Entrance to weir stream and mooring at Strodehne. No facilities. Depth uncertain.

135·5 Vehlgast. Possible mooring in old river entrance on right bank. Depth uncertain.

145·8 **Havelberg**. Entrance to Winterhafen Havelberg on right bank. Basic facilities only, but harbour is in pleasant village with all supplies.

146·0 Channel branches. Route to Elbe via Schleusenkanal straight on, entrance to Havel Mündungsstrecke on right. The Mündungsstrecke connects via Schleuse Quitzöbel (canoes only) to the Gnevsdorfer Vorfluter, which passes through another small lock, Schleuse Gnevsdorf, and joins the Elbe at Km 438·0. The depth of these waters can be less than 1m in dry seasons.

147·1 *Schleuse Havelberg*
Rise 1·5m.
VHF Ch 18.

148·5 Junction with Elbe Km 422·8.

Leisure-craft mooring place at Havelberg.

HAVELKANAL

Navigable length 34·9km
Maximum draught 2·00m
Maximum height 4·70m
Current Nil
Locks 1
Speed limit 6km/h

Following the division of Germany by the Allies after World War II, the East German canal link from the Elbe to the Oder required a passage through West Berlin. Cold War politics dictated that a new canal should be constructed to avoid this necessity, and therefore the Havelkanal came into existence in 1952, having taken only 13 months to build.

Being relatively straight and featureless, the canal is somewhat uninteresting to travel along. Nevertheless, it certainly provides the fastest route from the Elbe to the Oder, as not only is it shorter, but it also avoids a considerable wait during busy times at the Spandau lock. The advantage is now even greater, since the Spandau lock is being rebuilt, making a time-consuming detour via the Charlottenburg and Plötzensee locks necessary.

The canal is administered by WSD-Ost, and is free. Its only lock, Schönwalde, operates 0600 to 2000 Mon–Sat and 0700 to 1900 Sun.

Km

0·0 Junction with Havel-Oder-Wasserstrasse Km 10·5.

0·9 Mooring at Niederneuendorf on south bank. Clubhouse. Shops and restaurants in Hennigsdorf and Niederneuendorf.

8·8 *Schleuse Schönwalde*
Rise 2·0m.
VHF Ch 81.

18·1 Brieselang. Yacht harbour on west bank. Shops and restaurants nearby.

23·6 Commercial quay on west bank. No facilities for yachts.

30·3 Possible mooring on east bank.

34·4 **Paretz**. Entrance to old lock on right bank. Mooring possible against sloping bank. No facilities.

34·9 Junction with Untere-Havel-Wasserstrasse Km 32·6.

HAVEL-ODER-WASSERSTRASSE

Spandau Km 0 to Hohensaaten Km 93·0

Navigable length 93·0km
Maximum draught 1·85m
Maximum height 4·10m
Current Slight (westwards)
Locks 4 (including ship-lift)
Speed limit 12km/h from Km 0·0–10·4 (including lakes), 9km/h from Km 10·4–93.

Strictly speaking the Havel-Oder-Wasserstrasse comprises several connected waterways. The first 3·5km from Spandau is the Spandauer Havel. From Km 3·5 the Havel-Oder-Wasserstrasse cuts across to Hohensaaten (Km 93·0). At Hohensaaten the

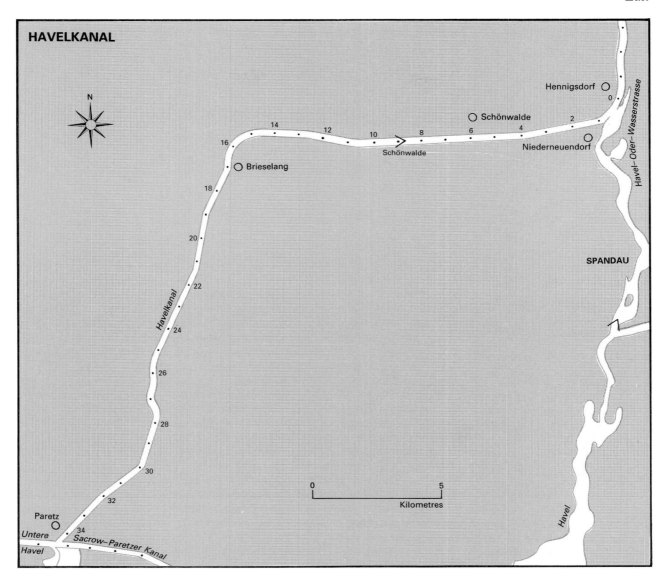

HAVELKANAL

notional direction of flow reverses, and the waterway becomes the Hohensaaten-Friedrichsthaler-Wasserstrasse, the end of which (Km 135·3) connects to the West-Oder close to the Polish border. For the sake of simplicity, the Hohensaaten-Friedrichsthaler-Wasserstrasse is described separately in this book, and the Havel-Oder-Wasserstrasse is considered to end at Hohensaaten.

Schleuse Spandau has long been something of a bottleneck in this very busy waterway, and waiting times for barges have often been very long – although smaller pleasure craft have usually been able to get through within a reasonable time by virtue of being able to tuck in behind larger vessels. It was therefore decided to rebuild the lock completely, and in 1993 it was closed. The new lock is not expected to be ready until 1998, and in the meantime it is necessary to make a diversion, either via the Havelkanal or via the Spree and the Spandauer Schiffahrtkanal (Hohenzollern-Kanal).

After leaving Spandau, which was part of West Berlin, the waterway is soon passing rusting factories at Hennigsdorf, in what used to be East Germany. Beyond this, however, open country is

reached and the canal lies amongst unspoilt rural countryside and woodlands.

The need to negotiate the massive ship-lift at Niederfinow (Km 77·9) in a small boat amongst the massive 1,500-tonne barges seems at first sight a fearsome prospect. In the event, however, the experience proves to be interesting rather than frightening, and on the whole less problematic than using one of the large commercial locks.

At Hohensaaten, where the waterway turns to the north to run parallel with the Ost-Oder (which is also the Polish border), storks nest on chimney tops, agriculture appears to be more primitive and the land seems wilder. Good places to stop for the night are few and far between in this stretch, but it is possible to find a comfortable mooring at Km 76·6 in the entrance to the disused lock staircase above the Niederfinow ship-lift. There are no official mooring places at either Oderberg or Hohensaaten, but there are places where with ingenuity it is possible to tuck away for the night.

If heading down the Oder towards Szczecin it is possible either to use the Ostschleuse and travel down the Ostoder, or to use the Westschleuse and

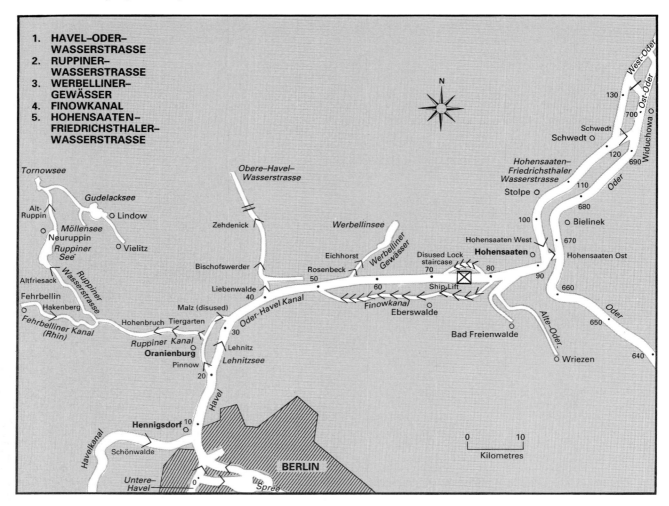

the Hohensaaten-Friedrichsthaler-Wasserstrasse. On the whole it is better to use the latter route because of more reliable depths.

The waterway is administered by WSD-Ost and the locks and the *Hebewerk* (ship-lift) are all equipped with VHF radio. The lock operating hours are given in the route description.

Junction of the Havel-Oder-Wasserstrasse with the Spree-Oder-Wasserstrasse and the Untere Havel-Wasserstrasse.

Km	
0·0	Junction with Untere-Havel-Wasserstrasse (Km 0·0) and Spree-Oder-Wasserstrasse (Km 0·0).
0·6	*Schleuse Spandau* (closed, to be rebuilt). *Rise* 1·8m.
1 to 10	The waterway is a series of interlinked lakes, but the through channel is well buoyed and navigation is straightforward. The banks and inlets are lined with yacht and boat clubs, although not all have space or facilities to cater for visitors.
3·4	Junction with Spandauer Schiffahrtkanal (Hohenzollern-Kanal) on east bank.
3·9	Entrance to Tegeler See on east bank. Navigable for 4km. Depth 2–4m. Many yacht clubs.
4·1	Fuelling berth on east bank at Tegelort.
10·5	Junction with Havelkanal (Km 0·0) on west bank.
12·3	Stadthafen Hennigsdorf on west bank. Commercial harbour. Mooring possible. Steelworks nearby.
20·8	Junction with Oranienburger Kanal on west bank, leading to Ruppiner Kanal.
25·0	Junction with Oranienburger Havel on west bank. No through passage. Depth 1·60m at entrance. Mooring possible.
25·5 to 28·0	Lehnitz-See. Channel well buoyed.
26·1	Staging on west bank of lake. Depth 1·50m. Also possible to anchor off. Shops and restaurants close by.

28·2	Waiting point for small boats behind dolphins on west bank below lock. Depth 1·30m. Provisions from small shop near lock.
28·6	*Schleuse Lehnitz* *Rise* 5·7m. *VHF* Ch 18. *Hours* Mon–Sat 0600–2100, Sun 0700–2000.
28·8	Waiting quay on west bank above lock. Depth 2·50m.
29·1	Waiting point for lock (with traffic lights) on east bank. Depth 1·00–1·20m alongside.
32·4	Entrance to (disused) Malzer Kanal. Mooring possible above Schleuse Malz.
40·5	Junction with Malzer Kanal (first section of Obere Havel-Wasserstrasse) on north bank.
41·5	Start of one-way traffic for commercial vessels.
50·4	Junction with Finowkanal on south bank.
54·7	Winterhafen Marienwerder. Quiet mooring away from traffic. Water, electricity. Shops and restaurants in village.
54·9	Junction with Werbellinkanal on north bank.
55·0	Yacht harbour on left bank.
57·8	Possible mooring on right bank.
71·0	Possible mooring place in entrance to old canal on north bank. Depth 2m.
78·0	*Schiffshebewerk Niederfinow.* *Fall* 36·0m. *VHF* Ch 22. *Hours* 0000–2400. Waiting point for small boats close to entrance above lift on north bank. Below lift it is possible to tuck into a corner out of the way of waiting barges. Contact lift on Ch 22 for instructions.
79·0	Junction with Finowkanal on south bank.
82·5 to *84·0*	Oderberger See. Buoyed channel along north side. Depth outside channel 1·00m.
84·6	Junction with Alte Oder on south bank.
85·5	Oderberg. No satisfactory mooring place.
91·9	**Hohensaaten**. Water authority harbour on north bank. Mooring not officially allowed, but possible if given permission.
92·6	Mooring to dolphins before Ostschleuse.
92·7	*Ostschleuse Hohensaaten* (to Oder river) *Rise* 2·2m. *VHF* Ch 20. *Hours* Mon–Sat 0500–2100, Sun 0700–1900.
92·8	Boats drawing under 1·20m can moor to staging on the right (west) bank above Westschleuse.
92·9	*Westschleuse Hohensaaten* *Fall* 0·8m. *VHF* Ch 20. *Hours* Mon–Sat 0500–2100, Sun 0700–1900.

Westschleuse and Ostschleuse Hohensaaten.

Niederfinow ship-lift, opened in 1934.

HOHENSAATEN-FRIEDRICHSTHALER-WASSERSTRASSE

Navigable distance 42·3km
Maximum draught 1·80m
Maximum height 5·00m
Current Negligible
Locks None
Speed limit 6km/h

This waterway, actually part of the Havel-Oder-Wasserstrasse, runs parallel to the Oder through pleasant agricultural countryside. The bird life in this area is very interesting: kingfishers, herons, storks, golden orioles, grebes and geese are much in evidence.

For vessels bound to or from Szczecin in Poland, this is an easier route than that via the Oder (Ostoder) itself, as there is less variation in depth. It should be noted that the direction of buoyage changes at Hohensaaten. From here northwards red buoys are to starboard and greens to port.

The Hohensaaten-Friedrichsthaler-Wasserstrasse near Stolpe.

Yacht harbour at Schwedt.

There are two options for vessels heading towards Szczecin. The normal route is to leave the Hohensaaten-Friedrichsthaler-Wasserstrasse at Schwedt and cross via the Schwedter Querfahrt to the Ostoder. This means using Schleuse Schwedt, as at this point the level of the Oder can be anything up to a metre above that of the Hohensaaten-Friedrichsthaler-Wasserstrasse. The alternative is to continue to the end of the Hohensaaten-Friedrichsthaler-Wasserstrasse at Km 135·3 and into the Westoder, clearing German customs (left bank) and Polish customs (right bank) at Mescherin. There are no locks to negotiate on this route. The Westoder route may be somewhat less busy with commercial traffic, but otherwise there is little to choose between the two options.

The operating times for Schleuse Schwedt are 0600 to 2000 on weekdays and 0700 to 1900 on Sundays. There are no fees.

Km
93·0   Junction with Havel-Oder-Wasserstrasse (Km 93·0). Kilometre markings continue.
95·8   Loading quay for gravel.
98·9   Possible bank-side mooring at Lunow on left bank. Depth 2m. No facilities.
105·6 Stolpe. Mooring on left bank in 1·80m. No facilities but restaurant nearby.
120·7 Schwedt. Possible mooring on left bank. Depth uncertain.
121·4 Bootshafen Schwedt. Yacht harbour on left bank. Depth 1·8m, but varies slightly. Water, electricity, showers, slip. Shops and restaurants nearby.

Schwedter Querfahrt
123·3 Junction with Schwedter Querfahrt (length 3·5km) on right bank. Connects to Ostoder via *Schleuse Schwedt*.
       Rise Around 1m, according to water level in Oder.
       VHF Ch 79.
       Hours Mon–Sat 0600–2000, Sun 0700–1900. Mooring on left bank after lock immediately before junction with Oder. Use stern anchor and tie bow line to tree. No facilities.

Hohensaaten-Friedrichsthaler-Wasserstrasse (continued)
125·0 Industrial quay on left bank.
128·0 Gatow. Possible mooring on left bank. Depth uncertain.
133·6 Friedrichsthal. Possible mooring on left bank. Depth uncertain.
135·3 Junction with Westoder (Km 3·0). 14km to German/Polish border. Speed limit on Westoder 12km/h.

RUPPINER WASSERSTRASSE

Navigable length 71·4km
Maximum draught 1·40m
Maximum height 3·00m
Current Negligible
Locks 5
Speed limit 6km/h, on Ruppiner See 25km/h, on Vielitz-See 12km/h.

The Ruppiner See and its connecting waterways form part of the original canal system of Germany, although nowadays, of course, there is no commercial shipping. It is an area of great charm and an excellent cruising ground.

The waterway system basically comprises the Oranienburger Kanal and the Ruppiner Kanal, leading to the Rhin river and continuing upstream through a series of lakes (including the 15km-long Ruppiner See) as far as Lindow. Boats drawing less than 1·10m can go 10km beyond Lindow to Vielitz. It is also possible to take the delightful lower part of the Rhin in a downstream direction; the river is navigable for 17km as the Fehrbelliner Kanal for boats drawing up to 1·3m. The old Rhin Kanal shown on some maps as an extension of the Fehrbelliner Kanal across to the Untere Havel at Garz is only a drainage canal.

Km
Oranienburger Kanal
20·8   Junction with Havel-Oder-Wasserstrasse Km 20·8.
22·5   *Schleuse Pinnow*
        Rise 2·4m.
        Hours 0730–1700.
28·8   Junction with Ruppiner Kanal Km 0·0 (and disused sections of Havel).

Ruppiner Kanal
0·0   Junction with Oranienburger Kanal Km 28·8.
2·1   *Schleuse Tiergarten*
        Rise 0·8m.
        Hours Mon–Thurs 0800–1200, 1400–1700. Fri–Sun 0800–1200, 1400–1900.
7·2   *Schleuse Hohenbruch*
        Rise 0·7m.
        Hours Mon–Thurs 0800–1200, 1400–1700. Fri–Sun 0800–1200, 1400–1900.
22·0   Junction with Rhin. Straight on upstream towards Ruppiner See and left for downstream Rhin and Fehrbelliner Kanal.

Fehrbelliner Kanal
0·0   Junction with Ruppiner Kanal.
8·0   *Schleuse Hakenberg*
        Fall 1·1m.
        Hours 0800–1800 on request (☎ 03391 3300)
17·5   **Fehrbellin**. End of waterway.

Ruppiner Wasserstrasse (continued)
28·7   *Schleuse Altfriesack*
        Rise 1·1m.
        Hours Mon–Thurs 0800–1200, 1400–1700. Fri–Sun 0800–1200, 1400–1900.
        Dangerous lock with high sill. Boats with a draught of over 1·00m should insist on using the third lock gate and should stay in the southern part of the double lock during locking.
29·6 to
43·5   Ruppiner See. Numerous possible mooring places and anchorages.
40·5   **Neuruppin**. Several possible mooring places on west bank.
43·7   Alt Ruppin.
45·1   *Schleuse Altruppin*
        Rise 2·0m.
        Hours Mon–Thurs 0800–1200, 1400–1700. Fri–Sun 0800–1200, 1400–1900.
45·3 to
47·0   Molchowsee. Possible anchorages.
47·5 to
49·7   Teetzensee. Possible anchorages.
50·3 to
53·0   Zermützelsee. Possible anchorages.
51·2   Entrance to Tornowsee (4km diversion).
59·5 to
60·5   Möllensee. Possible mooring place at southern end.
61·3 to
65·0   Gudelacksee. Mooring at staging on west side at Gühlen.
65·0   **Lindow**. Yacht harbour on lake.
65·3 to
66·6   Vielitz-Kanal. Maximum draught 1·00m.
66·6 to
71·4   Vielitz-See.
71·4   End of navigation.

FINOWKANAL

Navigable length 31·9km
Maximum draught 1·20m
Maximum height 3·80m
Current Negligible
Locks 12
Speed limit 6km/h

The Finowkanal, now closed due to the deterioration of Schleuse Stecher, was once the main route from the Elbe to the Oder. In 1890 over 15,000 ships passed through it, but it has not been used by commercial shipping since World War I. In consequence, for shallower-draught boats not pressed for time it is a beautiful, little-used waterway in which to linger, even though a through passage is no longer possible.

The remaining 11 locks are still in working order, but advance notice is required (☎ 03335 214) in order to use them. They operate only Mondays to Fridays from 0700 to 1400.

There are few problems in finding places to stop, either at locks or in the charming little villages through which the canal passes. There is a current, and although at normal times it is not significant, it can reach 3km/h in times of flood.

Km
50·5   Junction with Havel-Oder-Wasserstrasse Km 50·4.
59·2   *Schleuse Ruhlsdorf*
        Fall 1·8m.
61·1   *Schleuse Leesenbrück*
        Fall 2·5m.
63·3   *Schleuse Grafenbrück*
        Fall 3·6m.
67·5   *Schleuse Schöpfurt*
        Fall 3·6m.
71·0   *Schleuse Heegermühle*
        Fall 3·0m.
72·9   *Schleuse Wolfswinkel*
        Fall 2·6m.
73·5   Lift bridge.
73·9   *Schleuse Drahthammer*
        Fall 3·6m.
75·9   *Schleuse Kupferhammer*
        Fall 4·1m.
77·9   *Schleuse Eberswalde*
        Fall 3·6m.
81·0   *Schleuse Ragön*
        Fall 2·3m.
84·4   *Schleuse Stecher* (disused)
        Fall 3·0m.
86·3   Lift bridge.
88·9   *Schleuse Liepe*
        Fall 2·4m.
89·3   Junction with Havel-Oder-Wasserstrasse Km 79·0.

WERBELLINER GEWÄSSER

Navigable length 16·6km
Maximum draught 1·20m
Maximum height 4·00m
Current Negligible
Locks 2
Hours 0700–2000
Speed limit 6km/h (25km/h on lake if at least 100m from shore).

From Km 54·9 on the Havel-Oder-Wasserstrasse the attractive Werbellinkanal, 3·50m deep as far as the second lock, runs northwards to the Werbellinsee, a beautiful lake some 10km long and up to 50m deep. The waterway runs through woodland and heath rich in wildlife: kites, eagles, cranes, otters and beavers can all be seen from time to time. Much of the area is in fact a nature reserve. There are excellent anchorages and mooring places around the shores of the Werbellinsee, the largest being at the village of Altenhof (Km 14 on the east bank).

In the canal above Schleuse Eichhorst the depth of water can be a problem for deeper-draught boats, but a word with the friendly lock-keeper may well result in a temporary adjustment in level to overcome the problem.

Navigation on the lake is prohibited at night from 2200 to 0500. On Saturdays, Sundays and holidays from May to September motorboats are prohibited from navigating on the lake between the hours of 1200 and 1500.

Km	
3·4	Junction with Havel-Oder-Wasserstrasse Km 54·9.
6·0	*Schleuse Rosenbeck* *Rise* 3·1m.
8·5	*Schleuse Eichhorst* *Rise* 3·1m.
10·5 to 20·0	Werbellinsee.

Junction of Obere Havel-Wasserstrasse with the Havel-Oder-Wasserstrasse.

OBERE HAVEL-WASSER-STRASSE

Navigable length 94·4km
Maximum draught 1·20m
Maximum height 3·20m
Current Negligible
Locks 11
Speed limit 9km/h from Havel-Oder-Wasserstrasse to Km 23·5, 6km/h above Km 23·5.

The Obere Havel and its network of lakes, rivers and canals forms a major part of the beautiful area, generally known as the Mecklenburg lake district, to the north and northwest of Berlin which has become available to cruising boats since the reunification of Germany.

The main through route is basically the upper part of the Havel, which together with its major branches, the Wentow Gewässer, the Templiner Gewässer and the Lychener Gewässer, forms a magical waterway system set in an area of outstanding natural beauty. It is also an area rich in history, and the many picturesque towns and villages all have stories to tell, from mediaeval rivalries to the concentration camps of World War II. The northwestern end of the waterway links with the Müritz-Havel-Wasserstrasse, which in turn links with Lake Müritz and eventually, via the Müritz-Elde-Wasserstrasse, to the lower Elbe.

One of the attractive features of this area is that there are so many tranquil, out-of-the-way places in which to moor or anchor. There are a few yacht harbours, but such is the attraction of this little-known area that in the main most people find it preferable to lie in some peaceful corner of a lake, or perhaps at a quiet quayside above or below one of the locks.

The kilometering is a little confusing, as it still reflects some of the original waterway system, starting with 0·0 at the junction with the defunct northwest extension of the Finowkanal. The 2·9km section between this point and the Havel-Oder-Wasserstrasse is technically the Malzer Kanal, and is numbered from Km 44·0 at the junction with the Havel-Oder-Wasserstrasse to Km 46·9 at the junction with the old Finowkanal.

At normal times the main through route is available to boats drawing 1·50m, but in dry seasons the depth may be a little less than this.

Of the 17 locks in the area as a whole, 11 are on the through route and six are on branches. All operate from 0700 to 2000 daily. There are no fees.

Km	
44·0	Junction with Havel-Oder-Wasserstrasse Km 40·4.
45·3	*Schleuse Liebenwalde* *Rise* 1·9m.
46·9	Junction with old Finowkanal. Not navigable.
0·0	**Liebenwalde** Stadthafen at entrance to old canal on left (east) bank. Mooring possible.
4·5	*Schleuse Bischofswerder* *Rise* 3·3m.

The waterfront at Dresden.

Moritzburg castle, near Dresden.

Early morning on the Havel-Oder-Wasserstrasse.

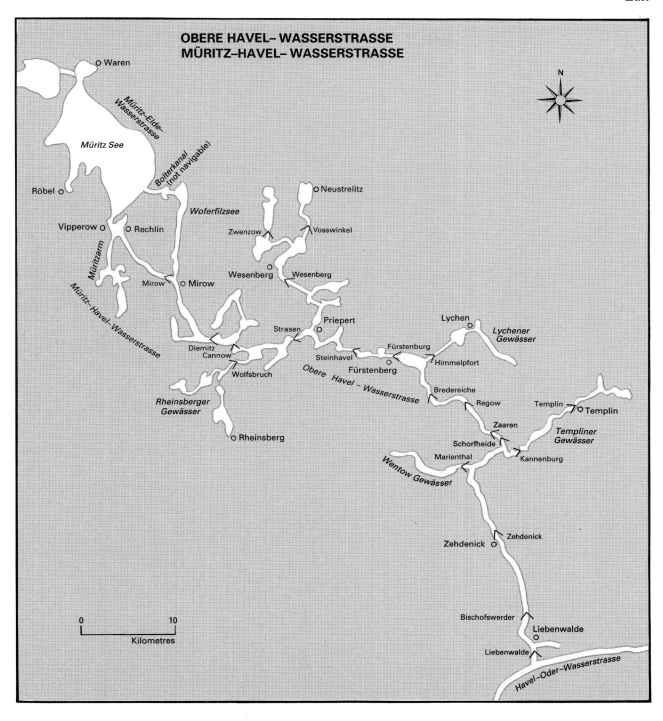

OBERE HAVEL– WASSERSTRASSE
MÜRITZ–HAVEL– WASSERSTRASSE

15·7	**Zehdenick**.
16·0	*Schleuse Zehdenick* *Rise* 3·0m.
16·1	Yacht harbour on left bank immediately above lock.
24·2	Burgwall. Possible mooring at camp site.
24·9	Junction with Wentow Kanal.

Wentow Gewässer
Navigable length 11·0km
Maximum draught 1·20m
Maximum height 3·9m
Current Negligible
Locks 1
Speed limit 6km/h

This short waterway, comprising the Wentow Kanal and the Wentowsee, lies amid very pretty countryside. There are several anchorages and mooring places.

Km	
0·0	Junction with Obere Havel-Wasserstrasse Km 24·9.
0·1	*Schleuse Marienthal* *Rise* 1·9m.
2·5 to	
7·9	Grosser Wentowsee.
9·5	Two bridges. Only small boats can continue beyond this point.
9·6 to	
11·0	Kleiner Wentowsee.

Obere Havel-Wasserstrasse (continued)

32·1   Junction with Templiner Gewässer.

Templiner Gewässer
Navigable length 21·0km
Maximum draught 1·20m
Maximum height 3·60m
Current Negligible
Locks 2
Speed limit 6km/h

The Templiner Gewässer are a string of small lakes connected together by canals. The countryside is very pleasant but the waterway passes through an area used for many years by Russian troops for exercises.

There are a number of places to moor or anchor.

Km
0·0   Junction with Obere Havel-Wasserstrasse Km 32·1.
3·6   *Schleuse Kannenburg*
         Rise 1·5m.
         Beware sloping walls.
5·8 to
9·8   Rödelinsee.
ca13   **Templin**.
13·3   *Schleuse Templin*
         Rise 4·0m.
         Note This lock has for some time been in a bad state of repair, and cannot be relied upon to be in operation.
14·0 to
17·1   Templiner See. Possible anchorages on both sides.
18·0 to
21·0   Fährsee, leading to Zaarsee. End of navigation.

Obere Havel-Wasserstrasse (continued)
32·7   *Schleuse Schorfheide*
         Rise 0·6m.
36·1   *Schleuse Zaaren*
         Rise 1·1m.
42·2   *Schleuse Regow*
         Rise 1·0m.
47·9   *Schleuse Bredereiche*
         Rise 2·6m.
48·0   Bredereiche. Two possibilities for mooring above the lock.
54·3 to
57·5   Stolpsee. Junction with Lychener Gewässer.

Lychener Gewässer
Navigable length 8·3km
Maximum draught 1·20m
Maximum height 3·50m
Current Negligible
Locks 1
Speed limit 6km/h

This is another pleasant detour from the main through route, suitable for boats drawing 1·20m. The Woblitz river leads through the pretty village of Himmelport into the Grosser Lychensee lake, at the northeastern corner of which lies the small holiday resort of Lychen. Although badly damaged by bombs in World War II, Lychen is still extremely attractive, and is a very pleasant centre from which to explore the surrounding neighbourhood. The Grosser Lychensee is generally around 5m in depth and has three small islands. Anchor in the lake or at the small staging on the foreshore at Lychen.

Km
0·0   Junction with Stolpsee Km 55·0.
0·2   *Schleuse Himmelpfort*
         Rise 1·2m.
0·3 to
1·7   Hausee.
4·3 to
7·0   Grosser Lychensee.
7·0   **Lychen**. Sailing club jetty.
7·2 to
8·3   Stadtsee. Possible mooring at staging on north side.
7·9   Railway bridge.
8·3   End of navigation.

Obere Havel-Wasserstrasse (continued)
54·3 to
57·5   Stolpsee.
59·4   Railway ferry, technical monument.
59·9   Junction with Schwedtsee. Yacht harbour at Fürstenberg on west side.
ca60   **Fürstenberg**.
60·3   Passage to Baalensee. Anchoring possible.
60·7   *Schleuse Fürstenberg*
         Rise 1·7m.
         Fuelling point beyond lock.
61·4 to
63·1   Röblinsee. Buoyed channel. Possible anchorages.
64·6   *Schleuse Steinhavel*
         Rise 1·6m.
66·6   Entrance to Menowsee on west bank. Possible anchorage.
67·3 to
68·5   Ziernsee. Mooring at camp site at northern end of lake.
68·8 to
74·1   Ellbogensee.
72·5   **Priepert**. Possible mooring to south of town. Junction with Müritz-Havel-Wasserstrasse (main route through to Müritz and the Elbe).
73·1 to
75·1   Grosser Priepert See. Possible mooring to north of Priepert.
75·3 to
75·5   Wangnitzsee. Motorboats forbidden to go east of marked channel.
77·8   Entrance to Drewensee on east side.
78·5   Ahrensberg. Covered bridge over Havel.
81·3   *Schleuse Wesenberg*
         Rise 2·4m.
82·7 to
86·7   Woblitzsee. Various anchorages and mooring places around shores.
86·2   Entrance to upper reaches of Havel river and Grosser Labus-See Km 90·3 to 92·9. Navigation further upstream by motor vessels forbidden.
86·8 to
92·0   Kammerkanal.
88·0   *Schleuse Vosswinkel*
         Rise 1·8m.
89·2   Railway bridge height 3·20m. Lowest bridge on waterway.
92·0 to
94·4   Zierker See. Buoyed channel. Possible anchorages.
94·4   **Neustrelitz**. End of waterway. Mooring at jetty to west of town.

MÜRITZ-HAVEL-WASSER-STRASSE

Navigable length 31·8km
Maximum draught 1·40m
Maximum height 4·00m
Current Negligible
Locks 4
Speed limit 6km/h

The Müritz-Havel-Wasserstrasse cuts through the heart of the Mecklenburg lake district. Although only 31km in length, it passes through a labyrinth of lakes, rivers and canals which are a paradise for boat owners. A large proportion of the gently rolling landscape is covered with woodland, and there are many charming and interesting small towns and villages. The small town of Mirow, for example, has a history which can be traced back to the 7th century.

The main branches from the main route are the Rheinsberger Gewässer to the south and the chain of small lakes leading north from Mirow (at one time with an exit via the Bolter Kanal to the Müritz sea).

There are four locks on the main route and a further one on the Rheinsberger Gewässer. They all operate from 0700 to 2000 daily. There are no fees.

Km	
0·0	**Priepert**. Junction with Obere Havel-Wasserstrasse Km 72·5.
2·7	*Schleuse Strasen* *Rise* 1·5m.
2·8	Strasen-Priepert. Mooring places immediately above lock in centre of village.
2·8 to 4·2	Grosser Pälitzsee. Channel passes through northern end of lake. 3km diversion to south end of lake possible. Opportunities for anchoring.
4·4 to 9·5	Kleiner Pälitzsee. Good anchorage on north side at Km 10·6.
7·4	Junction with Rheinsberger Gewässer on south side of lake.

Rheinsberger Gewässer

Navigable length 13·1km
Maximum draught 1·40m
Maximum height 3·50m
Current Negligible
Locks 1
Speed limit 6km/h, 12km/h on lakes

This is a short waterway which connects to the upper reaches of the Rhin at Rheinsberg. The Rhin becomes navigable lower down (see Ruppiner Gewässer), but at this point it is useable only by canoes.

The area has been somewhat developed for holiday homes, but there are still many pleasant anchorages and mooring places, especially in the Zechliner Gewässer, which branches off at Km 5·2.

Km	
0·0	Junction with Müritz-Havel-Wasserstrasse Km 7·4.
2·4	*Schleuse Wolfsbruch* *Fall* 0·4m.
5·2	Junction with Zechliner Gewässer on west side. The tree-flanked Zechliner Gewässer are 8·2km long, ending at the village of Flecken Zechlin. They can be used by vessels with a maximum draught of 1·40m and height 3·50m.
6·6	Zechliner Hütte. Small village on east side with mooring place.
6·8	Entrance to Dollgowsee on west side under bridge. The delightful Dollgowsee, which is a 3km diversion, is bordered by a nature reserve and provides good opportunities for secluded anchoring.
9·1 to 10·9	Rheinsberger See. Good anchoring places and a small yacht harbour at the southeastern corner. Depth uncertain.
11·6 to 13·1	Grienericksee. Small lake in front of the attractive and historic town of **Rheinsberg**, with its 18th-century castle. Mooring possible.
13·1	End of navigation.

Müritz-Havel-Wasserstrasse (continued)

Km	
9·5	*Schleuse Canow* *Rise* 1·3m.
10·0 to 12·5	Labussee. Channel turns west after leaving Canow. Interesting 8·5km diversion for small boats to the north through Oberbeck to the Gobenowsee and from here through the Drosedower Beck to the Rätzsee (officially closed to motorboats). The passage from the Gobenowsee eastwards under the bridge into the Klenzsee is probably no more than 0·50m deep.
13·2	*Schleuse Diemitz* *Rise* 1·4m. Anchoring/mooring above and below lock in Grosser or Kleiner Peetschsee.
14·0 to 15·5	Vilzsee. Channel passes through eastern end of lake. Can be choppy in strong westerly winds. A 2km diversion westwards along the lake is possible, and vessels drawing 1·40m can then enter the Schwarzer See (officially forbidden to motorboats).
18·0 to 19·7	Zotzensee.
21·8	Main route branches northwest as the Mirower Kanal. North branch leads to the waterfront of **Mirow**, with several mooring places and good services ashore. Continuing north, the route of the old Müritz-Havel-Wasserstrasse passes through several delightful small lakes and finishes in the Woterfilzsee, which was connected to the Müritz by the now defunct Bolter Kanal. Motorboats are forbidden to navigate on the Woterfitzsee.
22·3	*Schleuse Mirow* *Rise* 3·1m.
29·0 to 30·0	**Sumpfsee**. Buoyed channel.
31·0	End of waterway. Exit to Kleine Müritz Km 172·0.

MÜRITZ-ELDE-WASSER-STRASSE

Navigable length 183·0km
Maximum draught 1·20m
Maximum height 3·30m
Current Negligible
Locks 17
Speed limit 6km/h

This waterway provides an interesting and attractive route from the Elbe to the Müritz lake in the beautiful Mecklenburg lake district. From here it is possible to continue via the Müritz-Havel-Wasserstrasse and the Obere Havel to join the Havel-Oder-Wasserstrasse north of Berlin. The 44km Stör-Wasserstrasse, including the second-biggest lake in the area, the Schweriner See, makes an interesting detour.

From the Elbe, the first 120km of the Müritz-Elde-Wasserstrasse, to the Plauersee, the waterway is the canalised Elde river. It runs at first through very pleasant low-lying agricultural land, but from Parchim (Km 72) the landscape becomes more picturesque. There are few yacht harbours, but countless secluded places to moor or anchor and enjoy the scenery, to talk to the friendly East

Germans and to see the wildlife for which the area is famous. A major part of the shores of the Müritz is in fact a huge nature reserve, a breeding ground for white-tailed eagles and black storks as well as many other species. The woods abound with deer, and there are large numbers of interesting flora, including orchids and gentians. Müritz is famous for its water lilies during the summer months.

The towns of Waren, Malchow and Plau were all well established as health resorts by the middle of the 19th century. The beautiful old city of Schwerin has a 12th-century cathedral, many half-timbered houses dating from mediaeval times and a spectacular castle built on an island. The city was one of the few to escape damage from British bombs during World War II.

The 17 locks and the many opening bridges have survived the 44 years of Communist rule remarkably well and are generally in good working order. They operate from 0700 to 1800 daily during the summer months. The waterway is well buoyed where necessary; travelling eastwards from the Elbe is the upstream direction so reds are to port and greens to starboard, as convention dictates. It should be noted that in bad weather, owing to the size and shallowness of the Müritz (and other major lakes), danger-

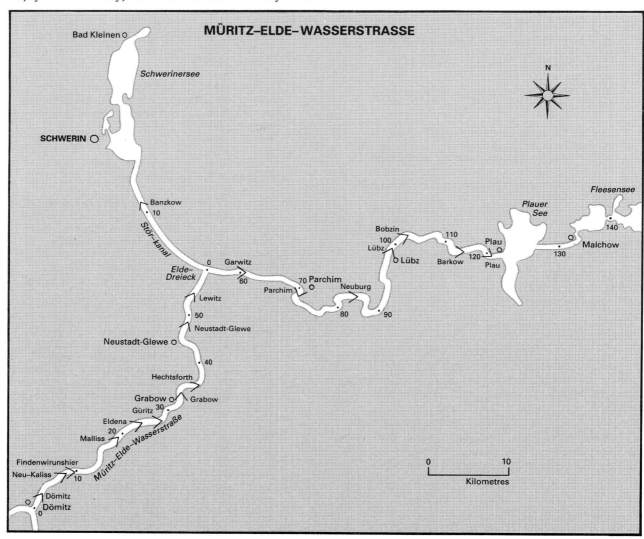

ous conditions can develop, often very rapidly. It is as well to be aware of the weather forecast before setting out to cross any of the larger lakes.

As might be expected, there are few places for repairs in this area. Should problems occur which call for professional assistance, the most likely places to find services are Dömitz, Grabow, Schwerin and Rechlin. There are no bunker stations on the waterway, but fortunately there are many places where roadside filling stations are within easy reach.

Km	
0·0	Junction with Elbe Km 504·1.
0·6	**Dömitz**. Mooring possible in harbour area before lock.
0·8	Swing bridge.
1·0	*Schleuse Dömitz* (with lift bridge). *Rise* 1·5m.
4·9	*Schleuse Neu-Kaliss Rise* 2·1m.
5·8	*Schleuse Findenwirunshier* (with lift bridge) *Rise* 2·1m.
9·5	*Schleuse Malliss Rise* 2·0m.
9·6	Mooring in inlet on right (west) bank. Depth uncertain.
18·0	*Schleuse Eldena Rise* 1·7m.
22·7	*Schleuse Güritz* (with lift bridge). *Rise* 3·3m.
ca30	**Grabow**.
30·8	*Schleuse Grabow Rise* 1·9m. Water authority harbour and boatyard.
34·8	*Schleuse Hechtsforth Rise* 3·2m. Good rural mooring below lock. No facilities.
ca46	**Neustadt-Glewe**.
46·2	*Schleuse Neustadt-Glewe Rise* 2·2m. Mooring below lock. No facilities, but convenient for town centre.
49·5 to	
55·5	Extensive fish farms on both sides.
50·6	*Schleuse Lewitz Rise* 3·7m.
56·7	Elde-Dreieck. Junction with Stör-Wasserstrasse (Störkanal). Müritz-Elde-Wasserstrasse turns southeast, Stör-Wasserstrasse turns northwest.

Stör-Wasserstrasse
Navigable distance 44·0km
Maximum draught 1·20m
Maximum height 3·90m
Current Negligible
Locks 1
Speed limit 6km/h

This waterway comprises the Störkanal and the Schweriner See. The first 10km of the canal are relatively straight and featureless, but then it takes a more meandering route and passes through several pleasant villages before entering the Schweriner See, which is a major centre for water sports and recreation. It is divided into two parts, north (Aussensee) and south (Innensee), which are separated by a narrow channel over which there is a road bridge with a height of 4·30m.

Yacht harbour at Schwerin.

The historic city of Schwerin has many interesting features, the most famous being the splendid castle and the 12th-century cathedral.

The single lock operates from 0700 to 1800 in summer.

Km	
0·0	Junction with Müritz-Elde-Wasserstrasse Km 56·7.
10·9	*Schleuse Banzkow Rise* 0·9m. Mooring above or below lock.
11·0	Swing bridge, operated by lock-keeper.
14·5	Plate. Mooring at restaurant Störkrug.
14·6	Lift bridge.
20·0	Raben. Entrance to Schweriner See. Mooring place on east side.
20·0 to	
30·0	Schweriner See – southern part. City of **Schwerin** on west side. Numerous mooring places, including the Schwerin sailing club close north of the castle. *Note* There is a well buoyed shallow patch in the centre of the lake. There are two islands, both nature reserves.
30·0	Paulsdamm. Bridge in northwest corner of southern half of lake leading to northern part of lake. Height of bridge 4·30m. Depth of water in channel at normal water levels 1·40m.
30·2 to	
44·0	Northern part of Schweriner See. *Note* There is also a shallow patch in the middle of this part of the lake, but again well buoyed. Several mooring or anchoring possibilities in northeast corner of lake, but access to nature reserve in extreme northeast corner is forbidden.

Müritz-Elde-Wasserstrasse (continued)
56·7	Junction with Stör-Wasserstrasse.
60·8	*Schleuse Garwitz Rise* 3·9m. Lock has two chambers. Lock-keeper will give guidance according to prevailing conditions.
61·3	Mooring possible at staging on south bank.
70·2	Landing stage on left bank.

ca72	**Parchim**.
72·1	*Schleuse Parchim*
	Rise 3·1m.
	Mooring above and below lock close to town centre.
82·0	Neuburg. Mooring place on left bank.
83·3	*Schleuse Neuburg*
	Rise 3·8m.
97·6	Mooring near camp site on outskirts of Lübz.
ca98	**Lübz**.
98·9	*Schleuse Lübz (with lift bridge).*
	Rise 2·9m.
99·9	Basin on right bank above town. Fuel.
103·8	*Schleuse Bobzin*
	Rise 6·9m.
	Strong turbulence due to water inlets in bottom of chamber.
108·5	Kuppentin. Mooring on right bank above bridge.
114·0	*Schleuse Barkow*
	Rise 3·2m.
ca120	**Plau**.
120·1	*Schleuse Plau*
	Rise 1·4m.

Schleuse Plau, on the Müritz-Elde-Wasserstrasse.

Malchow, on the Müritz-Elde-Wasserstrasse.

120·4 Lift bridge.

120·5 Mooring at sailing club just before junction with Plauer See.

121·0 Entrance to Plauer See. This 15km-long lake is a popular sailing centre and offers numerous quiet anchorages and mooring places, especially in the southern half. There are several shallow patches, but they are well marked.

126·0 Exit from Plauer See to Petersdorfer See. Mooring possible inside entrance to Petersdorfer See.

126·7 to
129·6 Petersdorfer See. Buoyed channel.

131·8 to
135·0 Malchower See. Divided in half by the opening road bridge in the centre of Malchow.

133·0 **Malchow**. Mooring either side of opening bridge in town centre. Bridge operates from 0700–1800.

135·0 to
139·8 Fleesensee. Popular for all water sports. Follow buoyed channel into open water, then head ENE for exit on east side of lake

140·2 to
147·2 Kölpinsee. 0·6km to the north of the entry point is a very narrow channel 1m deep leading through to the Jabelscher See, an idyllic lake for boats small enough to enter, although landing is forbidden. Otherwise follow wide buoyed channel across centre of Kölpinsee to exit on east side. Note that the south and east shores of the lake shelve very slowly and that anchorages, except in open water, are almost nonexistent. On the north side, however, anchorage may be possible in settled weather to the west of Schloss Schwenzin.

147·2 to
149·0 Reeck Kanal, leading to Binnen Müritz, a semi-enclosed bay about 2km wide at the northern extremity of the Müritz itself. Directly opposite the entrance lies the historic and beautiful town of **Waren**. There are several possible places to moor along the waterfront, but the 3m-deep town harbour is probably the most convenient.

151 to
169 **Müritz**. The second-largest lake in Germany, and a wonderful expanse of water for sailing on a good day, but it should be noted that storms can get up extremely quickly and create very dangerous conditions for small boats.
Apart from Waren, there are some very interesting places to visit around the shores of the Müritz. **Röbel** is not only a picturesque Scandinavian-style town with boathouses on stilts over the water, but it also has a very attractive small harbour. There are beautiful and secluded anchorages at Sietow and in the entrance to the shallow Bolter Kanal. Schloss Klink, dominating the western shore, should not be missed, and in the Kleine Müritz, the southern extremity of the Müritz, **Rechlin** has an excellent small marina (see opposite) in delightful surroundings.
Vipperow is also well worth a visit.
Unfortunately, most of the shoreline in between these harbours shoals gradually, leaving very few places to anchor safely close inshore. This problem is made clear by the line of offshore buoys guarding the shallows all round the lake. There are also a couple of shallow patches in the centre of the lake, but they too are well buoyed.

172 to
183 Müritzarm. This is the 11km-long and 300m-wide southern extension of the Müritz. It is flanked by low-lying marshland and woodland,

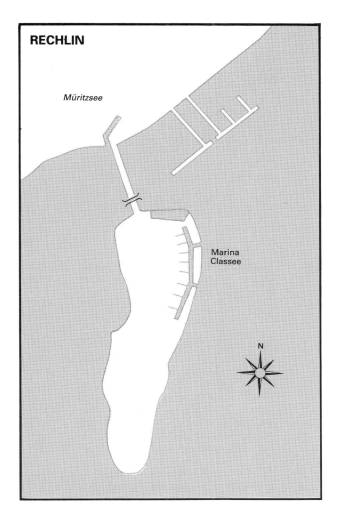

RECHLIN

Müritzsee

Marina
Classee

N

Berlin cathedral and television tower.

and is a glorious backwater to explore, especially for those interested in wildlife. It ends at the village of Buchholz, where there is a good mooring place.

172·0   Junction with Müritz-Havel-Wasserstrasse Km 31·8.

SPREE-ODER-WASSER-STRASSE

Navigable length 130·2km
Maximum draught 1·75m
Maximum height 4·00m
Current Negligible
Locks 7
Speed limit 9km/h (12km/h Km 0·0–6·3, 7km/h Km 6·3–23·5, 12km/h Km 33·3–45·0.

This waterway is the second main traffic route from Berlin to the Oder and the Polish waterway system, although compared to the Havel-Oder-Wasserstrasse it carries only a small volume of traffic. Starting at the point where the Spree links with the Havel at Spandau, the waterway is at first the Spree, but branches upstream into the Dahme where this runs into the Spree to the southeast of the city. After only a few kilometres the Oder-Spree-Kanal then cuts eastwards away from the Dahme, back to follow the course of the Spree for a short distance before leaving the river once again and heading

directly eastwards to the steel town of Eisenhüttenstadt, where it joins the Oder. In the Berlin area there are a number of branch and connecting canals forming a maze of waterways.

The first few kilometres downstream from the junction with the Havel are through a somewhat industrial area, but approaching the city centre the route becomes very interesting: Schloss Charlottenburg with its surrounding gardens, the Reichstag, so central to the recent history of Germany, and many other well known places. Continuing downstream after the Reichstag the route lies in what used to be East Berlin, passes Berlin Cathedral and continues through another relatively industrial area. At Köpenick, where the waterway leaves the Spree and turns up the Dahme, it becomes a wide lake (the Langer See) with yacht clubs, beaches and watersports centres of all kinds. At Wernsdorf the upstream part of the Dahme branches off southwards; the Spree-Oder-Wasserstrasse continues to the east as the Oder-Spree-Kanal, tree-lined but otherwise relatively featureless. At Schleuse Grosse Tränke, however, the downstream course of the Spree is rejoined and the waterway becomes alive again until it reaches Schleuse Kersdorf. Here it again leaves the course of the river, and its last 35km is somewhat lacking in character.

The pure canal sections of the waterway are not well endowed with suitable places to moor for the night, but where the route follows the Spree or the Dahme there is no shortage of places where a small boat can lie. In the centre of Berlin there are several attractive stretches of river bordered by parks, but although the authorities do not appear to object to mooring, in the interests of security it may be prudent to avoid such places.

The canal is administered by WSD-Ost and there are no charges for using it. All locks operate daily from 0600 to 2000, except Eisenhüttenstadt, which works from 0800 to 1800. The 7 locks listed on the main route of the Spree-Oder-Wasserstrasse include Grosse Tränke, although at normal times this stands permanently open.

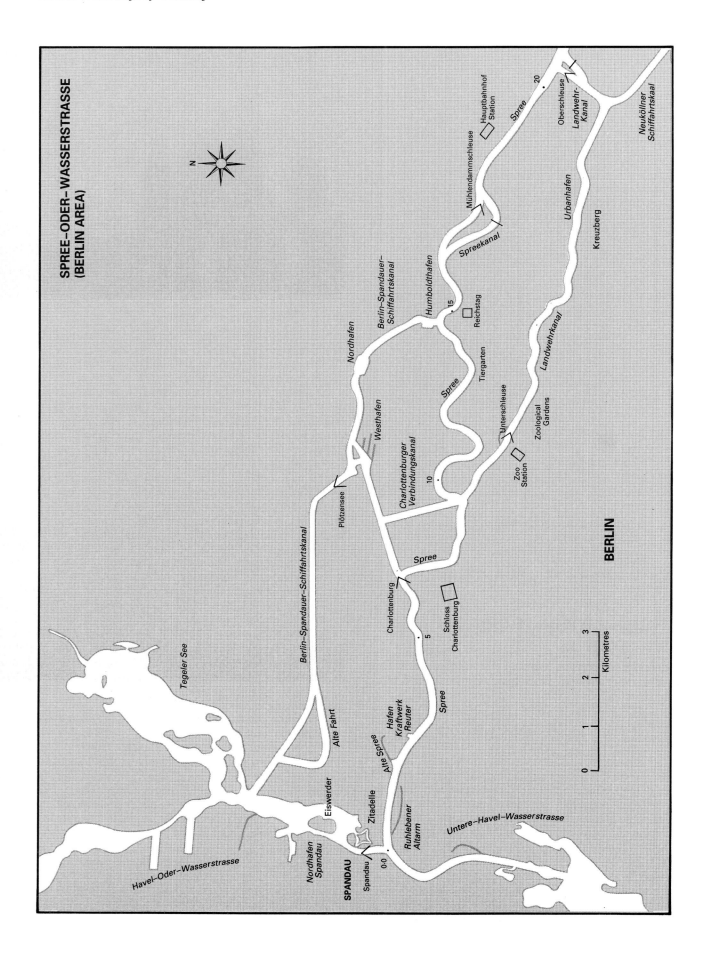

SPREE–ODER–WASSERSTRASSE
(BERLIN AREA)

N

Hauptbahnhof Station

Spree

20

Oberschleuse

Landwehr-Kanal

Neuköllner Schiffahrtskaal

Mühlendammschleuse

Spreekanal

Berlin–Spandauer-Schiffahrtskanal

Humboldthafen

15

Reichstag

Urbanhafen

Kreuzberg

Nordhafen

Tiergarten

Landwehrkanal

Westhafen

Spree

Unterschleuse

Zoological Gardens

Charlottenburger Verbindungskanal

10

Zoo Station

Plötzensee

Berlin–Spandauer-Schiffahrtskanal

Spree

BERLIN

Charlottenburg

Alte Fahrt

Schloss Charlottenburg

Tegeler See

5

Kilometres

0   1   2   3

Eiswerder

Zitadelle

Hafen Kraftwerk Reuter

Spree

Alte Spree

Nordhafen Spandau

Ruhlebener Altarm

Untere–Havel–Wasserstrasse

SPANDAU

Spandau   0.0

Havel–Oder–Wasserstrasse

Note that on the 25km stretch between Werns-dorf and Fürstenwalde it is forbidden to moor along the canal banks, but as there are no satisfactory mooring places anyway this is no great hardship.

Km

0·0   Junction with Untere-Havel-Wasserstrasse (Km 0·0) and Havel-Oder-Wasserstrasse (Km 0·0).

6·3   *Schleuse Charlottenburg*
        Rise 1·0m.
        VHF Ch 82.

6·5   Junction with Westhafenkanal on left (north) bank.

Westhafenkanal
Navigable length 3·1km
Maximum draught 2·00m
Maximum height 4·40m
Locks None
Speed limit 7km/h

This short canal connects the Spree and the Span-dauer Schiffahrtskanal. It is straight, partly tree-flanked and partly industrial.

Spree-Oder-Wasserstrasse (continued)
Km

7·7   **Schloss Charlottenburg** on left (south) bank.

9·1   Junction with Charlottenburger Verbindungs-kanal on right bank and junction with Landwehr-kanal on left bank.

Charlottenburger Verbindungskanal
Navigable length 1·7km
Maximum draught 2·00m
Maximum height 4·80m
Locks None
Speed limit 7km/h

Another connecting canal which is straight, mainly tree-lined and somewhat lacking in character.

Landwehrkanal
Navigable length 10·7km
Maximum draught 1·65m
Maximum height 3·30m
Locks 2
Speed limit 7km/h

This canal is a loop, with both ends connected to the Spree. It passes through the centre of West Berlin, between the Zoological Gardens and the Tiergarten.

Km

0·0   Junction with Spree-Oder-Wasserstrasse Km 9·1.

1·7   *Unterschleuse*
        Rise 1·4m.
        VHF Ch 81.

9·5   Junction with Neuköllner Kanal (see page 000).

10·6 *Oberschleuse*
        Rise 0·2m.

10·7 Junction with Spree-Oder-Wasserstrasse Km 21·2.

Spree-Oder-Wasserstrasse (continued)
13 to
14   **Tiergarten** on left bank.

15·0 **Reichstag** on left bank. Brandenburger Gate beyond it.

14·5 Junction with Berlin-Spandauer Schiffahrtskanal on right bank.

The Westhafen docks in Berlin.

Junction of Charlottenburger Verbindungskanal, Spree and Landwehrkanal.

Berlin-Spandauer Schiffahrtskanal (Hohenzollernkanal)

Navigable length 12·2km
Maximum draught 2·00m
Maximum height 3·90m
Locks 1
Speed limit 12km/h Km 0·0–7·5, 6km/h Km 7·5–12·2

This canal connects the Havel-Oder-Wasserstrasse directly to the Spree, avoiding the congestion at Schleuse Spandau. Part of it is flanked by trees and part of it is industrial.

The single lock works from 0600 to 2000 daily.

Km	
0·0	Junction with Havel-Oder-Wasserstrasse Km 3·5.
0·9 *and*	
2·8	Entrances to loop of old canal. Possible mooring. Depth uncertain.
7·5	*Schleuse Plötzensee* *Fall* 0·7m. *VHF* Ch 22.
8·0 *and*	
8·8	Junctions with Westhafenkanal.
12·2	Junction with Spree-Oder-Wasserstrasse Km 14·5. End of canal.

Spree-Oder-Wasserstrasse (continued)

16·3 *and*	
17·9	Entrances to Spreekanal (loop). No through passage.
17·8	*Schleuse Mühlendamm* *Rise* 1·5m. *VHF* Ch 20.
21·2	Junction with Landwehrkanal on left bank.
26·4	Junction with Britzer Zweigkanal (Km 31·8) on left bank.
28·5 *to*	
31·0	Possibility of mooring.
32·8	Waterway turns south into Dahme. Upstream Spree (Müggelspree) branches off eastwards.
33·6 *to*	
43·3	Langer See. Many possibilities for mooring and anchoring. Observe buoyage and markings.
35·2	Entrance to Teltowkanal on left bank. Not navigable. Use Britzer Zweigkanal Km 26·4.
43·1	Entrance to Grosse Krampe on right bank. Mooring possible at northern end. Depth 2m. Speed limit 12km/h on lake.
43·9	**Schmöckwitz.** Water-sports centre. Upstream Dahme branches south. Spree-Oder-Wasserstrasse continues in Seddinsee to entrance of Oder-Spree-Kanal. Seddinsee continues 3km beyond entrance of Oder-Spree-Kanal to start of Gosener Kanal (entry via buoyed channel).
45·1	Start of Oder-Spree-Kanal.
47·1	Entrance to Krossinsee on south bank, leading to Grosser Zug and hence to Dahme. Depth uncertain. Speed limit 12km/h on lake.
47·6	*Schleuse Wernsdorf* *Rise* 4·6m.
68·8	*Schleuse Grosse Tränke* *Rise* 0·0m (stands open).
73·5	Mooring at north bank.
74·8	*Schleuse Fürstenwalde* *Rise* 0·8m. Mooring place above lock.
89·7	*Schleuse Kersdorf* *Rise* 2·9m.
96·2	Junction with Obere Spree (via Speisekanal Neuhaus).
103·9	Yacht moorings on north bank. Fuel available. Shops and restaurants nearby. Last mooring place before Eisenhüttenstadt.
107·0	Junction with defunct Brieskowkanal, which at one time provided a direct route to Frankfurt.
125·1	**Eisenhüttenstadt.** Mooring place on south bank.
127·3	*Schleuse Eisenhüttenstadt* *Fall* 12·2m. Twin chambers operate alternately, with the same water being transferred backwards and forwards. Both locks are equipped for floating bollards, but they may not always be working. Check before entry.
127·9	Mooring place on east bank. Also possibility of mooring alongside water authority vessels stationed here.
130·2	Junction with Oder Km 553·4.

The Mühlendammschleuse, in eastern Berlin.

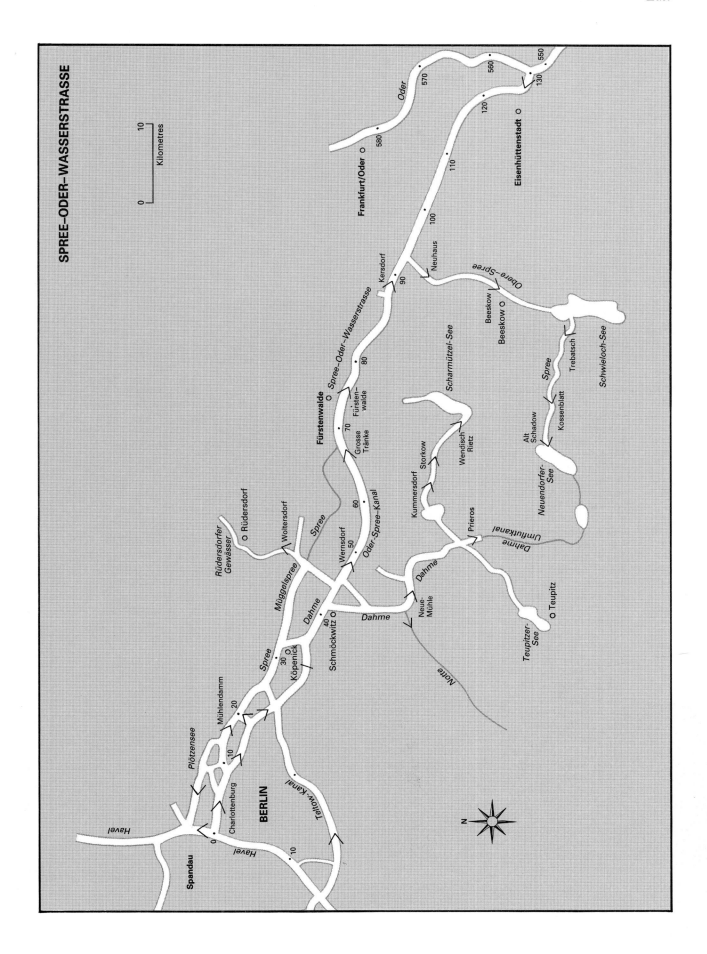

SPREE–ODER–WASSERSTRASSE

TELTOWKANAL

Navigable length 38·6km
Maximum draught 1·75m
Maximum height 4·40m
Current Negligible
Locks 1
Speed limit 7km/h (12km/h Km 0·0–3·1)

The Teltowkanal starts in the Glienicker Lake on the Potsdamer Havel and cuts across Berlin south of the city centre to join the Spree-Oder-Wasserstrasse via the short Britzer Zweigkanal. The Teltowkanal itself turns south at the junction with the Britzer and joins the SOW 9km south of the Britzer Kanal junction. However, the last 3km of this section are not navigable.

Apart from the first 3km, which are in a natural waterway, the canal is rather uninteresting. It is, however, the quickest route for a vessel wishing to get from the Untere-Havel-Wasserstrasse to the Spree-Oder-Wasserstrasse without spending time in Berlin.

The lock works from 0600 to 2000 daily. There are no charges.

Km	
0·0	Junction with Potsdamer Havel Km 28·4.
0·0 to	
3·1	Glienicker Lake and Griebnitzsee. Speed limit 12km/h.
3·3	Junction with Griebnitzsee-Kanal on north side. This is a short canal linking the Teltowkanal to the Grosser Wannsee. The maximum permitted draught is 1·30m and the maximum bridge clearance is 5·00m. The southernmost half-kilometre is subject to a one-way traffic system, alternating half-hourly. Speed limit 5km/h.
8·3	*Schleuse Kleinmachnow* Rise 2·7m. VHF Ch 18.
13·5	Zehlendorfer Stichkanal on north side. Industrial harbour.
16·7	Industrial quay on south bank.
18·7	Small industrial harbour on south side.
21·6	Small industrial harbour on south side.
23·4	Small industrial harbour on north side.
28·3	Junction with Britzer Zweigkanal and Neuköllner Kanal. Teltowkanal turns south, but no through route to the Spree-Oder-Wasserstrasse. The Britzer Zweigkanal is only 3·4km long, and is mainly tree-lined but otherwise featureless. Maximum permitted draught 1·75m and maximum height 4·60m. The Neuköllner Kanal is 4·1km long and connects to the Landwehrkanal. It can be entered by vessels with a draught of not more than 1·75m and a maximum height of 3·60m. It has one lock, *Schleuse Neukölln*, with a fall of 0·2m (going northwards). The lock works Mon–Fri 0630–1900, Sat 0630–1400 and is closed on Sundays except to groups of boats with advance booking (☎ 030 68092067). The canal is controlled by the *Land*, and a fee is likely to be charged. Speed limit 7·5km/h.

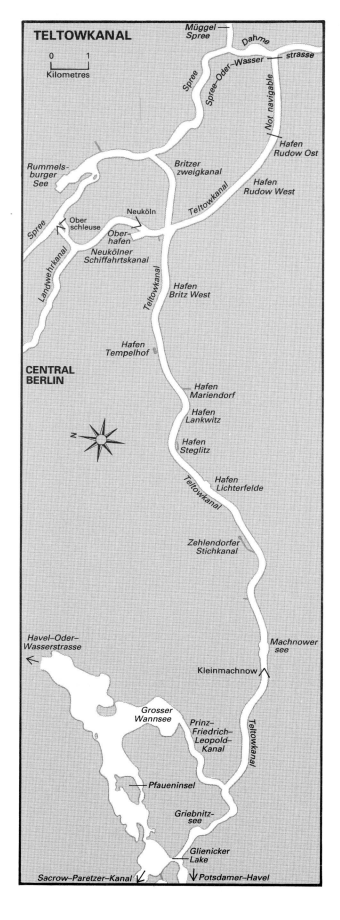

MÜGGELSPREE

Navigable distance 11·4km
Maximum draught 1·70m
Maximum height 4·70
Current Negligible
Locks None
Speed limit 7km/h (12km/h in Grosser Müggelsee,
  Km 4·0–7·0)

Although the main route of the Spree-Oder-Wasserstrasse through the Langer See (Dahme) is attractive, the alternative route via the Müggelspree, through the beautiful Müggelsee and then back south through the Gosener Kanal is even more so. It also offers the possibility of a diversion into the Löcknitz and the chain of pretty lakes which runs eastwards from the Rüdesdorfer Gewässer. The longer expedition to the northern part of the Rüdesdorfer Gewässer around Rüdersdorf itself is somewhat industrial and less interesting.

Km	
0·0	**Köpenick**. Junction with Spree-Oder-Wasserstrasse Km 32·8.
2·5	Friedrichshagen. Boatyard on north bank. Mooring possible.
3·8 to	
7·4	Grosser Müggelsee. Yacht harbour immediately south of entrance. Keep to buoyed channel across centre of lake. Motorboats are forbidden to leave the channel. Immediately north of exit is entrance to attractive small bay known as Die Bänke. Depth 1·20m. Beautiful yacht harbour.
7·8	Exit from Grosser Müggelsee.
11·4	Entrance to Dämeritzsee. Junction with Gosener Kanal immediately to starboard and access from eastern end of Dämeritzsee to Rüdersdorfer Gewässer.

Rüdersdorfer Gewässer
Navigable length 14·3km
Maximum draught 1·65m
Maximum height 4·00m
Current Negligible
Locks 1
Speed limit 9km/h (6km/h upstream of Km 9·8)

Km	
0·0	Entrance from Dämeritzsee.
2·6	Junction with Löcknitz and access for boats drawing up to 1·70m for a further 10·6km eastwards to Werlsee, Peetzsee and Möllensee. Various attractive mooring places and anchorages.
3·8	Schleuse Woltersdorf *Rise* 2·1m. *Hours* 0600–2000 daily.
9·7	Junction with Langerhans-Kanal to Kriensee. Industrial.
11·3	Entrance to Stienitzsee. Mooring places on each bank.
14·3	End of Stienitzsee.

Gosener Kanal
Navigable length 2·8km
Maximum draught 2·00m
Maximum height 4·30m
Locks None
Speed limit 8km/h

Km	
5·7	Exit from Dämeritzsee.
2·9	Entrance to Seddinsee. Speed limit 12km/h on lake.
0·0	Junction with Oder-Spree-Kanal Km 44·9.

DAHME-WASSERSTRASSE

Navigable length 26·0km
Maximum draught 1·60m
Maximum height 4·00m
Current Negligible
Locks 3
Speed limit 9km/h

The Dahme south of Schmöckwitz, together with its branches, forms an interesting network of natural waterways set in a pleasant, mainly wooded landscape, with many interesting places to visit and plenty of attractive spots in which to moor or anchor. Deeper-draught boats, however, need to take care in some of the remoter parts of the waterway, as depth can be a problem.

For the purposes of this book the waterway is assumed to end at Prieros, but except when water levels are low vessels drawing up to 1·50m could venture through Schleuse Prieros and Schleuse Hermsdorfer Mühle to Märkisch Buchholz.

There are two main side arms to the Dahme: the Storkower Gewässer, which give access to the Scharmützelsee, and the Teupitzer Gewässer, which lead to the Teupitzer See.

On the main route to Prieros there is only one lock, Neue Mühle. The Storkower Gewässer have three locks, but there are none in the Teupitzer Gewässer.

Km	
0·0	**Schmöckwitz**. Junction with Spree-Oder-Wasserstrasse Km 43·9.
0·5 to	
4·6	Zeuthener See. Numerous moorings on west bank.
4·5	Entrance to Grosser Zug and Krossinsee on east side. Very pretty alternative route back to Spree-Oder-Wasserstrasse, but depth of channel through Wernsdorf uncertain.
6·7	Entrance to Möllenzugsee on east side. Quiet anchorage.
7·0	Bunker station on west bank near ferry.
8·2	Königswusterhausen. Junction with Notte on west side. Small 22km river with depths around 1·00m and 1·10m-high bridge at Telz. It has a branch canal, the Galluner Kanal, which has depths of only 0·60m.
9·5	Schleuse Neue Mühle *Rise* 1·4m. *Hours* 0600–2000 daily.
10·3 to	
14·8	Krimnicksee and Krüpelsee. Follow buoyage. Interesting mooring places and anchorages, including the Zernsdorfer Lankensee, a superb 2km-long fjord with access through a railway bridge (height 3·5m) at Km 13·5. Speed limit on Krüpelsee 12km/h.
20·7 to	
23·3	Dolgensee. Follow buoyed channel.

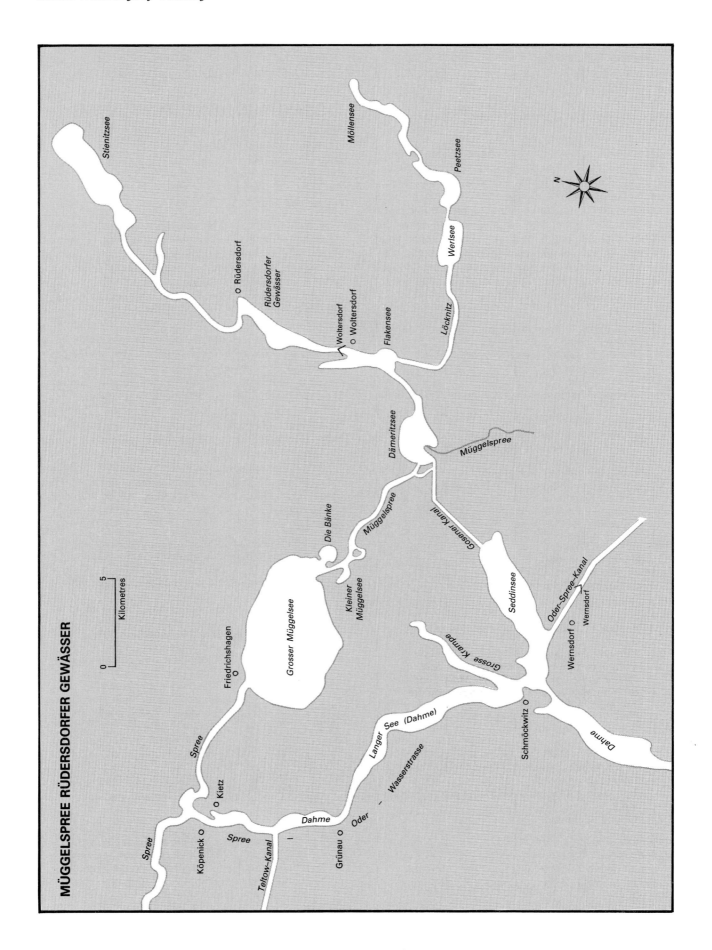

MÜGGELSPREE RÜDERSDORFER GEWÄSSER

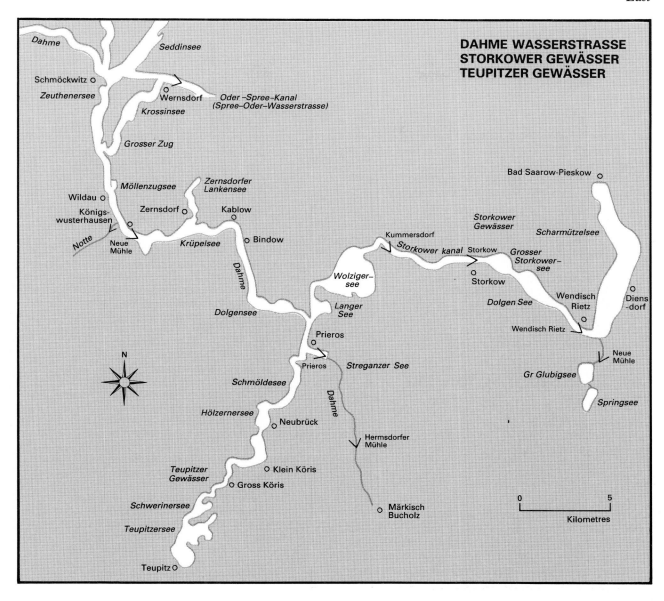

**DAHME WASSERSTRASSE
STORKOWER GEWÄSSER
TEUPITZER GEWÄSSER**

24·9   Entrance to Langer See and Storkower Gewässer on east side.

26·0   **Prieros**. Junction with Teupitzer Gewässer. Dahme continues eastwards through *Schleuse Prieros* and *Schleuse Hermsdorfer Mühle*, and (for canoes only) link to the Obere Spree via the Dahme-Umflutkanal. Schleuse Prieros and Schleuse Hermsdorfer Mühle operate 1000–1230 and 1330–1900.

Storkower Gewässer
Navigable length 33·6km
Maximum draught 1·40m
Maximum height 2·60m
Current Negligible
Locks 3.
Hours 0800–1200, 1300–1900
Speed limit 9km/h

Km
0·0   Junction with Dahme Wasserstrasse Km 24·9.
0·1 to
2·7   Langer See.
4·0 to
6·8   Wolziger See. Follow buoyage.

4·5   Blossin. Yacht harbour and water-sports centre on west bank of lake.

10·2   *Schleuse Kummersdorf*
Rise 1·2m.

15·6   *Schleuse Storkow*
Rise 1·9m.

16·2 to
21·1   Grosser Storkower See and Dolgen See.

22·6   *Schleuse Wendisch Rietz*
Rise 1·2m.

22·9   Wendisch Rietz. Harbour and several good anchorages near entrance to Scharmützelsee. The very attractive and secluded short canal to the south through Schleuse Neue Mühle is no more than 0·6m deep.

22·9 to
33·6   Scharmützelsee. Many places to moor or anchor towards northern end.

33·6   Bad Saarow-Pieskow. End of waterway.

Teupitzer Gewässer
Navigable length 18·2km
Maximum draught 1·40m
Maximum height 3·80m
Current Negligible
Locks None
Speed limit 9km/h

This waterway is a chain of small lakes which make it a wonderland for cruising, with many quiet anchorages.

There is a low lift bridge at Gross Köris which opens hourly from 0800 to 1800. Fee payable.

Km	
0·0	Junction with Dahme Wasserstrasse Km 26·0.
0·7 to	
6·7	Schmöldesee and Hölzerner See.
7·0 to	
10·0	Kleinköriser See. Observe buoyage.
8·6	Klein Köris. Mooring possible.
11·4	Opening bridge. See above.
14·0 to	
18·2	Teupitzer See.
18·2	**Teupitz**. End of waterway.

OBERE SPREE WASSER-STRASSE

Navigable length 40·9km
Maximum draught 1·30m
Maximum height 2·70m
Current 1–3km/h
Locks 5
Speed limit 6km/h

It is a great pity that depth limits the use of the Obere Spree to boats drawing only 1·30m, as it is a most attractive waterway in which to cruise. The Spree meanders lazily through swamp, moor and woodland, there are plenty of secluded anchorages and there is wildlife in abundance.

At Beeskow there are two locks side by side, but the smaller, the *Sportbootschleuse*, is not in operation. At the time of writing, Schleuse Kossenblatt is undergoing major repair and is likely to be out of action for some time. As Schleuse Trebatsch normally stands open, there are in effect only two locks on the waterway, Neuhaus and Beeskow. When Schleuse Kossenblatt is eventually back in action the waterway will extend a further 17·5km to Leibsch, the limit of navigation for all but very small boats. South of Leibsch lies the Spreewald, a labyrinth of swamp, woodland and waterway, famous for its wildlife and for the punts which are used to transport both goods and people. It is also an area which still has its own language, Sorbian, brought there by the Sorbs, a Slavic tribe which settled in the area many centuries ago.

Schleuse Neuhaus operates 0800–1600. Beeskow operates 0700–1900. Note that in dry summers the water level may fall below the designated minimum depth of 1·30m.

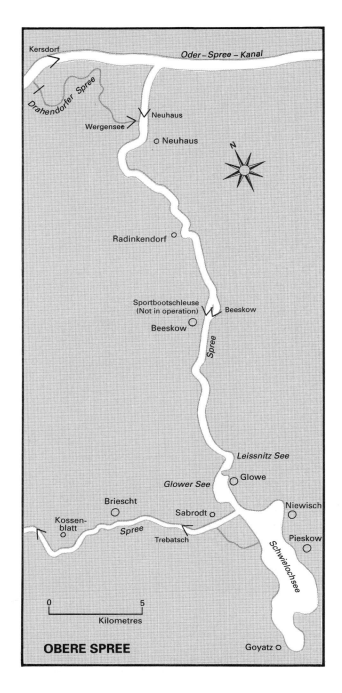

OBERE SPREE

Km	
0·0	Junction with Spree-Oder-Wasserstrasse Km 96·2.
2·8	*Schleuse Neuhaus* (with lift bridge). *Rise* 1·10m.
3·4	Drahendorfer Spree on west side via *Schleuse Wergensee*. Depth 1m. No through route.
16·9	*Schleuse Beeskow* *Rise* 0·40m. Boat lock out of operation.
25·2 to	
28·5	Leissnitz See and Glower See. Follow buoyed channel. Beware weeds.
28·5	Entrance southwards to Schwielochsee. 10km long. Several good anchorages at southern end. Yacht harbour at Goyatz.
31·6	*Schleuse Trebatsch* *Rise* Stands open.
35·6	Lift bridge.
40·9	*Schleuse Kossenblatt*. Temporary end of waterway.

ODER

Navigable distance 161·7km
Maximum draught 0·80–2·50
Maximum height 4·20m
Current 2–10km/h
Locks None

The potential of the Oder for cruising has not yet been fully explored. The river is navigable for 800-tonne barges from Kozle in southern Poland to its mouth at Swinoujscie on the Baltic Sea, around 850km. It also has a major link via the Warta and the Notec to the Wisła (Vistula), which flows into the Baltic near Gdansk; upstream the Wisła leads to Warsaw, and at one time it was connected to the Dniepr, which flows into the Black Sea.

The landscape along the Oder is undramatic, being mostly flat and either agricultural or wooded. Apart from the old Hanseatic town of Frankfurt/Oder, there are few towns of any size.

From Ratzdorf, to the southeast of Eisenhüttenstadt, to Widuchowa, a short distance south of Szczecin, the Oder is the border between Germany and Poland. This is the section described in this book, but it should be understood that there is much still to be learned about the river from the point of view of leisure cruising.

The timing of a cruise on the Oder is important. From Ratzdorf to Hohensaaten at mean water level the depth of water is normally sufficient for boats drawing 1·30m, and the current is likely to be in the region of 4km/h. During the second half of a dry summer, however, the depth in this stretch can reduce to well under a metre. In the spring, when the river is in flood, the depth may be considerably greater but the current may reach 9–10km/h (5kn). In the stretch from Hohensaaten to Szczecin at mean water level the depth is unlikely to fall below 1·50m, even in a dry summer, and the current is much less than higher up the river. Information on water levels can be obtained from Wasser- und Schiffahrtsamt Eberswalde, Grabowstrasse 1, 16225 Eberswalde-Finow 1 (☎ 03334–22053).

There are also water authority offices along the river at Frankfurt/Oder (Km 584·5), Gozdowice (Km 645·3) and Widuchowa (Km 701·8) where information on conditions may be available. Similar information is broadcast at 1155 daily over Polish radio. The official *Strecke* are:

Strecke 1   Ratzdorf–Frankfurt
Strecke 2   Frankfurt–mouth of Wartha
Strecke 3   Mouth of Wartha–Hohensaaten
Strecke 4   Hohensaaten–Widuchowa

Finding a place to moor for the night is a problem. There are no yacht harbours, and mooring is permitted only at certain designated points (listed below). There are also no refuelling points suitable for small boats.

The river is well buoyed, and in addition there are leading marks where the channel runs at an angle to the course of the river. Commercial traffic is relatively light, perhaps amounting to around 20 barges per day. The Oder is policed by the *Wasserschutzpolizei*, not by the Polish authorities. Navigation by

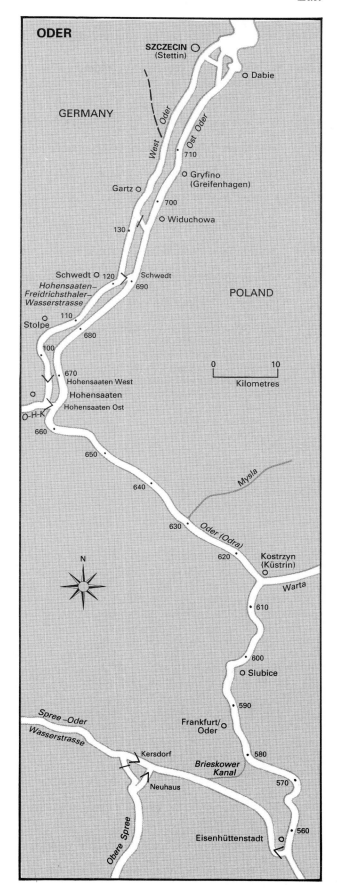

pleasure craft is prohibited between 1 November and 31 March and at night throughout the year.

Km

542·4	Junction with Lausitzer Neisse. Polish border.
542·8	**Ratzdorf**. Official mooring place on left bank.
553·4	**Eisenhüttenstadt**. Official mooring place in entrance to Spree-Oder-Wasserstrasse.
576·8	Official mooring place in entrance to Brieskower See.
582·6	**Frankfurt/Oder**. Official mooring place on left bank.
593·8	Lebus. Official mooring place on left bank.
617·1	Neu-Bleyen. Official mooring place on left bank.
617·5	Junction with Warta on right bank. Connects to River Wisła (Vistula).
632·8	Winterhafen Kienitz. Official mooring place at far end of harbour.
651·1	Zollbrücke. Official mooring place in inlet on left bank.
664·9	**Hohensaaten**. Official mooring place in inlet on left bank.
667·2	Junction with Havel-Oder-Wasserstrasse (Ostschleuse Hohensaaten).
697·0	Schwedter Querfahrt. Connects with Hohensaaten-Friedrichsthaler-Wasserstrasse. Official mooring place in entrance.
702·6	German customs post on left bank.
702·7	**Widuchowa**. Polish customs post on right bank.
704·1	Junction with West-Oder (weir – no through passage).

PEENE

Navigable length 98km
Maximum draught 1·80m
Maximum height 4·10m
Current Negligible
Locks None
Speed limit 12km/h

The Peene, with adequate depths, no locks, and interesting places to visit and to moor, is a very pleasant river to explore by boat. The rural countryside is a mixture of agriculture, swamp and woodland, and the visitor feels that nothing has changed in these parts for many years.

Although there are no locks, there are three opening bridges, at Anklam, Loitz and Demmin. The Peene continues upstream in a northwesterly direction from the Kummerower See, but only boats with a draught of less than 1·00m can reach Neukalen. The navigable route goes southwest through the Peenekanal to Malchin, the end of navigation for most cruising boats. Very shallow-draught boats can use the Dahmer Kanal and visit the charming Malchiner See.

Km

104·0	Mouth of Peene. Junction with Peenestrom. Nature reserve.
96·5 to 94·7	**Anklam**. Mooring places on right (south) bank (partly commercial harbour).
95·1	Railway lift bridge. Opens according to schedule, normally every 2–3 hours.
94·0	Yacht moorings on right bank.
85·7	Stolpe. Quay.

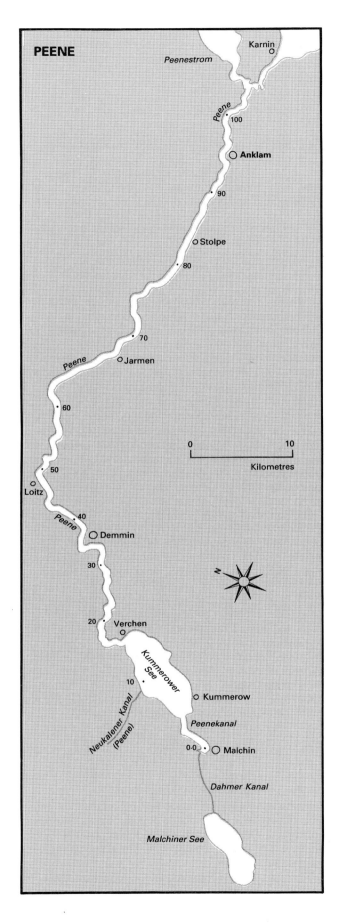

78 to	
71	Several isolated mooring places and anchorages.
67·7	Jarmen. Quay and boathouses.
57·0	Alt Plestlin. Quay.
52·9	Sophienhof. Quay.
48·9	Loitz. Quay.
48·8	Low swing bridge. Opens on request 0800–1600.
40·6	Ferry. Beware rope across river.
34·3	Entrance to Trebel. Navigable only by canoes.
34·0 to	
33·0	Demmin. Quay. Low lift bridge. Opens on request 0800–1600.
15·0	Entrance to Kummerower See. Several possible mooring places.
15 to	
4·7	Kummerower See. Buoyed channel across centre, but anchoring off possible near several small villages around lake. Depth questionable at several small jetties. Entrance to Neukalener Kanal leading to Neukalen. Depth 1·8m.
4·5	Entrance to Peenekanal.
3·0	Bank-side mooring place at restaurant.
0·0	**Malchin**. Several mooring possibilities on north side of canal. Canal continues as Dahme Kanal, leading to Malchiner See. Depth 1·0m.

Wolgast, on the Peenestrom.

UECKER

Navigable length 11·0km
Maximum draught 3·00m to Ueckermünde, 1·30m above Ueckermünde.
Maximum height Unlimited
Current Negligible
Locks None
Speed limit 6km/h

This small river is not dissimilar in character to the Peene. Flowing out into the Stettiner Haff (which lies half in Germany and half in Poland – it is known as Zalew Szczecinski in Polish) just inside the Polish border, the tree-lined river leads upstream 2·5km to Ueckermünde, where there is a *Stadthafen* in the town centre. 7km further upstream the Uecker itself swings southwest and the main route continues in the Randow for a further 1·5km to Eggesin.

There is an opening road bridge at Ueckermünde.

Km	
0·0	**Eggesin**.
1·5/	
26·2	Junction of Randow and Uecker.
33·2	**Ueckermünde**. Stadthafen on east bank.
34·2	Yacht harbour on west bank.
35·7	Entrance to Stettiner Haff.

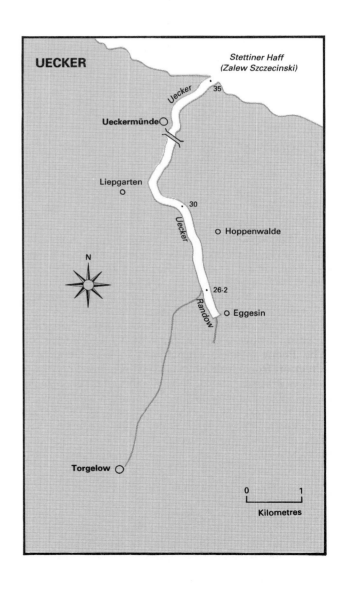

STRELASUND AND THE *BODDEN*

The northeastern corner of Mecklenburg-Vorpommern has always been remote and mysterious. An atmosphere of wildness pervades the air, and although the district is largely agricultural, there are large expanses of unspoilt saltmarsh and meadow where many species of flora and fauna flourish – and where it is easy to believe that secret activities are going on. It comes as no surprise that it was here, at Peenemünde on the island of Usedom, that the deadly V2 was developed during World War II.

After visiting Berlin, it is a very interesting cruise (for boats capable of navigating in coastal waters) to go down the Oder to Szczecin in Poland, cross into Germany in the Zalew Szczecinski (Stettiner Haff) and travel through the Peenestrom, the winding channel between the desolate island of Usedom and

the mainland. If time allows, it is worth diverting into the Uecker and the Peene and stopping to explore some of the interesting old towns and villages along the route. From the northern end of the Peenestrom a buoyed channel leads westwards across the huge Greifswalder Bodden and into the Strelasund. This channel divides the holiday island of Rügen from the mainland. Halfway along the Strelasund lies the lovely old Hanseatic city of Stralsund, which suffered considerable neglect during its 44 years of Communist government, but is now recovering rapidly.

Continuing northwards in the Strelasund, it is possible to branch either east or west into great expanses of enclosed and sheltered water forming a series of lakes known as *Bodden*. This whole area supports a great variety of wildlife, and part of it is a breeding ground for swans and geese, which can often be seen in thousands. Following several days

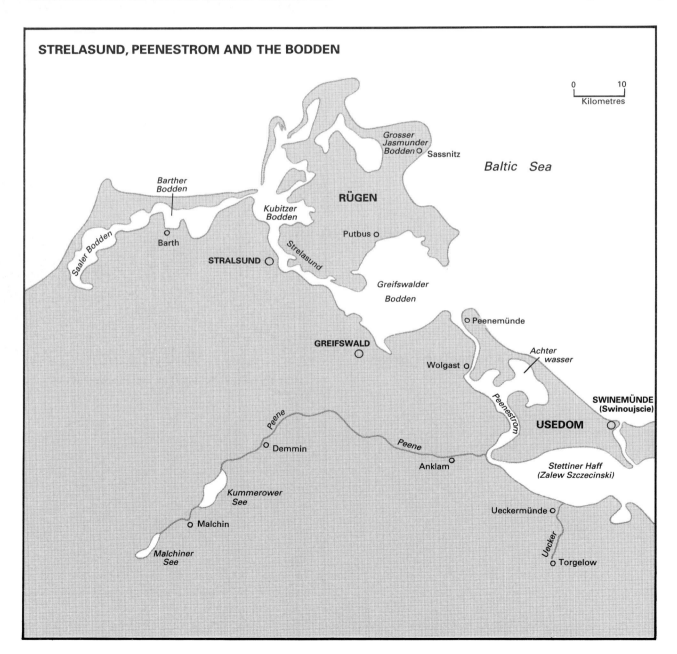

STRELASUND, PEENESTROM AND THE BODDEN

at least exploring the *Bodden*, a series of short coastal hops leads to Travemünde, and back into the inland waterway system via the Elbe-Lübeck-Kanal.

It is beyond the scope of this book to give detailed information on navigating in coastal waters, but appropriate charts and guide books are readily available.

Twin lift bridges over the Strelasund at Stralsund.

Rural scene near the World War II rocket-research centre at Peenemünde.

Appendix

I. GUIDES AND CHARTS

Guides in English
Slow Boat Through Germany Hugh McKnight Adlard
   Coles 1993
The Danube – A river guide Rod Heikell Imray 1991
The Baltic Sea Barry Sheffield (RCC Pilotage Foundation)
   Imray 1993
Through the German Waterways Phillip Bristow Adlard
   Coles 1976
Cruising Guide to Germany and Denmark Brian Navin
   Imray 1994

Guides in German
Series: German Waterways (Edition Maritim, Hamburg)
   Der Rhein
   Main – Main-Donau-Kanal – Donau
   Die Mosel mit Saar
   Vom Rhein zur Nord- und Ostsee
   Die Weser
   Binnengewässer zwischen Elbe und Oder
   Die Elbe mit Saale
   Von der Elbe zur Müritz
   Von der Elbe nach Berlin
   Nebenflüsse der Elbe
   Von Berlin zur Müritz
   Gewässer in und um Berlin
   Gewässerführer Berlin
Series: By boat through the valley of ... (Squarra,
   Bensheim)
   Mit dem Boot durchs Rheintal
   Mit dem Boot durchs Neckartal
   Mit dem Boot durchs Maintal
   Mit dem Boot durchs Altmühltal (Main-Donau-Kanal)
   Mit dem Boot durchs Donautal
   Mit dem Boot durchs Lahntal
   Mit dem Boot durchs Moseltal
   Mit dem Boot durchs Saartal
   Mit dem Boot vom Rhein sur Elbe
   Mit dem Boot durchs Heideland (Elbe-Seitenkanal and
      Elbe-Lübeck-Kanal)
   Mit dem Boot von der Elbe zur Oder

Others
WESKA (Westeuropäischer Schiffahrt- und Hafenkalender)
   Annual Binnenschiffahrts-Verlag
Führer für Binnenfahrtensport, DMYV
Signale der Binnenschiffahrt, Binnenschiffahrts-Verlag

Charts
Karte der Wasserstrassen in Deutschland und Benelux,
   1:1,000,000
Rheinkarte Bodensee – Nordsee, 1:600,000
Karte der nordwestdeutschen Wasserstrassen, 1:400,000
Schiffahrtskarte Neckar, 1:130,000
Schiffahrtskarte Mosel – Saar, 1:200,000
Wasserstrassenkarte Ost-Deutschland und Umgebung,
   1:500,000
Elbe-Atlas, 1:50,000
Verkehrskarte, 1:10,000
   Main, 4 volumes
   Main-Donau-Kanal, 2 volumes
   Donau, 2 volumes
   Elbe-Seitenkanal
   Saar
Wasserstrassen-Atlas Berlin-Brandenburg, 2 volumes,
   1:50,000
Wasserstrassen-Atlas Mecklenburg-Vorpommern, 1:50,000
Wasserstrassen-Übersichtskarten
   Elbe-Müritz-Havel, 1:250,000
   Havel-Spree-Oder, 1:175,000
Gewässerkarten, 1:25,000
   Seengebiete zwischen Berlin und dem Spreewald, 4 charts
   Seengebiet um Potsdam
   Seengebiet um Brandenburg
   Seengebiet um Neuruppin
   Seengebiet um Rheinsberg
   Schweriner See und Umgebung
   Die Müritz
   Plauer See, Fleesen – und Kölpinsee
   Mecklenburger Kleinseenplatte
Der Nord-Ostsee-Kanal (Kiel canal) 2 charts, 1:55,000
Sportschiffahrtskarten binnen, 1:35,000
   Berlin und Märkische Gewässer
   Berlin und Mecklenburger Gewässer
   Nördliche Oder und Peene
   Elbe (and canal connections)

II. USEFUL ADDRESSES

German National Tourist Office, 65 Curzon Street London W1Y 7PE ☎ 0891 600 100 *Fax* 0171 495 6129

German Embassy 23 Belgrave Square, London SW1X 7JT ☎ 0171 235 8080

For general enquiries and information on yacht and sailing clubs

Deutscher Motoryachtverband eV Gründgensstraße 18, 22309 Hamburg ☎ 040 630 80 11, *Fax* 040 632 21 15

Deutscher Segler-Verband (DSV), Gründgensstraße 18, 22309 Hamburg ☎ 040 632 009 0, *Fax* 040 632 009 28

For technical enquiries relating to specific waterways

Wasser-und Schiffahrtsdirektion Nord, Hindenburgufer 247, 24106 Kiel ☎ 04 31 33 94 0

Wasser- und Schiffahrtsdirektion Nordwest, Schloßplatz 9, 26603 Aurich ☎ 0 49 41 6 02 0

Wasser- und Schiffahrtsdirektion Ost, Werderscher Markt, 10117 Berlin ☎ 030 20 38 35 00

Wasser- und Schiffahrtsdirektion Mitte, Am Waterlooplatz 5, 30169 Hannover ☎ 05 11 91 15 0

Wasser- und Schiffahrtsdirektion West, Cheruskerring 11, 48147 Münster ☎ 02 51 27 08 1

Wasser- und Schiffahrtsdirektion Südwest, Brucknerstraße 2, 55127 Mainz ☎ 0 61 31 9 79 0

Wasser- und Schiffahrtsdirektion Süd, Wörthstraße 19, 97082 Würzburg ☎ 09 31 41 05 0

For information on licensing

Bundesverkehrsministerium, Abteilung Wasserstraßen, Postfach 20 01 00, 53170 Bonn

Bookshops

Bade and Hornig GmbH, Herrengraben 31, 20459 Hamburg ☎ 040 37 48 110 *Fax* 040 36 64 00

Eckardt and Messtorff GmbH, Rödingsmarkt 16, 20459 Hamburg ☎ 040 37 48 42 22 *Fax* 040 37 30 28

III. CHARTER COMPANIES ON GERMAN WATERWAYS

Arns Charteryachten, Postfach 10 01 31, 42801 Remscheid ☎ 02191 92 62 40 *Fax* 02191 2 38 03 (Rhein, Mosel, Lahn, Main, Berlin, Mecklenburg)

Barone Yachting, Unterlinden 11, 79098 Freiburg ☎ 0761 38 06 30 *Fax* 0761 27 31 93 (Rhein, Mosel, Lahn, Main, Berlin, Mecklenburg)

Bodingbauer Yachtcharter, Zapfweg 18, 81241 München ☎ 089 83 06 91 *Fax* 089 820 12 05 (Mecklenburg)

Brenneisen Yachtcharter, Gottenheimer Strasse 19, 79224 Umkirch ☎ 07665 5 12 80 *Fax* 07665 54 81 (Berlin, Mecklenburg)

B & R Yachting, Hauptstrasse 70, 12159 Berlin ☎ 030 8 59 25 21 *Fax* 030 8 59 2069 (Berlin, Mecklenburg)

Charterhanse, Auf den Schwarzen Bergen 26, 21224 Rosengarten ☎ 040 7 96 76 51 *Fax* 040 7 96 76 61 (Mecklenburg)

DERTOUR Bereich Bootstouren, Emil-v-Behring-Strasse 6, 60439 Frankfurt ☎ 069 95 88 00 *Fax* 069 95 88 10 10 (Mosel, Lahn, Berlin, Mecklenburg)

Intermarin Yacht Charter, Postfach 22 30, 45752 Marl ☎ 02365 4 40 13 *Fax* 02365 4 43 65 (Rhein, Mosel, Lahn, Main, Elbe, Berlin, Mecklenburg)

Kuhnle Tours, Nagelstrasse 4, 70182 Stuttgart ☎ 0711 16 48 20 *Fax* 0711 1 64 82 60 (Berlin, Mecklenburg)

Sarres-Schockemöhle Yachting, Hubert-Underberg-Allee 2, 47495 Rheinberg ☎ 02843 1 70 31 *Fax* 02843 1 70 04 (Berlin)

Windrose Yachtcharter, Tangstedter Chaussee 2, 25462 Rellingen ☎ 04101 2 22 37 *Fax* 04101 20 79 54 (Mecklenburg)

IV. SPEED AND DISTANCE TABLE

Time to cover 1km	Speed over the ground	
min:sec	km/h	knots
2:00	30	16·2
2:30	24	13·0
3:00	20	10·8
3:30	17	9·2
4:00	15	8·1
5:00	12	6·5
6:00	10	5·4
7:00	8·6	4·6
8:00	7·5	4·0
10:00	6	3·2
12:00	5	2·7
15:00	4	2·2
20:00	3	1·6
30:00	2	1·1

V. GERMAN VOCABULARY

German English

Abwasser sewage
Abwassertank holding tank
Anhalten to stop
Anker anchor
Ankerplatz anchorage
Anlegestelle mooring place
Ausfahrt exit
Backbord port side
Bake beacon
Benzin petrol
Berg mountain
Bergfahrer upstream vessel
Betreiben to operate
Binnengewässer inland water-
    ways
blau blue
Bodden saltwater lagoons
Boje buoy
Boot small boat
Bootshöhe über Wasser height of
    boat
Bootstankstelle filling station for
    boats
Bootstreppe boat ramp
Bootsvermietung charter
    company
Bootswerft boatyard
braun brown
Breite width
Brücke bridge
Bug bow
Bundeswasserstrassen national
    waterways
Bunkerboot bunker boat
Burg castle
Charterfirma charter company
Dalben dolphin
Diesel diesel
Doppelschleuse double lock
Durchfahrthöhe headroom
Duschen showers
Einfahrt entrance
Eisenbahnbrücke railway bridge
Fähre ferry
Fahren to travel
Fahrrinne channel
Fahrrinnentiefe channel depth
Fahrt journey
Fallhöhe fall of lock
Fender fender
Festmachen to tie up
Flagge flag
Fluss river
Führer guide
Führerschein permit
Funk radio
Gasthof guesthouse
Gaststätte pub/restaurant
Gelb yellow
Geschwindigkeit speed
Gesperrt closed
Gewässer waterways
grün green
Hafen harbour
Hafenbecken harbour basin
Hafenverwaltung harbour
    administration
Hebewerk ship-lift
Heck stern
Hinweise reference material
Hochwasser high water
Höhe height
Hubhöhe rise of lock
Insel island
Jacht yacht

Kai quay
Kanal canal, VHF channel
Karte map
Knoten to tie
Kraftstoff fuel
Kraftwerk power station
Kran crane
Land state or region
Länge length
Langsamer slowly
Lebensmittel groceries
Liegebühren mooring fees
Liegemöglichkeit possibility of
    mooring
Liegeplatz mooring place
Liegeverbot mooring forbidden
Liegezeit mooring period
Mast mast
Müll garbage
Mündung mouth of river
Niedrigwasser low water
Nord north
Notfall emergency
Nullpunkt zero point
Öl oil
Ost east
Pegel depth gauge
Pegelstand water level at *Pegel*
Poller bollard
Propeller propeller
rot red
Rückwärts astern
Ruhig quiet
Rundfunk broadcast radio
Schachtschleuse shaft lock
Schiff ship
Schiffahrt shipping
Schiffsbedarf chandlery
Schleppzug convoy
Schleuse lock
Schleusengruppe multiple lock
Schleusenkammer lock chamber
Schleusentor lock gate
Schleusenwärter lock-keeper
Schloss castle
Schnell fast
Schutzhafen safety harbour
schwarz black
Schwimmen to swim
Schwimmpoller floating bollard
Schwimmweste lifejacket
Segel sail
Sicherheit safety
Sperrtor flood barrier
Sportboot pleasure craft
Sportboothafen yacht harbour
Sprechfunk radio telephone
Stadt town
Stark strong
Steganlage staging
Steuerbord starboard side
Stoppen to stop
Strassenbrücke road bridge
Strassentankstelle roadside
    filling station
Strecke stretch of river
Strom electrical current
Stromabwärts downstream
Stromaufwärts upstream
Strömung current in river
Süd south
Supermarkt supermarket
Tal valley
Talfahrer downstream vessel
Tankstelle filling station
Teilstrecke stretch of river

Tief deep
Tiefe depth
Tiefgang draught
Toiletten toilets
Tonne buoy
Treibstoff fuel
Trinkwasser drinking water
Ufer bank of river or canal
UKW VHF
Umschlagstelle loading place
Unbefahrbar unnavigable
Untief shallow
Verbindung connecting
Verboten forbidden
Verein association
Versorgung provisions
Wassersportler pleasure boater
Wasserstand water level
Wasserwanderer person who
    cruises
WC WC
Wehr weir
weiss white
Wendestelle turning place
Werft dockyard
West west
Zoll customs
zu Berg upstream
zu Tal downstream
Zweigkanal branch canal

English German

anchor *Anker*
anchorage *Ankerplatz*
association *Verein*
astern *Rückwärts*
bank of river or canal *Ufer*
beacon *Bake*
black *schwarz*
blue *blau*
boat ramp *Bootstreppe*
boatyard *Bootswerft*
bollard *Poller*
bow *Bug*
branch canal *Zweigkanal*
bridge *Brücke*
broadcast radio *Rundfunk*
brown *braun*
bunker boat *Bunkerboot*
buoy *Boje, Tonne*
canal, VHF channel *Kanal*
castle *Burg, Schloss*
chandlery *Schiffsbedarf*
channel *Fahrrinne*
channel depth *Fahrrinnentiefe*
charter company *Bootsver-
    mietung, Charterfirma*
closed *Gesperrt*
connecting *Verbindung*
convoy *Schleppzug*
crane *Kran*
current in river *Strömung*
customs *Zoll*
deep *Tief*
depth *Tiefe*
depth gauge *Pegel*
diesel *Diesel*
dockyard *Werft*
dolphin *Dalben*
double lock *Doppelschleuse*
downstream *Stromabwärts, zu
    Tal*
downstream vessel *Talfahrer*
draught *Tiefgang*
drinking water *Trinkwasser*
East *Ost*

electrical current *Strom*
emergency *Notfall*
entrance *Einfahrt*
exit *Ausfahrt*
fall of lock *Fallhöhe*
fast *Schnell*
fender *Fender*
ferry *Fähre*
filling station *Tankstelle*
filling station for boats
    Bootstankstelle
filling station in street
    Strassentankstelle
flag *Flagge*
floating bollard *Schwimmpoller*
flood barrier *Sperrtor*
forbidden *Verboten*
fuel *Kraftstoff, Treibstoff*
garbage *Müll*
green *grün*
groceries *Lebensmittel*
guesthouse *Gasthof*
guide *Führer*
harbour *Hafen*
harbour administration *Hafen-
    verwaltung*
harbour basin *Hafenbecken*
headroom *Durchfahrthöhe*
height *Höhe*
height of boat *Bootshöhe über
    Wasser*
high water *Hochwasser*
holding tank *Abwassertank*
inland waterways *Binnen-
    gewässer*
island *Insel*
journey *Fahrt*
length *Länge*
lifejacket *Schwimmweste*
loading place *Umschlagstelle*
lock *Schleuse*
lock chamber *Schleusenkammer*
lock gate *Schleusentor*
lock-keeper *Schleusenwärter*
low water *Niedrigwasser*
map *Karte*
mast *Mast*
mooring fees *Liegebühren*
mooring forbidden *Liegeverbot*
mooring period *Liegezeit*
mooring place *Anlegestelle,
    Liegeplatz*
mountain *Berg*
mouth of river *Mündung*
multiple lock *Schleusengruppe*
national waterways *Bundes-
    wasserstrassen*
North *Nord*
oil *Öl*
to operate *Betreiben*
permit *Führerschein*
person who cruises *Wasser-
    wanderer*
petrol *Benzin*
pleasure boater *Wassersportler*
pleasure craft *Sportboot*
port side *Backbord*
possibility of mooring
    Liegemöglichkeit
power station *Kraftwerk*
propeller *Propeller*
provisions *Versorgung*
pub/restaurant *Gaststätte*
quay *Kai*
quiet *Ruhig*
radio *Funk*

radio telephone *Sprechfunk*	ship-lift *Hebewerk*	supermarket *Supermarkt*	water level at *Pegel Pegelstand*
railway bridge *Eisenbahnbrücke*	shipping *Schiffahrt*	to swim *Schwimmen*	waterways *Gewässer*
red *rot*	showers *Duschen*	to tie *Knoten*	WC *WC*
reference material *Hinweise*	slowly *Langsamer*	to tie up *Festmachen*	weir *Wehr*
rise of lock *Hubhöhe*	small boat *Boot*	toilets *Toiletten*	west *West*
river *Fluss*	South *Süd*	town *Stadt*	white *weiss*
road bridge *Strassenbrücke*	speed *Geschwindigkeit*	to travel *Fahren*	width *Breite*
safety *Sicherheit*	staging *Steganlage*	turning place *Wendestelle*	yacht *Jacht*
safety harbour *Schutzhafen*	starboard side *Steuerbord*	unnavigable *Unbefahrbar*	yacht harbour *Sportboothafen*
sail *Segel*	state or region *Land*	upstream *Stromaufwärts, zu Berg*	yellow *gelb*
saltwater lagoons *Bodden*	stern *Heck*		zero point *Nullpunkt*
sewage *Abwasser*	to stop *Anhalten, Stoppen*	upstream vessel *Bergfahrer*	
shaft lock *Schachtschleuse*	stretch of river *Strecke, Teil-strecke*	valley *Tal*	
shallow *Untief*		VHF *UKW*	
ship *Schiff*	strong *Stark*	water level *Wasserstand*	

VI. NAVIGATIONAL MARKS, SIGNS AND SOUNDS

LOCK SIGNALS

No entry

Opening soon

Enter now

Lock not in operation

BRIDGE SIGNS

Red/White diamonds

Yellow diamond

Yellow diamonds

SOUNDS

▬ ▬	Attention
•	I am turning to starboard
••	I am turning to port
•••	I am going astern
••••	I am incapable of manoeuvring
•••••	Danger of collision
▬▬ ▬▬	(repeated) Distress signal
▬ ▬ •	I am turning round to starboard
▬ ▬ ••	I am turning round to port

WARNING SIGNS (RED)

No entry · No overtaking · No passing · No long-term mooring · No anchoring · No mooring · No turning · Making waves forbidden · Pleasure craft forbidden · Rowing boats forbidden · Motor boats forbidden

Mandatory direction sign · Stop · Speed limit (km/h) · Sound horn · Danger · Major waterway ahead · Height (m) · Depth (m) · Width (m) · Keep away from bank (m)

OTHER SIGNS (BLUE)

Entry allowed (Green) · Electricity cable · Weir · Ferry · Mooring place (long term) · Turning place · Side turning · Anchoring place · End of prohibited area · Advisory direction sign

Index